UNDERSTANDING JONESTOWN AND PEOPLES TEMPLE

UNDERSTANDING JONESTOWN AND PEOPLES TEMPLE

Rebecca Moore

PRAEGER

Westport, Connecticut
London

Library of Congress Cataloging-in-Publication Data

Moore, Rebecca, 1951-
  Understanding Jonestown and Peoples Temple / Rebecca Moore.
    p.   cm.
  Includes bibliographical references and index.
  ISBN 978-0-313-35251-5 (alk. paper)
  1. Jonestown Mass Suicide, Jonestown, Guyana, 1978. 2. Peoples
Temple–History. I. Title.
  BP605.P46M66   2009
  988.1–dc22   2008045489

British Library Cataloguing in Publication Data is available.

Library of Congress Catalog Card Number: 2008045489
ISBN: 978-0-313-35251-5

First published in 2009

Praeger Publishers, 88 Post Road West, Westport, CT 06881
An imprint of Greenwood Publishing Group, Inc.
www.praeger.com

Printed in the United States of America

The paper used in this book complies with the
Permanent Paper Standard issued by the National
Information Standards Organization (Z39.48–1984).

10 9 8 7 6 5 4 3 2 1

CONTENTS

ACKNOWLEDGMENTS

I wish to thank first and foremost my husband Fielding McGehee for being an unfailing source of strength, support, and wisdom.

I would also like to extend my deep appreciation to Tanya Hollis, Laura Johnston Kohl, John V. Moore, and Denice Stephenson for taking the time to read and comment upon the manuscript. Their suggestions have made the book stronger, clearer, and better in every way.

I appreciate the generosity of Eugene V. Gallagher and Douglas E. Cowan for taking the time to read a preliminary draft of the manuscript.

I am grateful for the help and advice from the staff at Greenwood Press, especially Suzanne Staszak-Silva. I also appreciate the work of Frank Scott at Aptara who helped so much in the production of this book.

This book could not have been written without the help of many survivors—defectors and loyalists alike—who have deepened my own understanding of Peoples Temple. Telling their stories to a skeptical and at times unforgiving public has taken great courage and much trust. All of us are indebted to them for speaking out of the truth of their experiences.

AUTHOR'S NOTE

I have been studying Peoples Temple and Jonestown for more than thirty years. My interest is both personal and professional. My personal interest began when my older sister, Carolyn Layton, joined Peoples Temple in 1968, and continued when my younger sister, Annie Moore, joined in 1972. And of course, when they died in Jonestown on 18 November 1978, I experienced the same grief, shock, and horror felt by people worldwide, since their deaths were completely unexpected by me or by my family.

The deaths of my sisters and my four-year-old nephew, Kimo, initially led me on a personal quest to learn what happened exactly and why. I wanted to understand my sisters, the lives they led, and the choices they made. Because my parents and I had personal knowledge of some of the Jonestown victims, we were unable to accept pop psychological analyses of "brainwashed fanatics" and "crazed cultists." These descriptions did not apply either to my sisters or to other members of Peoples Temple that we knew.

In addition, I am sure that this quest was my personal way of addressing the grief and loss I experienced. My parents, John and Barbara Moore, had lost two daughters and a grandson, and they dealt with their bereavement differently than I did as a middle daughter who lost two sisters. I wanted answers, and I was not satisfied with those provided by news stories or government officials. Looking back upon that time, I realize that I was asking existential questions as well as factual questions: How could people kill their own children? Why did they punish each other in public humiliation sessions? Were they murdered by mysterious government forces?

Although I was never part of Peoples Temple, I did visit the facilities in Northern California on one occasion in 1975. My older sister, Carolyn, had become part of the leadership group in Redwood Valley. She had moved to Talmage, near Ukiah and Redwood Valley, with her husband, Larry Layton, who was performing alternative service in the state mental hospital as a conscientious objector to the Vietnam War. She and Larry divorced, however, and she began a relationship with the leader of Peoples Temple, Jim Jones, who—throughout the affair—remained married to his wife, Marceline. My younger sister, Annie, was enrolled in the nursing program at Santa Rosa Junior College. During my visit I saw extensive facilities for mentally retarded youth, for mentally ill adults released from the state hospital, for senior citizens, and for the wider community. I toured the Temple's print shop and laundromat, as I recall, and though I saw the exterior of the church building, I did not go inside, nor did I attend a worship service.

I was living in Washington, D.C., in the 1970s while my sisters were part of Peoples Temple, first in California and then in Guyana, so I did not have much contact with them except for occasional trips. My parents, however, frequently visited the Temple in San Francisco, and hosted Jim Jones and some of his children at their house on Ashby Avenue in Berkeley. They had reason to: Carolyn and Jim Jones had a son, called Jim-Jon or Kimo. Jim seemed to think that my father, John, had some political weight and authority because he was a District Superintendent in the United Methodist Church. He included my parents at public events in large part because of this perceived influence.

My parents, however, especially my mother, did not want to alienate my sisters, so they stifled their concerns and criticisms for the sake of family harmony. They had unique access to the Temple that other families lacked, and were in a relatively privileged position. While they were aware of the side that Temple members presented to the public, they were not privy to events that occurred within the Temple, however, with one or two exceptions.[1]

I mention this background because it helps to explain how personal concerns progressed into a professional interest in Peoples Temple in particular and new religions in general. In my initial writings about Peoples Temple, my primary purpose was to humanize those who had lived and died in Jonestown in order to counteract the books and articles that demonized them. I wrote to understand and explain the beliefs of Temple members, their motives, and their actions, though not to justify them. Advanced studies in new religions gave me the tools and language to write in a different style for a different audience: scholars. While my earlier writings emphasized the voices of those who died, my later writings have attempted to analyze all the voices of Jonestown.

Part of my own process of understanding and interpreting those voices led to the creation of a website called *Alternative Considerations of Jonestown and Peoples Temple* in 1998, on the twentieth anniversary of the deaths. In the decade since its inception as an alternative to what I believed were biased accounts, the site has grown into a forum for a variety of viewpoints about Peoples Temple and Jonestown. In addition, under the direction of my husband, Fielding McGehee, the site has grown into a repository of primary source data: from audiotape transcripts to articles written by survivors of Jonestown to documents generated by the Temple itself. Much of the source material cited in this book can be found online at http://jonestown.sdsu.edu.

Thirty years of research and reflection have gone into this book. Nevertheless, I still write out of the experience of being a relative. This gives me a feeling of sympathy for the victims, but also a sense of empathy for the perpetrators. A song written by Ken Risling, a high school friend of my sister Annie, poetically described the situation of people like me:

> There's really just one question now,
> that lingers on my lips:
> Had I walked that final mile
> inside your shoes
> Would I do the same damn thing
> if I were you?[2]

I am convinced that given the right time, the right leader, and the right circumstances, I too might have joined a movement like Peoples Temple. Although I had numerous opportunities to join the Temple, and my sisters encouraged me to become part of the group to which they were dedicated, I never did. And so I live to tell the tale.

INTRODUCTION

Framing the Subject

I can be expected to look for truth but not to find it.
　　　　　　　—Denis Diderot, *Pensées Philosophiques**

On 18 November 1978, more than 900 Americans died in the small South American country of Guyana. A congressman was assassinated on a remote jungle airstrip, journalists were shot and killed, a woman slit her three children's throats and then her own, and hundreds of men, women, and children died in what appeared to be the largest mass suicide in history. This is where most Americans would begin the story of Peoples Temple, for it was the community at Jonestown, and the events that occurred there, that brought Peoples Temple to the attention of the world. Little was known about the religious group that emerged from Indiana in the 1950s, moved to northern California in the 1960s, became a political force in San Francisco in the early 1970s, and established a utopian commune in Guyana in the mid-1970s. For most people, the story also ended when the last bodies were removed from the jungle community. The treatment of the remains at Dover Air Force Base, the government investigations, the dispersal of Temple assets, even the few criminal trials were all relegated to the back pages of newspapers. As a result, for many the history of Peoples Temple began and ended in violence during a single week, the week of Thanksgiving in 1978.

CONSTRUCTING THE NARRATIVE

The news media quickly tried to tell the story of the group despite an insurmountable obstacle: the people about whom they were writing were all dead. Only a few remained to chronicle the life and death of Peoples Temple. These included a small number of Jonestown residents who escaped the deaths, several dozen who survived by being in Guyana's capital city on 18 November, some journalists who had previously reported on the group, and a vocal cohort of critical ex-members. With a U.S. congressman dead, three reporters killed, and a dozen wounded in the attack on the congressman, initial accounts of Peoples Temple were somewhat lopsided, representing the views of people who, for the most part, were quite hostile to the group.

It is no wonder, then, that preliminary news accounts framed the story of Jonestown as a story of good versus evil: the noble congressman versus the evil cult leader; the courageous defectors versus the brainwashed followers; sanity versus insanity. Journalists constructed the story as a morality play, especially since three of their own lay dead. This is the way most people remember Jonestown.

A brief summary of the narrative established in 1978 helps to set the stage for the rest of this book, which will relate the story very differently.

The narrative begins with a charismatic, but deranged, prophet named Jim Jones who founded an interracial church in Indianapolis in the 1950s, challenging both segregation and capitalism with a social gospel that called for racial equality and just distribution of wealth among group members. The group, called Peoples Temple, moved to Ukiah, in Northern California, following Jones' prediction of nuclear holocaust—undoubtedly based upon *Esquire* magazine's 1962 inclusion of the small town in its listing of the top nine safest places to live in case of a nuclear attack. The group grew under an aggressive proselytizing program and expanded to San Francisco and Los Angeles. Although free social services such as housing, legal aid, meals, healthcare, and welfare advocacy were provided to members and non-members alike, church members also conducted abusive practices within an inner leadership cadre called the Planning Commission. In addition, faith healings were faked in order to draw in more members.

Concern about the safety of its members, given the political environment in the United State in the 1970s, led the group to establish a community in the Northwest District of Guyana. An Afro-Guyanese government saw advantages to settling a group of 1,000 Americans in a territory disputed by Venezuela. In Guyana, the workers at the Peoples Temple Agricultural Project cleared hundreds of acres of jungle to create a community, which came to be called Jonestown. Negative publicity about the Temple in San Francisco, however, forced a rapid migration to the project in the summer of 1977, where people were kept in a virtual concentration camp.

In November 1978, California Congressman Leo J. Ryan courageously visited the isolated jungle community to investigate conditions there, accompanied by journalists and relatives of Peoples Temple members who sought to liberate their children. On 18 November 1978, fifteen residents of Jonestown asked to join Ryan and his party as they left. While they waited to board two small aircraft, a few young men who had followed the party from Jonestown began firing upon it, killing Ryan, three newsmen, and one defector. A dozen others were wounded, some quite seriously.

Back in Jonestown, more than 900 residents gathered in the central pavilion, where Jones told them what had happened and exhorted them to drink a cyanide-laced fruit punch. A tape recording of the incident reveals that the few residents who protested were shouted down by the majority. Eyewitness accounts are conflicting, with some saying that people were coerced into taking poison, and others saying that people willingly drank the mixture. By the end of the day, 918 Americans in Guyana were dead: 909 in Jonestown; five on the airstrip; and four in the Temple's residence in Georgetown, the capital of Guyana.

While this synopsis imparts the bare facts about the history of Peoples Temple and the events in Jonestown, it suggests a particular framework as well. Several loaded words indicate a spin that judges Jim Jones (deranged) and group members (abusive), and that valorizes Leo Ryan (courageous). The use of adjectives and value-laden nouns is never neutral, however, and news accounts that discussed religious fanatics, brainwashed cultists, or courageous members of Congress suffered from a lack of objectivity.

WHERE'S THE APOSTROPHE?

A note on the spelling of Peoples Temple is in order. The earliest news reports about the group spelled it "People's Temple." When we examine the Temple's own literature, we find it both with and without an apostrophe. What is clear, however, is that the group used it with less frequency once it relocated to California, and dropped it entirely with the move to Guyana. The group in Redwood Valley, for example, identified itself as "Peoples Temple Christian Church" on signage and stationery.

Moreover, the group did not seem to identify itself as *the* Peoples Temple, but simply Peoples Temple. Yet we observe news accounts, books, and even a play calling it The Peoples Temple or The People's Temple.

For these reasons, I will be calling the group Peoples Temple; and when I use "Temple" as an adjective—such as the Temple's facilities or the Temple's philosophy—I will capitalize Temple since it is the name of the group, not the identification of a building. I will also present direct quotations that use "People's" without a [sic] to indicate original spelling, for ease of reading and in recognition of all the variants that exist.

THE ANTICULT NARRATIVE

The times in which the Temple arose influenced early news reports. The 1960s and 1970s saw the rise of many new religions in the United States.

A major reason for this was the development of a counterculture that challenged the assumptions and values of society at large. Well-educated young adults, predominantly white and affluent, were drawn to New Religious Movements (NRMs) because of their readings in philosophy and their study of Zen Buddhism, because of their drug use, and because of their interest in alternative lifestyles. Drug use in particular created a desire for ecstatic experiences, either through chemicals or through religious ritual. An unpopular war and a militant civil rights movement also led many to question the values with which they had grown up. Another element that explains the rise of new religions was the repeal of the Asian Exclusion Act in 1965. Abolition of this act, promulgated in 1924 and aimed at limiting all immigration from Asia, enabled many religious leaders to come to the United States. These leaders brought with them a variety of new religions that attracted rebellious young adults who sought deeper meaning and a more involved spiritual practice than they had found in their parents' faith. All of these factors contributed to the willingness of young adults to try out new religions.

Those who joined these alternative groups dramatically altered their lifestyles. They grew their hair or they shaved it off. They lived in communes and shared sexual partners or they became celibate. They dropped out of school or they stopped taking drugs. They proselytized in public places like airports or they disappeared into ashrams. One thing they all seemed to have in common was a rejection of the lives their parents led, discarding worldly success and traditional markers of middle-class achievement such as careers, homes, and families.

These vivid changes produced a widespread horror of "cults," and groups like the Unification Church (also known as Moonies), the International Society of Krishna Consciousness (also known as Hare Krishnas), and the Children of God (now called The Family International) were feared and reviled. Ad hoc groups of parents, supported by psychological professionals, believed their children were programmed to follow depraved gurus and brainwashed into selling flowers on street corners. The 1970s saw a wave of kidnappings in which desperate parents abducted their adult children and paid for them to be deprogrammed by nonprofessional and unscrupulous "exit counselors." An organized anticult movement arose in order to protect people from these dangerous pseudo-religions.

This anticult movement helped shape the eyewitness and first-person accounts of life in Peoples Temple that emerged immediately after the deaths. These accounts presented the firsthand experiences of critical ex-members and of relatives of members who died in Jonestown. They depicted Peoples Temple as a dangerous cult guided by a cynical and conniving leader who misled and betrayed his trusting followers. These works are useful in gaining insights into life inside Peoples Temple and the activities of former members once they left. Yet they are somewhat incomplete, as they tell only part of the story: that is, they describe former members' unhappiness in Peoples

Temple, but they downplay, or ignore, what attracted them in the first place, and what kept others there.

Later anticult literature used Jonestown and Peoples Temple to signify the danger of cults. The events in Jonestown legitimized public concerns about new religions, and justified parents' fear for their own children. Jonestown became a code word that evoked a range of negative images and emotions: from the vat of poison and the bloated bodies surrounding it, to feelings of fear and disgust. Rather than placing Peoples Temple within the paradigm of cults, anticult rhetoric located all new religions within the paradigm of Jonestown. Perhaps the best, or worst, example of this was cult expert Rick Ross's conjuring the specter of Jonestown and shaping the Bureau of Alcohol, Tobacco, and Firearms' views about the Branch Davidians in Waco, Texas, in 1993. The tragic standoff that led to the burning of Mount Carmel and the deaths of more than eighty people stemmed directly from miscalculations borne out of federal agents' fears about "another Jonestown."[1]

CHALLENGING THE CULT STEREOTYPE

Scholars who study new religions try to avoid using the word "cult." Cult is never a value-neutral word since it always carries an implicit criticism. We do not call Baptists or Catholics or Jews cultists; we only call religions of which we disapprove cults. To avoid making a value judgment when discussing various religious groups, scholars have come up with several alternatives to the word, including NRM, alternative religions, and emerging religions. None of these terms is completely satisfactory, yet none carry the negative freight that the word cult does. Journalists today have become aware of the implications of their choice of words when referring to new religions, and many do use the term NRM in place of cult. But in the 1970s, American society in general understood all new religions to be cults.

In many ways, however, Peoples Temple challenged the cult stereotype. It began as a Christian church in Indianapolis, Indiana, in the 1950s, and became a member of the Disciples of Christ denomination. Though its leader was a white charismatic preacher, its membership was predominantly working-class and overwhelmingly African American. Children and senior citizens made up the majority of members, with a relatively small number of able-bodied adults supporting them. Throughout its twenty-five-year history, until the move to Guyana, Peoples Temple practiced the Christian Social Gospel. That is, it justified political activism on biblical grounds, making Jesus' parable of the Last Judgment its watchwords:

> For I was an hungered and ye
> gave me meat;
> I was thirsty, and ye gave me
> drink;

> I was a stranger, and ye took
> me in;
> Naked, and ye clothed me;
> I was sick, and ye visited me;
> I was in prison, and ye came
> unto me. (Matthew 25:35–36,
> King James Version)

Far from dropping out, Peoples Temple members were engaged in the world, and tried to make concrete differences in individuals' lives and in society as a whole.

With the migration to the agricultural project in Jonestown, the group changed, becoming a utopian commune. Following a long tradition of American utopian experiments—from the nineteenth-century community of Oneida in New York to the many agricultural communes in California— Peoples Temple attempted to become self-sufficient and live off the land. Like many of these groups, the Temple found self-sufficiency a difficult goal to achieve. Religious language and ritual were absent in Jonestown, replaced by collective concern about livestock, crops, world affairs, and potential threats to the community's survival coming from the United States.

In short, Peoples Temple differed greatly from the majority of new religions that emerged in the 1960s and 1970s. Indeed, Peoples Temple was a home-grown religion and, at its heart, reflected American institutions.

ALTERNATIVE NARRATIVES

While journalists and critics initially framed the analysis of Peoples Temple as a discussion of cults, a range of alternative perspectives offers new insights today. John R. Hall described the Temple's American roots in *Gone from the Promised Land*, in which he showed its affinity with three streams of U.S. culture: the Social Gospel of Protestant Christianity, black messiahs, and American Communism. He charted the Temple's course in California, arguing that it succeeded largely because it was a "distinctly American social movement." He concluded by noting that "in diverse ways, the growth of Peoples Temple was fueled through its relations to our society."[2]

We might also consider the group in the context of black religion in America.[3] Peoples Temple had many of the earmarks that scholars use to define black religion, such as having a charismatic leader, being engaged in social transformation, and longing for exodus from exile into the Promised Land. Its large African American membership, coupled with its message of social justice and racial equality, all reflected the activism of urban black churches in the 1960s and 1970s.

Another approach is to examine Peoples Temple comparatively, evaluating it in light of other instances of religious violence. In the mid-1990s scholars took note of the differences between Peoples Temple and the Branch Davidians. They also contrasted the Temple with Aum Shinrikyo, the group that waged a sarin gas attack on the Tokyo subway in 1995. A number of studies took into account the social contexts in which different groups arose, the diverse demographics, the internal leadership dynamics, and the external forces impinging upon the groups.[4]

Stories from loyalists, just beginning to emerge in the twenty-first century, are starting to provide new accounts of life in Peoples Temple. Loyalists are members who survived the deaths, but who had been so traumatized by the events that they remained closeted for a generation. In the last decade they have started to tell their side of the story. They do not necessarily disagree with critics on the facts of what happened, but their interpretations differ greatly. The same trip up the Kaituma River, for example, viewed as a nightmare according to a defector, is transformed into heaven on earth according to a loyalist.

An important narrative not available in 1978 is that of those who lived and died as part of Peoples Temple. We can hear their voices on some of the 900 audiotapes recovered from Jonestown. We can read their writings and learn their thoughts in thousands and thousands of documents which various government agencies retrieved from the defunct organization. Primary sources generated by Peoples Temple members—letters, memos, newspapers, even shopping lists—show what life was like inside and give insights into the nature of the community.[5] What is most significant about these items is the fact that they were not created looking backward: Jonestown was ahead, not behind, and so they are not colored by the deaths of hundreds of people.

A final alternative narrative comes from those who offer artistic renderings and interpretations of the events. Painters, playwrights, musicians, authors, and others have been intrigued by the questions raised by Jonestown. Their impressions and conceptions, while not always literal or representational, enlarge the boundaries within which we think about the meaning of Peoples Temple and Jonestown.

Jonestown is enormous, by which I mean it looms large in the repository of human consciousness, in the history of religions, in the study of new religions, in the understanding of religion in America, and in the consideration of ethics and morality. Obviously it remains a defining occasion for those who lost loved ones. But its immensity explains the enduring fascination it holds for a new generation of young adults, as well as for people who have memories of the events themselves. This book, then, introduces readers to a movement of enormous scope. One way to indicate the enormity is to allow all of the voices of Jonestown to be heard—skeptics, critics, and true believers—thereby constructing a sufficiently large frame in which to consider the subject. While many questions will have been answered by the end of this volume, understanding Jonestown and Peoples Temple means appreciating that some questions have no answer.

For Further Reading

The first books that came out after Jonestown were two paperbacks written by journalists who were traveling with Congressman Ryan in Guyana: *Suicide Cult* by Ron Javers and Marshall Kilduff, and *The Guyana Massacre* by Charles Krause. These were followed in short order by accounts by former members or their families, such as *Six Years with God*; *Peoples Temple, Peoples Tomb*; *The Broken God*; and *The Cult That Died*. These accounts reflect the anticult perspective described in this introduction.

CHAPTER 1

Beyond White Trash

All evil begins in the mind. If the mind is pure all else is pure.
—Jim Jones, *Notes for Bible Study**

The story of a poor boy, born on the wrong side of the tracks, who educates himself and rises above his background to become an influential religious leader, is quintessentially an American story. Intelligent, clever, sensitive, and manipulative, Jim Jones was destined for great things, one way or another. Peoples Temple was his brainchild, and at its height, was a large, integrated organization that mounted successful opposition to a racist society. Jones moved with presidents and politicians: his church in San Francisco and his agricultural project in Guyana served as the backdrops for photo opportunities with the powerful and mighty. Yet he threw it all away, taking 900 people with him, in a self-destructive act reminiscent of other American tragedies.

An understanding of Jim Jones illuminates the history and theology of the Temple, although it doesn't tell the whole story. His background and personal conflicts served as the foundation from which his religious, moral, and political positions emerged. It is difficult to piece together his childhood, adolescence, and young adulthood in Indiana, however. Sources include an autobiographical monologue he gave in 1977, biographies his mother Lynetta and his wife Marceline wrote in the 1970s, personal remembrances from people who knew him as a child, and news accounts and documentary evidence (such as a birth certificate, ordination certificates, and other historical items).[1] While these sources depict a strange little boy who grew up to be an unusually intense young man, they fail to capture the ultimate enigma of Jim Jones, the man who went from poor boy to prophet of God to mad messiah.

Moreover, sources are open to interpretation, and a single story may be interpreted in markedly different ways. Compare the following two accounts:

> Even before he was toilet-trained, Jimmy would toddle around unsupervised with a dirty face and bare bottom...Jimmy's nudity was perhaps his first attention-getting device. Once he did it in front of cattle drivers, with his mother chasing him. Another time, he marched into a church bottomless, accompanied by a troop of dogs, and presented the minister with a bouquet of flowers.[2]

> One time, [Lynetta] remembered, Jim wandered into a church "half naked and with all his dogs and animals behind him" and presented flowers to a congregation that rippled with laughter at the gesture. "The preacher got so confounded mad, he says, 'I don't want to hear any more funny business...There's more religion in one little finger of this child than there is in the whole town...You have something in your midst that's a crackling gift from heaven'."[3]

These two stories illustrate the difficulty of writing a biography, especially when using secondary sources. Accounts of Jones's childhood say as much about the writer as they do about Jones. Was he a bad seed from the beginning? Or did life experiences mold and then warp him? The answer depends upon who tells the story.

JIMBA

James Warren Jones was born 13 May 1931 in Crete, Indiana. His parents were James Thurman Jones and Lynetta Putnam Jones. It was the Great Depression and times were tough. Within a few years of Jim's birth the family farm failed, and the three moved to Lynn, Indiana, a nearby town of almost 1,000 people. James T. was a World War I veteran whose lungs had been damaged by mustard gas. He frequented V.A. hospitals when he wasn't picking up occasional jobs on railroad construction. But his war injury—which caused breathing difficulties—made him a failure rather than a hero in the 1930s since he could not work much and could not support his family on his disability pension. His habit of removing himself to the town's pool hall mirrored an emotional withdrawal from his family, and he became a remote and distant father to his only child.

It was his wife who supported the family. Lynetta had gone to college for two years and attended business school for another two years, but she worked at whatever jobs she could get: field work, canneries, factories, waitressing. She even worked as a labor organizer in her off hours during World

War II. By all accounts Lynetta was a tough, straight-talking woman who said what she thought. She was critical of hypocrisy, class distinctions, and social inequity. She wore her work clothes into town—pants or overalls—which shocked the more genteel members of the community. She smoked cigarettes in public and drank beer in her own home. Lynetta and James T. separated in the late 1940s, and he died soon after, in 1951.

As an adult, Jim Jones constructed a narrative about himself that described a little hell-raiser, a troublemaker right from the start. This portrait is somewhat corroborated by his childhood friends, though it seems more colorful than the bleak life he really had. He lived near the railroad tracks in the poor section of town, and was acutely aware of the injustices in his life. In the absence created by a working mother and a disabled father, little Jimba, as his mother called him, surrounded himself with animals and kept a menagerie that attracted visits from neighborhood children. Jones said he felt deeply alienated from his peers. He said he was considered white trash, and as a result, he was ready to kill by the end of the third grade. "I mean, I was so fucking aggressive and hostile, I was ready to kill."

Despite his later recasting of himself as a rebel with a cause, Jones nonetheless excelled in school. He was a voracious reader and he had the vocabulary to prove it, even at an early age. His IQ was in the 115 to 118 range, and in high school he was ranked fifth or sixth in a class of forty. He read widely in medicine, religion, and current events. He was nicely groomed, and looked older than he was.

Jones's parents did not go to church or attend school functions, a noticeable deficiency in a small town the size of Lynn. Lynetta had little use for organized religion, although she did believe in spirits and possessed a type of animistic belief in animals and nature. She reported a number of visions and dreams that persuaded her to take certain actions. Perhaps most oddly, her son looked like her elderly foster father, Lewis Parker, whom she admired greatly. He had Parker's brown eyes, rather than the blue eyes of both Lynetta and James T. She considered this a good omen.

It was from Jones's neighbor, Myrtle Kennedy, that he first received formal religious training. Mrs. Kennedy belonged to the Church of the Nazarene, and she took young Jones with her to services. He also visited the local Methodist church and the Quaker meeting. It was the Pentecostal Church, however, that attracted Jones, and more particularly, a Pentecostal woman preacher who saw in the ten-year-old boy the makings of a child evangelist. Lynetta put a stop to his involvement in that church, but Jones had got religion, and after his Pentecostal experience, he set up a little church that he called "God's House" in the loft above the family garage. He held services for children in the neighborhood, preaching for hours and holding them spellbound, at least when it was cool outside. He also conducted funeral services for dead animals, saying prayers and giving eulogies like a professional. His interest in religion grew, and at sixteen he took to hitch-hiking to Richmond, about seventeen miles south of Lynn, to preach in a predominantly African American neighborhood. Waving his Bible and talking about the need for brotherhood, he would collect small crowds of two dozen people, both white and black, and some spare change as well.

THE PREACHER MAN

Jones got himself a job as a part-time orderly in Reid Memorial Hospital while he attended high school. He met Marceline Baldwin at the hospital, where she was completing training as a nurse. After a few initial social gaffes, Jones was able to win over the Baldwin family, despite the age difference between him and their eldest daughter. They married 12 June 1949, when he was 18 and she was 22, after he had completed his first semester at Indiana University in Bloomington. In 1951 the couple moved to Indianapolis where Jones could enter the Indiana University Law School as an undergraduate, but he never completed his studies there. Eventually, he graduated from Butler University in 1960.

The Baldwins were a typical Hoosier family: conservative, hard-working, down-to-earth, and Republican. Walter Baldwin, Marceline's father, had served on the Richmond City Council. They were also Methodists who raised their daughters in the Methodist tradition. Jones ridiculed Marceline's faith in God and her organized religion. But when he read the Methodist social creed in the spring of 1952, it was a life-changing experience. Here was a church that supported the alleviation of poverty, the right of collective bargaining, free speech, prison reform, full employment, and racial integration. Like many in the American underclass, Jones found religion to be the way out of poverty. He decided to become a minister, and by that summer he was working as a student pastor in the Sommerset Southside Methodist Church. He apparently served the church for two years, but his Pentecostal preaching style, which mixed holiness spirituality with a message of racial equality, eventually led to a parting of the ways. By some accounts, he was kicked out because of his integrationist activities. By others, he left after attending revivalist meetings in Columbus, Indiana; Cincinnati, Ohio; and Detroit, Michigan, seeing greater opportunities for growth and development.

By 1954 Jones had set up his own church, Community Unity, on Hoyt and Randolph streets in Indianapolis. Some of the members of the Laurel Street Tabernacle—an Assemblies of God Pentecostal denomination—heard the dynamic young preacher at a Detroit convention, and visited him at the Hoyt Street church. One of the ministers at Laurel Street, the Rev. Russell Winberg, invited Jones to give some guest sermons at the Tabernacle, since church elders were considering a replacement for the senior pastor who was retiring. Jones brought his interracial congregation to the Tabernacle, and the leadership decided not to hire him. But a few members of the Laurel Street congregation followed the dynamic preacher back to Community Unity.

Some of the pilgrims from Laurel Street Tabernacle, such as Jack and Rheaviana Beam, became leaders in a new religious group, Wings of Deliverance, incorporated by Jim and Marceline on 4 April 1955. The organization moved the congregation to a larger building, which could seat 700, at 15th and New Jersey streets in Indianapolis, and called itself Peoples Temple. A second move, to 975 Delaware Street in 1957, saw the group change its name to Peoples Temple Apostolic Church. Finally, when the congregation voted in 1959 to affiliate with the Disciples of Christ denomination, it became the Peoples Temple Christian Church Full Gospel. It was not until 1960, however, that Peoples Temple officially became part of the Disciples of Christ, a mainline denomination known for its commitment to progressive social action.

Peoples Temple in Indianapolis was in most respects a Pentecostal church, with a message that appealed to working-class whites and African Americans. Services were lively and energetic, featuring healings, glossolalia—or speaking in tongues—and a biblical message. "I was a Methodist preacher, before God took a little of the starch out of me," Jones admitted to the congregation, adding that he could speak in tongues. "But yet I would rather speak five words with the understanding of what Pentecost performs. I would rather have five words of the reality of the proof of Pentecost, than 10,000 words in an unknown tongue."[4] Notes that Jones prepared for Bible study, which he headed "Bible Interpretation," reiterated familiar themes in evangelical Christianity: creation and fall, sin and redemption, personal evangelism. He listed the qualifications for "soul winners" in lesson 3, which included knowing oneself, being a man of prayer, desiring to see souls saved, and having confidence in the power of the Word of God.

As the church grew, so did the family of Jim and Marceline Jones. In June 1953, they adopted a little girl, Agnes, the first of many children. Their earlier attempt to adopt Ronnie Baldwin, Marceline's ten-year-old cousin, fell through when the boy was reunited with his birth mother. In 1958, the Joneses adopted two Korean children, Stephanie and Lew. Stephanie died in a car accident in May 1959, an event which profoundly affected both Jim and Marceline, in part because Stephanie was buried in the African American section of the cemetery, a swampy, water-logged section of lowland. "That fucking vault, the water half-filling it," Jim exclaimed in his autobiography. "I pulled Marceline back because I knew there was no use to stand there and watch that."[5] A few weeks after Stephanie died, Marceline gave birth to their only biological child, a son they named Stephan Gandhi Jones. The couple then adopted another Korean child whom they named Suzanne. Two years later they adopted James Jones Jr., and became the first white couple in the state of Indiana to adopt an African American child. Their "rainbow family," as they called it, would continue to grow as other children and teenagers came and went.

RELIGION AND RACE

Peoples Temple was a product not only of Jim Jones, but of its membership as well. To neglect the people who formed the initial core of Temple leaders and members is to overlook the power of hope that people had for a better life in this world and to disregard their belief that Christianity promises social equality for all people in the here and now. Jim Jones's use of biblical texts to insist on the necessity of justice, including integration in the churches and in society, was as persuasive as the reality of black and white together that he mandated in his own congregation and family. Missionaries from the church would invite African Americans to attend services, and they came. Whites, like blacks, were attracted by the gospel message and Jones's healing abilities. Edith Cordell, for example, left Laurel Street Tabernacle and joined the Community Unity congregation when Jones healed her arthritis. But unlike blacks, whites had to make a conscious decision to abandon the race prejudice that permeated the culture in which they lived. Jack Beam, another emigrant from Laurel Street, described the dilemma that whites faced:

> What [Jones] wanted to say, but they was religious people, [was] "God damn it, you want the fuckin' healing, well stick your fuckin' money up your ass, if you don't love these black people." And he'd have to coin it in all loving biblical words. [The whites] were in awe; they would'a liked to kill him, but they thought that they would be touching God's anointed, and at that time, that was one of the scriptures that was used: "touch not my anointed; do my prophets no harm."[6]

The whites who joined—for the most part poor and working-class like their black counterparts—accepted integration in exchange for the signs and wonders they saw Jim Jones perform. They also found a haven from the racism that imprisoned both black and white. For example, when Archie Ijames, an African American carpenter who quickly rose to Temple leadership, complimented Rheaviana Beam, a white woman who worked as chief cook in the Peoples Temple restaurant, Beam was moved to tears by his kindness. A different kind of world seemed possible in the Temple, one in which people were human beings laboring in common cause rather than fighting each other because of the color of their skin.

Many members of the Cordell family, who were white, joined the Temple in Indianapolis, beginning with Edith Cordell, who met Jim Jones when he was selling live monkeys door-to-door to raise money for the church. Edith's nephew Harold Cordell joined when he was in high school, and he encouraged his younger brother to attend. Richard was impressed with the warmth that Jim and Marceline projected. Although Jones was preaching the

Bible and conducting healings, "back then ... he was saying the same thing that he is now, he was just saying it in a different way," according to Rick. "His message was always very stark, since I knew him it's Brotherhood, all races together."[7]

Demographic figures are uncertain, with one source claiming that the congregation was one-fifth African American by 1960, and another asserting it was more than fifty percent African American. Although the smaller figure is likelier, in either case a mixed congregation was rare in the 1950s. "In the beginning, [Jones] had a hard time making black people believe that he was sincere," Marceline Jones wrote. "He and his workers knocked on the door of every black family in Indianapolis, Indiana."[8] Archie Ijames and his family responded to Jones's invitation, and Jones, recognizing Ijames's abilities, recruited him as an assistant pastor to demonstrate his authentic commitment to integration. Archie and his wife Rosie, children of sharecroppers, sought a religious institution that could address the very real problems of racism they experienced. The couple and their children felt welcomed. Archie committed himself to working full time for the Temple when it opened its restaurant in 1960.

Catherine Hyacinth Thrash and her sister Zipporah Edwards, also African Americans, joined the Temple after seeing the integrated choir perform on television and hearing the charismatic preacher say, "God is no respecter of persons." In an account of her life in Peoples Temple, Hyacinth Thrash said that:

> We were impressed with Jim and the church. He invited us back. A month passed. Then one day a flyer appeared on the doorstep. It said Jim and twelve of his members would be on our block Wednesday night, calling. Well, he came, held our hands and had prayer. It was wonderful.[9]

Hyacinth and Zippy joined in 1957 and volunteered for the church, preparing food baskets for the needy and working in the kitchen to feed those who came to Sunday services.

Another African American family, the Cobbs, joined in Indianapolis after Jones called out seven-year-old Jim Cobb during a service and told him he had an ear problem. This was, in fact, true: Jim Cobb did have an ear problem that needed surgery. Jones's psychic abilities coupled with the warmth James and his mother Christine experienced in the Temple persuaded Christine to abandon her Baptist church on the other side of town.

THE SINCEREST FORM OF FLATTERY

The growth that Peoples Temple witnessed during its first decade can be attributed to Jim Jones's charisma, energy, and passion; the support and leadership of his wife Marceline; and the power of an integrationist message backed by biblical teachings. It can also be attributed to the successful and conscious emulation of another integrationist religious movement: the Peace Mission led by Father Divine, a charismatic and flamboyant African American spiritual leader and capitalistic entrepreneur. Born George Baker around 1880, and the son of former slaves (or sharecroppers, depending upon the account), Father Divine established an interracial ministry in Saybrook, Long Island, before moving to Manhattan, where it flourished during the 1930s. The key to Divine's success was his support for black business operations, including restaurants, barbershops, hairstyling salons, and hotels. He espoused both black capitalism and cooperative ventures at the same time, encouraging members to live in mission-owned rooming houses and to contribute their wages to the mission in exchange for room and board.

Father Divine inspired thousands of black and white Americans with his can-do message of self-help. He also preached and practiced a message of racial integration, although his insistence on the celibacy of his members was well-considered in a time of anti-miscegenation laws and fears about race-mixing and sexual misconduct. Despite his integrationist message, his leadership group was predominantly white, while the majority of his members were African American. The Peace Mission moved to Philadelphia in 1942, and at its height had branches around the country where a weekly sumptuous banquet gave poor people a taste of what an integrated society of plenty might be like.

Father Divine also inspired Jim Jones, who made several visits to the Peace Mission in the 1950s and came away deeply impressed by Divine's message and methods. A twenty-eight-page booklet Jones probably composed in 1957 summarized his experience this way: "How a pastor of a large full gospel assembly was more consecrated to Jesus Christ by his contact with the Rev. M. J. Divine Peace Mission movement."[10] The booklet reported on his and Marceline's careful investigation of the group, in which they checked with nearby businesses, observed the morals of members, and left quite satisfied that people practiced what was preached. The Peace Mission's communalism greatly impressed the young pastor.

> It is refreshing to see that the Kingdom principles of cooperative communalism is [sic] no longer in the realms of Biblical theory. The Divinites have perfectly fulfilled the Scriptural principle: from each according to his ability to each according to his need. They have sincerely put into practice Acts 2 which required that the believers live together and hold all things in common.

Jones took additional notes on Divine's operations, however. He encouraged his congregation to call him "Father," as Divine's followers called him, and he asked them to call his wife Marceline "Mother," just as Mother

Divine was called by Peace Mission members. He began a housing and feed-ing program—which started in his own home in Indianapolis and spread throughout the membership—just as Father Divine had operated a housing and feeding program. He visited the mission a few years after Divine's death in 1965, but Mother Divine asked him to leave when he attempted to take over the organization. On a return visit, Peoples Temple members recruited and proselytized Peace Mission members who might be interested in joining the Temple. Although they did not gain as many defectors as they'd hoped, they did attract others in Philadelphia and elsewhere in Pennsylvania.

The key to the success of Father Divine's mission was the financial security the movement had by maintaining profitable business ventures. Commerce, and not just an offering plate, subsidized the many charitable endeavors that the Peace Mission offered. Jim Jones might have been taking notes on this model as well, and he began a number of enterprises which supported church activities. Around 1955 a middle-aged white woman, Esther Mueller, moved into the Jones's household. With Marceline's training as a nurse, the assistance of Esther Mueller, and the upgrading of the parsonage to meet state certification standards, the Jones family began to take in elderly nursing home patients. The couple formed the Jim Lu Mar Company and church-run nursing homes expanded, providing income and employment for the Jones family and for church members. When Marceline's parents retired, they moved to Indianapolis and became part of the nursing homes' management team. Known for their cleanliness and their superior care, the homes had excellent reputations in the community.

In 1960 the Temple opened a free restaurant and social service center in the basement of the church. It quickly began serving thousands of meals a month, and served as an outreach agency, providing employment services, clothing, and food. Many of those who came were single men, alcoholics, or unemployed. The Rev. Winberg—now one of the Temple's associate ministers—provided drug and alcohol counseling. Others who came were simply families in need, and they received social services without proselytizing. Volunteers from the Disciples of Christ—which had its headquarters in Indianapolis—worked at the Temple and directed people to appropriate agencies for help.

LEAVING THE HEAT

The meal program and the Temple's other charitable endeavors, as well as the group's affiliation with the Disciples of Christ, brought Jim Jones and his church to the attention of Indianapolis city officials. In January 1961, the mayor of Indianapolis asked Jones to accept an appointment as the director of the Indianapolis Human Rights Commission. Jones used the position as a platform to press for integration in many places: churches, restaurants, movie theaters, and hospitals. In one instance, Jones dispatched Ross Case, a new associate minister formally trained and ordained in the Disciples of Christ, and Russell Winberg to witness a case of racial discrimination reported by a black patron of a lunch counter. After the two observed a waitress refusing to serve the black man, they reported the incident to the police. The restaurant manager relented and began to serve blacks, as did other Indianapolis eateries.

Jones himself was involved in another step toward integration. An ulcer and other health problems sent him to Methodist Hospital in October 1961. Because his physician was African American, Jones was placed in the "colored" ward. When the nurse realized her mistake, she offered to move the patient, but Jones insisted then and there that the hospital be integrated. The Temple's integrationist stance led to a number of attacks. A woman spit upon Marceline as she was carrying their adopted son Jim Junior. Jones received hate mail, and swastikas were painted on the parsonage and the church door.

The harassment took its toll on Jones, and led to a breakdown and hospitalization. When his doctor recommended a two-month leave of absence, Jones visited Guyana. This was not his first foray into the Caribbean. He and Marceline had traveled to Cuba in 1960, shortly after Fidel Castro's revolution, in the hope of recruiting some Afro-Cubans disaffected with the new regime, but left without success. Jones returned from the 1961 trip to Guyana more critical than ever of churches in the United State. He remained in his post as human rights director for only a few days before he resigned in December.

Jones and his family then left Indianapolis for Hawaii, and soon began a two-year sojourn in Brazil, putting the fate of the church in the hands of his associate pastors: Russell Winberg, Ross Case, Jack Beam, and Archie Ijames. Jones had had a vision of a nuclear holocaust in October 1961, and had discussed the possible relocation of the Temple with his associates in light of the potential disaster. An article in the January 1962 *Esquire* magazine listed the nine safest places to be in case of an attack: one of the places was Belo Horizonte, Brazil. Jones took his family there, and then to Rio de Janeiro, embarking on a mission program which introduced him to the poorest of the poor in the world.

Shortly after his arrival in Belo Horizonte, Jones met the Rev. Edward Malmin, an ordained Pentecostal minister who had been a missionary in Brazil with his family for more than three years. The Malmins mentored the Jones family, and their sixteen-year-old daughter Bonnie lived for a time with the Joneses. Writing under her married name, Bonnie Thielmann later described their modest lifestyle:

It was a simple home, without rugs on the floor...There were no bedspreads; each bed had only a pair of sheets and a single blanket. The only income came from the church back in Indianapolis; as a result our usual diet was bread and rice, sometimes with beans or another vegetable. Meat was the exception.[11]

Marceline cooked rice in a large five-quart pot in order to feed an extra ten to fifteen street children who lined up at their doorway each night. But Thielmann noticed an absence of prayer in the household, and wrote that she became the official "pray-er" for the family.

Jack and Rheaviana Beam joined the Joneses in October 1962, during the Cuban missile crisis when the world was on edge about an American attack on the Soviet Union. They worked in local orphanages alongside Jones. But after the Beams returned to the United State in the spring of 1963, the Jones family relocated to Rio de Janeiro, where they moved into a rather posh apartment. Jones taught English parttime, and worked with the poor who lived in the favellas in the cliffs behind the city. According to Thielmann, he also dabbled in Afro-Brazilian religions, drawn to their spiritism and interested in developing his own occult powers.

BACK IN THE U.S.A.

Things at the church in Indianapolis were falling apart in Jones's absence. Finances were shaky and the church was in debt, although the care homes and church property remained in the hands of the Baldwins and Lynetta Jones. The Winbergs, who led the congregation in Jones's absence, had alienated the social activists. Jones asked Ed Malmin to take over, and after thinking about it, the minister agreed to go to Indiana. This caused further divisions in the church, and the Winbergs left, taking about two dozen members of the congregation with them. Ross Case and his family departed for California. Even though they had only recently returned from Brazil, the Beams moved to California to scout a location for a possible move there. Although Malmin restored financial stability, his old-time gospel message further distanced longtime activists, especially Archie Ijames. The Jones family left Rio for Indianapolis at the end of 1963 to rescue the Temple from impending collapse.

Despite Jones's return, the Temple in Indianapolis never regained the glory it had seen before his departure. In 1964 he moved the reduced congregation to the Broadway Christian Center, at 17th and Broadway, the same year he received his ordination by the Disciples of Christ. There were a number of reasons the church failed to thrive upon Jones' return. He had left Indianapolis exhausted, worn-out by the challenges he faced as Human Rights Director. He returned having missed a tumultuous time in American history, which included the assassination of President John F. Kennedy and the turn of the civil rights movement from nonviolent protests to civil rebellions in the cities. He remained convinced that nuclear war was on the horizon, and that an attack on Chicago would destroy Indianapolis as well. Jones was now out of touch with American politics, and others failed to see the threat of thermonuclear destruction as clearly as he did.

FROM PASTOR TO PROPHET

Although Jones's theological beliefs also appeared to have changed while he was in Brazil, it is more likely that they had slowly evolved over several decades. The approbation of his mother Lynetta undoubtedly contributed to a sense of self-importance when he was a child. His contact with Father Divine throughout the 1950s introduced him to notions of his own divinity. His study of Afro-Brazilian religions reinforced his interest in psychic phenomena and the occult, which he had used as a Pentecostal preacher and healer to discern members' problems and to foretell the future. He began his abandonment of the Bible and Christian dogma, although he retained the message of the social gospel. In some Christian broadcasts, he made on WIBC radio in 1965, he even criticized the Bible and praised Mahatma Gandhi, which led to his expulsion from the airwaves.

His gradual desertion of biblical principles corresponded to his embrace of Communist, or rather communalist, ideals. He claimed to have been a Communist from an early age, and that he worked for the Communist Party, U.S.A. (CPUSA) during the McCarthy era.[12] His will, dated October 1977, left everything to CPUSA. He said that in high school he had admired Josef Stalin, though he explained that it was the bravery of the Soviet people under Stalin's leadership in World War II that he actually appreciated. He said that he wept when Julius and Ethel Rosenberg, who were convicted of passing classified information to the Soviet Union, were executed in 1953. Jones also said that his Christianity was a ruse by which he was able to spread the message of Communism. Yet some of his claims seem to be a revision of his own past, a rewriting of history in order to make himself appear more radical than he had been. What does seem clear is that Jones's commitment to communalism—that is, the pooling of resources for the common good and the distribution of those resources as needed—was growing, and that a refuge, away from the possibility of nuclear disaster and the reality of racial discrimination, was needed.

All of these factors combined with a new confidence in his own powers and persona. The deification of the beloved pastor as a second incarnation of God seemed to have occurred after Jones' return from his two years in Brazil, and coincided with his vision of a nuclear holocaust. A move to California would require members of Peoples Temple to accept Jim Jones not just as pastor, but also as prophet. A letter from Harold Cordell to Ross Case dated 18 February 1965 asserted that, although the Bible contained fabrications, God was speaking through Jim Jones today. "He is a prophet of the first degree whose prophecies always come true to the minute detail."[13] Cordell added, "James Jones is certainly a deliverer and the same Anointed Spirit or Christ spirit that we know resided in Jesus. . . . [He is] one of the greatest prophets and messengers that have [sic] ever appeared on this earth."

Ross Case's "Dear James" letter of 3 March 1965 indicated the shift that had occurred in the leadership of the Temple, and his own discomfort with that change.

> When Archie [Ijames] was here, I discussed with him Harold Cordell's letter. Archie said, "Brother Case, in the past we have believed in respecting each others' differences of opinion. We can't do that anymore. If we have these differences we are bound to speak them. For myself, I have come to the position that I must submit my mind completely to the mind of Jimmy." . . . After I had reaffirmed my faith in Jesus Christ, Archie also said (again no exact quotes), "Brother Case, you know why we're having this talk, don't you?" I replied in some indirect manner as "No, what do you have in mind?" He stated, "We would not want you to work with us with your beliefs, and I'm sure you would not want to work with us with our beliefs."[14]

Case's handwritten draft stated that he would "submit my mind to Jesus, but to no mere mortal." He expressed a willingness to work with Jones on human service projects, "as a friend," but that "I will not work on a religious basis under any circumstances where I cannot work in the name of Jesus for his glory." Not only did Case's letter mark the end of his relationship with Peoples Temple, it also marked the shift that had occurred in people's attitudes towards Jim Jones. No longer was he a mere mortal. In California, he would begin as a prophet, God's newly-anointed one.

For Further Reading

Hyacinth Thrash gives an account of joining the Temple in Indianapolis in *The Onliest One Alive*, while Bonnie Thielmann describes Jones' life in Brazil in *The Broken God*. CDs released by the FBI under the Freedom of Information Act (FOIA) include a wealth of information. The FBI's FOIA release contains ten items, identified as "HH-6 History of JJ." Other biographical information comes from Marceline and Lynetta Jones, in "BB-18 Marcelline [sic] Jones." Lynetta Jones' remembrances are on FBI Audiotape Q 762, and Jim Jones gives his own account on Q 134. Tim Reiterman and John Jacobs, in *Raven*, and John R. Hall, in *Gone from the Promised Land*, provide extensive biographical material on Jones, and describe the rise of Peoples Temple in Indianapolis. *Dear People*, edited by Denice Stephenson, also sheds light on the Indianapolis years.

CHAPTER 2

California Dreamin'

We shared a passionate idealism to make the world a better place.
—Tim Carter, *The Big Grey**

"The ideas float like ghosts," wrote Shiva Naipaul about San Francisco and California in the 1970s. "So do the men and the women who cling to the ideas. A swirling vapor of assorted 'idealisms'—ecology, feminism, heightened consciousness—clouds the brain. The gurus wait with open arms."[1] Naipaul—novelist, social critic, and younger brother of V. S. Naipaul—attributed the rise of Peoples Temple to a decadent California culture that was already "shop-soiled, eaten up with inner decay." Naipaul's extremely bitter view took particular aim at 1960s Flower Power and San Francisco radical chic. "Jim Jones built his movement on the debris of the sixties; on its frustrations, failures and apostasies."

Yet ascribing the expansion of Peoples Temple and the deaths in Jonestown to what Archie Smith Jr. called the "Only in California" explanation misses some key points about both California and Peoples Temple. "The idea behind the 'Only in California' thesis," he wrote:

> is the notion that California represents individualistic hedonism, a retreat from reality, a playground, or perhaps it is the insane ward; that out west a peculiar ethos of normlessness has emerged which puts certain groups and kinds of folk at high risk for all kinds of exploitative adventures.[2]

Smith argued that it would be a mistake to claim that Peoples Temple could have emerged *only* from California culture.

Yet another analysis of the Temple's success in California, by Duchess Harris and Adam John Waterman, focused on the group's shift "from the margin to the center of the struggle for racial justice in the U.S., just as in 1965 when the most visible sites of struggle moved from the rural South to the urban North."[3] If Indianapolis represented the conservative heartland, then California signified the progressive frontier. This account suggested that Jim Jones was a political visionary who wanted the Temple to adopt a more radical stance than it had in Indianapolis, and perhaps even to become a player upon the world stage, like the Black Panther Party in Oakland, California. If this were indeed the case, however, the group should have gone directly to San Francisco. Instead, it moved to an isolated and rural part of northern California—Ukiah and Redwood Valley—about 110 miles north of San Francisco.

Three factors are critical for understanding the migration from the Indiana heartland to the California frontier. First was Jones's vision of a nuclear holocaust, a revelation that felt so real to him that he moved his family to Brazil for two years before returning to Indiana to take his flock to California. Second was the dramatic shift in Jones's self-understanding—from pastor to prophet—that occurred. While we cannot determine whether this new identity was real or calculated, we nevertheless can observe a decisive alteration in Jones's rhetoric about himself and about Christianity. The third factor was the tightening of Jones's grip on the movement. Content to leave Peoples Temple in the hands of others while he was out of the country, Jones never again relinquished control, either of the organization or of its individuals. The migration strengthened members' dependence upon their leader, and the movement thus began to focus more on Jim Jones and less on Jesus Christ.

REDWOOD VALLEY

Several Temple members had scouted possibilities in California in the early 1960s while the Jones family was in Brazil. Ross Case had moved to Ukiah. Jack and Rheaviana Beam had moved to Hayward. In 1965 the Jones family and about eighty-five members moved from Indianapolis to Ukiah and nearby Redwood Valley. Work was hard to get, and the early settlers did whatever they could find, which included picking fruit and working at the local Masonite factory, while Jim Jones held teaching jobs at some area high schools.

The absence of people of color in rural northern California also made life difficult for the multiracial movement. Stephan Jones described the shock of the move:

We lived in Indianapolis in a poor area, in a black area, so I went to school with black children. But there was nobody black in Redwood

Valley's school. It was unbelievable. They acted like they had never seen a black person before. They acted like they were inhuman . . . We were all unacceptable. My brothers and sister were unacceptable because of their color and I was unacceptable because I accepted them.[4]

Racial incidents occurred frequently, and the children of Peoples Temple hung out together for protection and self-affirmation.

Outside threats as well as the need for survival led to a more intentional and successful form of cooperative life in Redwood Valley. In addition, the Temple's association with Christ's Church of the Golden Rule—a communal religious group with several ranches and businesses located in nearby Willits—shaped its collective outlook. One Peoples Temple member, Carol Stahl, had grown up in CCGR.

When I met Jim Jones in 1965, he and few people came to visit one of our meetings at Ridgewood Ranch, where we shared a few ideas. The Golden Rule had a large property, about 16,000 acres that would have been very well put to use . . . Jim had tried to worship with various churches in the Ukiah-Redwood Valley area and he had been turned down by all of them because of the fact that they were an integrated church.[5]

The CCGR elders agreed to worship together with members of Peoples Temple. This worked for about three years, and the two groups even discussed a merger. Things came to a head with Stahl's engagement to a Temple member, however, and she was forced to choose between the CCGR and the Temple: she could not maintain membership in both churches. At that point, Jim Jones and Temple members staged a walkout, went back long enough to remove their organ from the church, and never returned.

After the separation, Temple members met in Jones's garage and then outside the home of other members while a church building was erected in Redwood Valley, according to Rheaviana Beam. "February 2, 1969 we moved into the current Peoples Temple for the first meeting," by which she meant the large church in Redwood Valley.[6] Within a few years, the Temple established its own print shop, laundry, group homes, and agricultural projects, both farming and ranching. These efforts were aimed at developing a self-sufficient, collective economy by which the Temple and its members could become independent and self-contained.

Hyacinth Thrash and her sister Zipporah, for example, purchased a care home from retirees who had taken in patients evicted from Mendocino State Hospital when Governor Ronald Reagan shut down California's mental hospitals. "We bought a lovely four-bedroom ranch house on one and a quarter acres of land and took in four lovely ladies as 'care' patients," Thrash wrote.

I was just crazy 'bout our home . . . We loved it in the Valley. We had
our own grape arbor by the house. And pears! Zip and I put up 150
quarts of pear stuff . . . And we canned peaches, pretty as a picture. We
even made zucchini pickles.[7]

Did the Temple's communal orientation reflect a deliberate theological
position, or did it simply indicate Jim Jones's growing efforts to isolate
the group from the larger world? The former seems more likely, given the
eventual expansion to San Francisco and Los Angeles. Jones's message was
growing more revolutionary even in Redwood Valley, where he preached
that "all separation comes from class." If money were equalized, there would
be no rich, no poor, no racism, and no religion. Paraphrasing the Bible,
he said that love of money is the root of all evil, but then added, "That's
called capitalism."[8] The Temple had well-established Christian precedent for
"going communal," as they called it. Even in Indianapolis, Jones had pointed
to the example of the early church, noting its communalism as described in
Acts 2:44–45 and 4:34–35. With biblical precedent and political analysis
behind it, the church moved toward a collective economy.

One of the first steps was to help members and nonmembers alike navigate the social welfare system. This not only fulfilled the group's charitable
mission but also helped its missionary goals by adding new members to
the rolls. Several social workers in the Mendocino County welfare office
who joined the Temple—including Garrett Lambrev, Jim Randolph, Sharon
Amos, Barbara Hoyer, and Laurie Efrein—helped make this possible. Still
other Temple members were eligibility workers who processed applications.
All of those who worked at the welfare department made themselves available to explain forms and requirements and to organize and collect medical
or financial information as needed. This ability to steer people through the
social welfare system—to receive the services they needed and to which they
were entitled—became the hallmark of Temple service activities throughout
its years in California.

Young college-educated whites from California joined the working-class
members who had migrated from Indianapolis. They saw in Peoples Temple what they believed was the realization of their political aspirations and
responded to the appeal of Peoples Temple and the turbulent times from
which it emerged: the civil rights movement, antiwar protests, and anticolo-
nial struggles of the 1960s and 1970s. Garrett Lambrev captured some of
this when he wrote:

[What] an extraordinary Aquarian family we comprised, a microcosm
in many ways of these United States, at least in the 1970s, a source
of potentially transformative power by virtue or vice of our collective
commitment to the vision of a radically changed, once again revolutionary America, whose egalitarian model many of us—and not just

white middle-class intellectuals like myself—thought we could provide
to a world in need of salvation from multinational corporate greed.[9]

The whites who joined the Temple in Redwood Valley became some of the
most important leaders of the organization: Tim Stoen, an assistant district
attorney for Mendocino County; Grace Stoen, his wife, who became head
counselor in the Temple; Michael Prokes, a news reporter from Stockton
who joined the Temple after he investigated it for a story; Elmer and Deanna
Mertle; Maria Katsaris, a leader in Jonestown; and my sisters, Carolyn Layton, a high school teacher, and Annie Moore, who became a registered nurse;
and many more. Some of these same people—Tim and Grace Stoen and the
Mertles (who changed their names to Al and Jeannie Mills)—defected and
were instrumental in the oppositional group, the Concerned Relatives.

EXPANDING TO THE URBAN CORE

Even while the church was establishing itself in Redwood Valley in the
1960s, Jones was also actively proselytizing up and down the West Coast.
Bus trips regularly took members to participate in services led by Jones as
far north as Seattle, and as far south as Los Angeles, where the Temple
purchased a former Christian Science church building at the corner of Al-
varado and Hoover streets, and opened it in 1972. Assistant pastors based
in Los Angeles met day-to-day needs, while the group from Redwood Valley
made the eight-hour trip for services in Los Angeles every other weekend on
Temple-owned buses.

The primary mission target, however, was San Francisco. As early as
1970, the church rented space for Sunday services at Benjamin Franklin
Junior High School on Geary and Scott Streets. In 1972 it purchased a
building at 1859 Geary and started holding services there. Four years later
the Temple moved its headquarters from Redwood Valley to San Francisco.

Outwardly the church in San Francisco still appeared to be a church in
the Pentecostal tradition. Flyers distributed in the predominantly African
American Fillmore District of San Francisco emphasized healings and miracles, and accounts of resuscitations filled the leaflets: one even claimed that
no deaths had occurred among the Temple's members. The mimeographed
publications also emphasized the Christian Social Gospel, that is, the justification for social action based upon the life and teachings of Jesus. One
declared that "if a person doesn't believe in racial justice or total equality,
he shouldn't attend our services." Another said that "thousands have been
moved by Pastor Jones' message of Apostolic Equality," while yet another
asked people to send money for social services rather than for healings. In
addition to the special revelations given at meetings, the services were described as "an opportunity to learn of the beautiful concepts of apostolic
social justice."[10]

It is clear that social justice became an important and perhaps central element of Peoples Temple's theology. In a "Message from the Prophet" titled "Who Are the Real Radicals," Jim Jones argued that the real radical was not someone who engaged in violence for social justice. "No, the real radical is one who is engaged in a determined struggle to break out of the vicious cycle of violence that is a part of our everyday life... A Christian radical attempts to transform society not by hate, animosity and fear... but by a positive activism, protest and dissent and non-violent participation in the electoral process."[11]

The promotional materials departed from traditional Christianity, however, when they depicted Jim Jones as a prophet and more. "Please read every word for this letter contains many vital messages and prophecies, warnings, and a special message from this unique God-sent prophet, Jim Jones." One mimeographed sheet went even further: "This Divine Compassion gives precise revelations that no man could possibly know, often of events that took place many years in the past or that are currently taking place many miles from the meeting."

The flyers also showed how Jones was reinterpreting scripture. One of the Prophet's "Messages" clarified some of deeper biblical truths by saying that Jesus' sacrificial death proved his heroism, "but no more does away with man's sin than a school boy volunteering to be flogged for another would eliminate the negligence or irresponsibility of the other student." The Message went on to analyze Isaiah 7:14, which states that a virgin shall conceive, and what that prophecy would have meant historically to the Israelites. Another leaflet invited those who would like back issues of "Jim Jones' outstanding sermons on reincarnation, power of positive thinking, and errors in the King James of England's translation," to just write.

Jones had begun to point out the inconsistencies in the Bible as early as 1963, but it was probably in San Francisco that he published a twenty-four-page booklet, titled "The Letter Killeth," in order to denigrate the Bible's legitimacy by exposing its errors and inconsistencies. Paradoxically, the booklet also provided the biblical basis for the Peoples Temple ministry and justified Jones's position as an anointed prophet.[12] "God and Jesus are as reincarnatable as a child's smile," Jones wrote, "God never appears the same way twice." Although the booklet began with a brief listing of the "great truths of the Bible," the bulk of the copy was devoted to deriding "errors." For example, God says you must not kill (Exodus 20:13), then commands the Israelites to kill (Exodus 32:27). Jesus dies at the third hour in one gospel (Mark 15:25), and at the sixth hour in another (John 19:14-15). One section of the booklet was devoted to the biblical defense of slavery, and others to "absurdities," "atrocities," and "indecencies" in the Bible. Jones had abandoned his biblical beliefs, although not his use of biblical language, even if the majority of his followers had not.

PRACTICING THE SOCIAL GOSPEL

From 1972 to 1975 members continued to commute between services in Redwood Valley, San Francisco, and Los Angeles. The Southern California church had its own team of ministers and active church leaders. Redwood Valley continued to serve as the home office. But members began moving to San Francisco, and many of the Redwood Valley transplants lived communally in the city. Carlton Goodlett, publisher of the *Sun-Reporter*, the Bay Area's African American newspaper, said that Jones was following Father Divine's example of encouraging communal living. Church records show that at least 500 members were living in communal apartments, including units within the Geary Street facility.[13] It is clear that the group focused on human service ministries rather than social justice or political action at this time. "Peoples Temple mainly addressed issues of drug rehabilitation, medical care, child care, and feeding the hungry, all of which bolstered its standing as an organization committed to meeting the immediate needs of an impoverished community in what the Temple termed 'the ghetto,'" according to Tanya Hollis.[14]

Numerous files housed at the California Historical Society attest to the Temple's concrete help to people in need. Letters to Pastor Jim made requests for money or legal assistance, sought help in fighting evictions and support for gaining welfare benefits.[15] More than one document was a letter from Temple lawyers—to a probation officer, a warden, or family member whose relatives were in prison. One note indicated a welcome-home group gathered to greet a member being released from prison. A Temple member in Los Angeles sent a news clipping to Jones with a note attached: "Enclosed is the story of a woman who needs your help. It seems to me justice should be done." The story described a mentally ill woman in poor health who faced further incarceration; Temple lawyer Eugene Chaikin followed up with a letter to the woman. Another item listed the people who agreed to attend the trial of a member's son, with a notation of those who actually went and an account of the reasons some people failed to show up. The Temple organized massive letter-writing campaigns to judges prior to court appearances scheduled for members and relatives in order to gain sympathetic hearings.

The congregations in both San Francisco and in Los Angeles were dominated by a large African American presence. Eighty to ninety percent of the members of Peoples Temple in California were African American. Part of this demographic profile undoubtedly stemmed from the Temple's social service commitment and its concrete activities to help the poor. But this does not tell the whole story. Mary Maaga gave an indication of how the Temple drew in African Americans:

> Individuals would be attracted to the Pentecostal-style healing services,
> or interracial congregation and social activism, or social services and

supportive community. Individuals would then invite family members and close friends to participate in this wonderful church they had found. Even the most negative accounts of Peoples Temple generally start with an account of the excitement at having discovered such a lively, committed and caring congregation.[16]

Archie Smith Jr. provided an anecdote that a black pastor related to him about a member who had joined Peoples Temple, where she found "a family-like atmosphere, a sense of belonging on a daily basis in ways that she could not find in her own church."[17] In fact, black ministers in the Bay Area felt the effects of Jones' "sheep-stealing," as their members drifted to a church that promoted this-worldly salvation. J. Alfred Smith noted the problems inherent in an upwardlymobile African American church establishment that had little outreach to the underclass:

> They had no ministries to address the needs of the hurting people who made the sidewalks of San Francisco their beds and used yesterday's newspapers as blankets. Their followers did not want to be bothered with the huge numbers of disenfranchised and disaffected people around them.[18]

The miraculous and wondrous also appealed to people. Bea Alethia Orsot recalled "that electrifying moment" when she saw Jim Jones for the first time:

> He called me out from the audience of hundreds: "Bea Orsot from Savannah, Georgia, come up to the podium." When I did, I noticed he had tears in his eyes as he looked down upon me with the words, "You've suffered long enough, my child." When he told me the contents of a note I'd written to God 37 years earlier, I knew he wasn't an ordinary man, and that I would be with him forever.[19]

Other African Americans, as well as white liberals, found the clear message of racial equality appealing, and joined by the hundreds. In addition, many mixed-race individuals obtained a level of acceptance not available from either the white or black communities outside the Temple.

A POLITICAL PLAYER

Although Temple members in California had heard militant messages for years, it was not until the 1975 mayoral race between liberal George Moscone and conservative John Barbagelata that the public saw an apparent turn from a progressive church in the Disciples of Christ to an activist political organization. During the planning stages of the Moscone campaign, "someone suggested that [California Assemblyman Willie] Brown line up Peoples Temple volunteers. Soon the Temple was being bandied about as one of the community groups needed to pull together a winning liberal coalition."[20] While Temple members probably provided "no more than a few hundred voters," their volunteer effort to get out the vote apparently succeeded. Moscone won, and San Franciscans believed that Peoples Temple made the difference.

The election seemed to shift the focus from human services to direct political action and involvement. Human needs continued to be met in hundreds of small, but significant, ways that dramatically changed people's lives: what the Black Panther Party called "survival programs," which "contributed to the well-being of poor and working-class racial and ethnic minorities."[21] But the political arena offered a new platform from which Jones and the group could espouse their views. The Temple's success was evident when, during the 1976 presidential campaign, Rosalynn Carter, wife of Democratic Party candidate Jimmy Carter, visited the Temple. Other signs of the group's growing importance included Jones's appointment to the San Francisco Housing Commission, first as a member, then as its chair, in the wake of the Moscone victory; and the January 1977 Martin Luther King Day celebration held at Peoples Temple with a battery of Democratic political heavyweights.

In addition to participating in Democratic Party events, the Temple engaged in more revolutionary politics. The 1976 African Liberation Day celebration at Peoples Temple featured officials from Tanzania and the People's Republic of Angola, and from liberation movements in southern Africa, such as the Zimbabwe African National Union and South Africa's Pan African Congress. Temple members showed up at rallies in support of the Wilmington 10, the Camp Pendleton Four, and other defendants in raciallymotivated prosecutions. A handwritten calendar listed all of the events Temple members planned to attend or support.[22] The causes ranged from protesting the Bakke decision (which ruled that affirmative action is unconstitutional) to circulating petitions to free South Africa's Nelson Mandela. Meetings were held with representatives of the Chilean consulate to protest the repressive regime of Augusto Pinochet. Political fundraisers, a reception for civil rights leader Andrew Young, a meeting for American Indian Solidarity, and more were on the schedule. It is no wonder that Peoples Temple became the church that political activists strongly endorsed and turned to for support in those years.

The pages of *Peoples Forum*, the Temple's newspaper, which started as a four-page newsletter in 1976, charted the ideological shift occurring within the Temple as it moved from rural to urban California, and from religious to political organization. Initial issues carried articles on subjects as diverse as killer bees, Muhammad Ali, freedom of the press, and Jim Jones hosting a TV show. An editorial from an issue in May 1976 asked:

> Are you an activist yourself? Do you believe in the practical approach to resolving human problems? Do you have any spare time or energy? Is there anything you can or would like to do to help out? If you want to put your resources into something that gets results or simply want to become part of a warmly integrated community dedicated to human service, call.[23]

The cover stories in the September 1976 issue described a miracle experienced by Jack Beam—and predicted by Jim Jones—and a description of a high school class experiment on regimentation. The November issue included an ad promoting "spiritual healing," as well as an open letter from Mayor George Moscone.

By the end of 1976, *Peoples Forum* had gone to tabloid size, and page one of the new format featured articles on Chilean torture, California Nazis, the FBI's role in the death of Black Panther Party leader Fred Hampton, the CIA's role in the Kennedy assassination, and operations of the Korean CIA in Los Angeles.[24] A March 1977 issue had a cover photo of Jim Jones shaking hands with Huey Newton, leader of the Panther Party. There was also a page one story on Zimbabwe, Nazis, and the problem of child abuse. It wasn't until page four that church and community notes appeared.

Perhaps the most unusual announcement noted the Temple's cooperation with the Nation of Islam (NoI). An article in the *Bilalian News* from 5 March 1976 reported the church's support for Minister Nathaniel Muhammad— brother of Wallace D. Muhammad, the NoI leader at the time—who was accused of drug trafficking. The next month the Nation of Islam and Peoples Temple held a joint worship service in San Francisco. The Los Angeles Temple was also meeting with the mosque in Southern California, and organized a rally in May with Wallace D. Muhammad. Edith Roller—a white, middle-aged Temple member who kept an extensive diary of life inside the Temple—reported that "everyone to whom I spoke expressed massive boredom with Wallace D.'s speech."[25] While Jones criticized the Nation of Islam inside the Temple, he also understood the significance of the joint meetings.

A NEW CONSCIOUSNESS, A NEW FAMILY

Jim Jones did not just preach a new society; he encouraged and indeed required the Temple congregation to live it. Members set out to recreate themselves by abandoning elitist and bourgeois attitudes, and by restructuring the traditional nuclear family. While most adults stayed in monogamous relationships, children did not necessarily remain with their biological parents. Sibling groups and unrelated children might live in a stable household with nonrelated guardians or adoptive parents. Part of the process of creating a new, more inclusive family consisted of regular public confession meetings called "catharsis." These sessions were designed to create a collective consciousness that put the group before the individual.

As early as the Indianapolis days, the congregation engaged in a "corrective fellowship," in which members were criticized by a group of their peers for not living up to expectations.[26] In Redwood Valley, the congregation held Tuesday night "Deeper Life Catharsis Meetings," in which members engaged in public confrontation, confession, and repentance. Patricia Cartmell, a white transplant from Indianapolis, described catharsis as an experience

> in which each member of the body was encouraged to stand and get off his chest everything that was in any way a hindrance to fellowship between himself and another member or between himself and the group, or the leader even, Jim in his utter honesty not desiring nor seeking immunity from the exposure of his own faults... We are reminded that catharsis is not a new approach to the solution of human problems, there being an old but seldom obeyed biblical injunction, "Confess your faults one to another and pray one for another that ye might be healed."[27]

By the time the group moved to California, the catharsis sessions involved both public confession and criticism of anticommunal behaviors that the group wished to eradicate. Edith Roller's journal revealed that members of all ages were publicly praised for hard work, generosity, and having "good attitudes," but they were also censured for stealing, lying, being rebellious, and having "bad attitudes." Her entry for 21 April 1976 stated:

> Little Ronald Campbell was brought on the floor, even though he had been up all night with a toothbrush—he bit a little girl today. J. assigned him to work again all night. J. had Dave Garrison bite him so that he would know what it feels like.[28]

Miscreants were often assigned to clean out moldy bathroom tile with a toothbrush. Extra work duties, or more volunteer hours, usually comprised consequences, but corporal punishment also occurred. Violence against others warranted physical punishment in the Temple, although taking dope, smoking, or driving without a license also earned it. One young man who had made sexist remarks was sentenced to fight against a girl, who knocked him out, "which exhilarated the feminine portion of the audience," according to Roller.

Public humiliation and punishment sessions served as the means by which Temple leadership attempted to develop a collective consciousness. They also functioned as the means by which leaders could control members. Other controlling mechanisms included confessing to outrageous crimes—such as assassinating President Kennedy and his brother Robert, being a violent revolutionary, and disclosing that they were pedophiles—or admitting to assorted misdemeanors. "Dad, I steal quarters from Mom and Lew," confessed "Your son, Jimmy Jones." "I, K—— B——, was a member of the S.L.A. [Symbionese Liberation Army] and helped them with their bank robberies, kidnapping, and murders," said one note. Another confession note admitted to raping a little girl, cutting her up, and burying her in the woods.[29]

Temple leaders and members also used positive methods, however, to foster a new sense of family. First, they completely integrated senior citizens into the life of the organization. Seniors continued to play important roles—from letter writers to greeters to bake-sale producers—and were publicly praised and commended. Temple medical staff provided regular health exams that included blood pressure checks for seniors at every worship service and periodic sickle-cell anemia tests for African Americans, members and nonmembers alike. Communal living apartments, as well as state-licensed senior care homes, not only provided a source of income for the Temple and room and board for senior citizens but also offered a meaningful intergenerational experience for society's elders.

Similarly, foster care and guardianships supplied income to Temple members, room and board for the children, and meaningful and productive opportunities for society's throwaway kids. Many of these arrangements were made between relatives, with aunts and grandmothers caring for related children. The Temple celebrated Christmas and birthdays with equality of expectations and gifts being the rule. Adoptions were encouraged and families were enlarged, all of which were supported by the church in various ways.

Communal and group homes also generated a collective consciousness among young adults and other members who had to share living quarters, bathrooms, and housekeeping chores. Few Temple members in San Francisco lived on their own in individual apartments. One might see the communal arrangements as yet another type of restriction, a way to keep tabs on people. Temple members saw them differently, however, viewing their cooperative activities as the first step toward transforming self-centered, destructive, capitalist individuals into other-centered, constructive family members.

A final way an expanded sense of family was produced came when members "went communal," which meant they either turned over their paychecks to Peoples Temple and were given room, board, and a small allowance for personal needs, or when they worked full time for the Temple itself, serving as lawyers, medical assistants, or administrative staff. In all of these ways, the Temple became a way of life in which a new consciousness of "others first" was encouraged, and even demanded, of those who made the commitment.

BEHIND CLOSED DOORS

The public face of the Temple—compassionate, concerned, active—contrasted markedly with what occurred behind closed doors. A system of rewards and punishments kept people in a state of tension and confusion. Catharsis sessions focused on sexuality and created a sense of guilt about love and desire. Declarations about sex, and sexual acts, served as mechanisms to control members' feelings about each other and about Jim Jones. Members affirmed that they practiced sodomy and engaged in oral sex, that they were molested as children or that they had molested their own children, and that they were homosexual. David Wise, a Temple survivor, argued that Jones's lewd conduct arrest in Los Angeles in 1973—he exposed himself in a public restroom to an undercover police officer—prompted an emphasis on homosexuality.

> He was forced to find outlets for his sexuality within the church to avoid being destroyed from without. He used the preposterous notion that he had to "relate" to other men's homosexuality, to reach them on their level, or he would propose to introduce men to their inner homosexuality. Although Jim was the one who was actually guilty, the arrest led him to spread a new ideology: that all men were latently homosexual except for him.[30]

Male Temple members would admit to having sex with Jones whether they had or not, in order to protect Jones, according to Wise. While the focus on homosexuality may have increased after Jones's arrest, some documents show that his obsession existed well before this.

Eventually, everyone admitted to being homosexual. Scores of handwritten notes recovered in Jonestown after the deaths revealed members confessing homosexual and bisexual feelings, and listed the names of both women and men to whom they were attracted. In one catharsis session in San Francisco, Roller noted that Jones accused his teenage son Lew of being attracted to another boy. "Attention was shifted to all males in the congregation and an effort made to convince them that all are homosexual," she wrote. Lew then admitted to having homosexual feelings.[31] In *A Lavender Look at Peoples Temple*, Michael Bellefountaine analyzed Temple attitudes toward gays and lesbians and found many contradictions. He discovered a rhetoric of disgust and condemnation, and yet a reality—as reported by survivors—that accepted and encouraged different orientations.[32]

Sex was an important way Jim Jones controlled individuals. He arranged marriages between couples, some of which encouraged procreation—especially among African American or mixed-race couples—and others that encouraged celibacy. Above all, Jones made himself the principal object of members' sexual desire, encouraging them to confess to their physical need for him. "He was a power-seeker and used sex as his way to gain additional power over a person—in a very personal way," observed Laura Johnston Kohl, another survivor. "He didn't discriminate. He didn't want ANY young vibrant person infatuated or involved with anyone but him."[33] His circle of female secretaries was intimate in all senses of the word. He openly conducted these relationships while remaining married to Marceline, and admitted that he fathered two sons through these affairs: John Victor Stoen and Jim-Jon (Kimo) Prokes. He also forced women he impregnated to get abortions. Jones's management of relationships was not about sex, but about power, and he used this power to control all aspects of life inside the Temple.

THE SOCIAL PYRAMID

In return for long hours and grueling schedules, Temple members believed they had found an alternative to a racist society full of class distinctions and discrimination. Nevertheless, class distinctions continued to exist in the movement, and top leadership positions revolved around Jones. Peoples Temple had a hierarchical structure by which power and knowledge were managed. The situation for members in the Los Angeles Temple and the ranches and care homes in Redwood Valley differed from that in San Francisco. Members experienced Peoples Temple in a variety of ways, depending on where they lived and where they were located on a social pyramid. At the top of the pyramid, at highest levels of power, many members found themselves in a nightmare. But most members did not experience the Temple in this way.

The broadest level—the base of the pyramid—encompassed those who attended church services on Sundays. Those who went to services or other events saw one aspect of the movement: a large interracial progressive Christian group that was engaged and socially active. While this group might hear Jones criticize the Bible, claim to be divine, or challenge other churches to get involved, they did not see the Temple in its entirety. This is why many politicians and public figures could claim to know so little about what was really going on: access and information were granted only on the appropriate and authorized levels. Moreover, as fears about repression and enemies grew, entrée even to the Temple's public arena was not always unconditional. Temple greeters at all services and in all locations would scrutinize strangers and decide whether to grant admittance.

Catharsis and self-criticism meetings occurred at the next level on the pyramid. These sessions were reserved for members who had "gone communal"; who were engaged in Temple businesses (such as care homes or foster care); who regularly participated in rallies, meetings, and letter-writing campaigns; or whose commitment went beyond Sunday morning worship. Members would write their concerns and give them to Jones, or they might inform on someone in the meeting. Catharsis generally occurred at least one evening a week in all three locations.

A Planning Commission (PC) served as the forum for discussing major decisions, with Jim Jones retaining ultimate authority. It superseded "The Board (of Elders)" Jones had in Redwood Valley, a loose advisory group of his closest associates, all of whom were men. (The expression of "elders" was quickly dropped.[34]) The PC grew from about 37 members in 1973 to about 100 members by 1977. The majority of people in positions of leadership—financial officers, counselors, public relations—were white. According to Mary Maaga, "It was almost impossible for black persons to make their way into positions of influence in the Temple."[35] While the PC comprised professionals, personal secretaries, and the most dedicated workers, it also included those whom Jones distrusted so that he could keep an eye on them. Working with Jones, the PC made decisions on who might become part of Temple staff, and who could advance through the ranks. It was clear that young, white women advanced faster than anyone else.

Several inner circles existed within the Planning Commission. They included people who participated in fake healings, arranged questionable property transfers, knew about dirty tricks (like going through people's garbage for information and making harassing phone calls to critics), and managed a complicated financial network. In Jonestown a small circle knew about the poison. Membership in these overlapping circles did not guarantee complete knowledge of the internal workings of the organization, but rather only of one small part. One woman was apparently the secretary in charge of arranging Jim Jones's liaisons, according to some survivors. At the pinnacle of the pyramid was the most intimate and most powerful inner circle, comprising several women, among them my sister Carolyn Layton, Jones's wife Marceline, and a few men. The seven members of the Board of Directors of the Peoples Temple of the Disciples of Christ—incorporated in California in 1965 with just the Joneses and Archie Ijames—consisted of Jim and Marceline Jones, Archie Ijames, Carolyn Layton, Linda (Sharon) Amos, Tim Stoen, and Mike Cartmell in 1973. This small group knew the most about the entire operation, at least in California.

DEFECTIONS

Many people came and went in Peoples Temple over the years. At one point in its history, the Temple boasted a membership of 20,000, though this inflated figure undoubtedly reflected the number of people who simply walked through the doors, rather than those who actually became members. A better barometer of membership—those who had identification cards— puts the number closer to 5,000. Those who left the Temple were called defectors, and the language of defection reveals the attitude that existed in the Temple: one didn't quit or leave, one defected, that is, one went to the other side. Scholars identify those who leave new religions and become visible opponents, dedicated to revealing the flaws and dangers in the group they once embraced, as "apostates." While very few Temple defectors became apostates, those who did had a profound impact on the group.

The first major defection came from a group of college students, who became known as the "Gang of Eight." The racial makeup of the Planning Commission and various inner circles, coupled with the emphasis on sex, led the Gang of Eight to take collective action by writing a letter to Jim Jones and then leaving as a group in 1973. Their very important letter began by exculpating Jones, and then went on to blame Temple staff for the lack of a sufficiently revolutionary attitude.

You said the revolutionary focal point at present is in the black people. There is no potential in the white population, according to you. Yet, where is the black leadership, where is the black staff and black attitude?[36]

The group pointed out that whites advanced more rapidly in the Peoples Temple organization than did blacks. Most importantly, "for the past 6 years all staff have concerned themselves with have been the castrating of people, calling them homosexual, sex, sex, sex. What about Socialism?" The letter asserted that the charge of male chauvinism, while important, was overemphasized. Grace Stoen, who left the church three years later, confirmed this charge. Men were routinely "put down and cut down," and women were praised as stronger, "both physically and emotionally."[37] The letter from the Gang of Eight concluded: "We want it known by you and staff that we don't believe in religion, we don't believe in God, we don't believe in reincarnation, we don't believe in impossible [sic]. We are not concerned with the beginning, the end, or the hereafter. We are only concerned about today."

This first major defection created grave concern within the group about its security and safety. The Gang of Eight seemed poised to commit violent acts that neither Temple leaders nor members condoned. According to Jeannie Mills, a member who herself left the Temple two years later, Jim Jones broached the possibility of suicide—or "translation" as he had called it in the past—for the Planning Commission the day after the eight defectors departed, but no one was very eager.[38] The group discussed contingency plans, escape routes, and other options, including making a move to the

Caribbean island of Grenada. On 8 October 1973, the board of directors of Peoples Temple adopted a resolution to establish a mission in Guyana.

The Gang of Eight had abandoned the movement for political reasons: the Temple was insufficiently revolutionary. Other defectors said that they had been physically abused, theologically misled, financially defrauded, or all three. As early as 1972, reports of cruelty surfaced. Lester Kinsolving, an ordained Episcopal priest and a religion reporter for the *San Francisco Examiner*, wrote a series of articles that foreshadowed a number of themes that would re-emerge in 1977. The first four articles ridiculed Jones's claims of divinity and his ability to raise the dead, criticized questionable financial dealings, and disapproved of the involvement of Mendocino County employees and public officials in Temple affairs. Temple members mobilized to write letters to the editor of the *Examiner* and picketed the newspaper's offices in protest. It is possible, but unlikely, that Temple pressure persuaded the *Examiner* to drop the final four articles slated for the series. Kinsolving's unpublished articles alleged that Temple members were responsible for the death of a member, that Jones defamed an African American pastor by alleging he had propositioned two young girls, and that the Temple had armed guards in Redwood Valley.[39] Kinsolving also reported that members were punished in group meetings for crimes and misdemeanors, noting the example of a young boy being forced to eat his own vomit.

Several high-profile members who defected from the Temple between 1973 and 1977 became apostates, including Al and Jeannie Mills in 1975, Grace Stoen in 1976, and her husband Tim in 1977. The Stoens in particular troubled the leadership because they filed a custody suit to recover John Victor Stoen from Temple guardianship (see Chapter Four for details). The apostates became known to the San Francisco community in 1977 when *New West* magazine published two extremely critical articles about Jim Jones and Peoples Temple. Written by Marshall Kilduff, a *San Francisco Chronicle* reporter, and Phil Tracy, a reporter for *New West*, the articles described catharsis sessions in which severe beatings had occurred, revealed that miraculous healings of some people were faked—with "cancers" turning out to be chicken parts—and documented property transfers and financial dealings that seemed questionable to the public. The *New West* articles prompted other apostates as well as family members concerned about their relatives in Peoples Temple to talk to the media. Throughout 1977 and 1978 stories circulated about several suspicious deaths, with news accounts questioning the ways in which Maxine Harpe, Robert Houston, John Head, and Chris Lewis had died. (Police and coroner investigations confirmed that Harpe and Head had committed suicide. Chris Lewis was murdered in San Francisco in what looked like a revenge-style execution, according to the police. Bob Houston, who suffered from narcolepsy, died in an accident at the Southern Pacific train yards where he worked. None of those who died played significant roles in Temple life, nor had they become apostates.) No Peoples Temple member was ever charged, indicted, or convicted of murder or any other crime in connection with these deaths or other accusations made in the press. Nevertheless, suspicion about the Temple and its practices remained high among critics.

As with its earlier attempt to suppress Lester Kinsolving's articles, the Temple tried to prevent publication of the *New West* exposé. Indeed, its efforts to stop the damaging story became a story itself, according to John R. Hall, and resulted in an article appearing in the *San Francisco Chronicle* on 7 June 1977. Ten days later, *New West* staff reported a burglary of the magazine's editorial offices. The very next day, apostates spoke with Phil Tracy. Although it turned out that a *New West* staff member had locked himself out of the office and tried to get back in, the belief that Peoples Temple had burglarized the office stuck. In short, *New West* and the reporters created the opportunity for defectors to go public.[40] By the time the article actually appeared in print, however, many Temple members, as well as Jim Jones, had moved to Guyana.

Although traditional analyses of the movement state that it was the *New West* article that sent Temple members scurrying to Guyana, Hall argued that rejection of the Apostolic Corporation's application for tax exemption by the Intesnal Revenue Service served as the impetus for the major migration in 1977. The Apostolic Corporation would have provided nonrelated business income through life-care contracts for senior citizens: in other words, it would have been a major source of revenue for Peoples Temple.

Despite the negative publicity from *New West*, the Temple's political allies remained steadfast, refusing to desert what had become an institution in San Francisco politics. Temple functionaries compiled endorsements from various dignitaries and published them in July 1977. Laudatory comments came from the lieutenant governor of California, the director of the San Francisco Council of Churches, the president of the San Francisco NAACP, the majority whip for the California State Legislature, and many others. Nevertheless, the emigration from the Bay Area, which began in spring 1977, continued through the summer and fall.

A skeleton operation remained in Redwood Valley, with Claire Janaro maintaining the ranch and others maintaining some care homes. A congregation continued in San Francisco under the leadership of Archie Ijames. A second congregation carried on in Los Angeles with David Wise and Hue Fortson as its ministers. The stateside contacts supported the agricultural project abroad, providing logistical, financial, and political support. Members in San Francisco handled media inquiries and spearheaded resistance to opposition that increased throughout 1977 and 1978. The heart and soul of the movement had moved to Guyana, however, with the 1,000 members who began what they hoped would be a new and better life.

For Further Reading

Jeannie Mills describes life in Redwood Valley in *Six Years with God*, as does Hyacinth Thrash in *The Onliest One Alive*. *Dear People*, edited by Denice Stephenson, gathers many primary sources about Peoples Temple contained in the collection at the California Historical Society. Excerpts from Edith Roller's journal are available online at http://jonestown.sdsu .edu/AboutJonestown/JTResearch/eRollerJournals/index.htm; the original Roller journal appears on CDs released from the FBI as part of a FOIA request. A number of other primary sources appear online at http:// jonestown.sdsu.edu/AboutJonestown/PrimarySources/primary_resources. htm/, including the letter from the Gang of Eight. *Peoples Temple and Black Religion in America* has essays by Milmon Harrison, J. Alfred Smith, Archie Smith Jr., and Duchess Harris and Adam John Waterman that shed light on the San Francisco Temple.

CHAPTER 3

The Promised Land

Dear Dad, I was outside the other night and I looked up at the stars, I never saw such a beautiful sight in my life. They all twinkling as though they were saying to me, "Welcome."
—Zipporah Edwards, *Letter to Jim Jones**

When Peoples Temple moved from Indiana to California in 1965, it grew in numbers and influence. The small Christian sect from the Midwest became an important mainline Protestant congregation in San Francisco. When the Temple relocated again, however, moving from California to Guyana in 1977, it contracted in size and status. That is because members turned inward, focusing on the survival of their own community. The concern of the organization shifted to supporting and maintaining the Peoples Temple Agricultural Project. Members no longer could actively participate in various political events and causes in California because so many had left the country. Although some remained in Redwood Valley, San Francisco, and Los Angeles, Jim Jones, the group's leadership, and its most committed members had migrated to Guyana.

The rejection of the United States revealed a number of concerns that leaders in the Temple had. They feared that the IRS might freeze the Temple's assets. They worried that the results of a child custody battle might remove one of the children from the community. They responded to Jones's prophecy that a fascist takeover was imminent in the United States A dualistic us-versus-them mentality fed the desire for a pure environment away from crime, drugs, unemployment, and all of the problems that accompany urban life. But members believed they were not just deserting something worse but also moving *to* something better. They set the goal of creating a community without racism, in which all children would be free and equal. They wanted to start their own society, but to do so, they needed to find a place where they could live and work in peace.

WHY GUYANA?

There were a number of reasons, therefore, that Temple leaders decided to pursue a communal experiment in Guyana, a cooperative socialist republic located on the north coast of South America. The Caribbean was always a sort of El Dorado for "the soldier of fortune, the pirate, the profit-seeking merchant, the sugar planter, the 'poor white,' the slaver, the merchant prince, and all the rest," according to the Caribbean scholar Gordon K. Lewis.[1] Guyana in particular functioned as the escape route for convicts and rebellious slaves, with the interior symbolizing freedom and independence. In addition to serving as a symbol for literal escape, however, the Caribbean represented spiritual escape, with its acceptance of new gods and antislavery religions. Moreover, despite its location on the South American continent, Guyana "is a part of the English-speaking Caribbean, both for historical and cultural reasons." The fact that Guyana is a multiracial nation and the only country in South America in which English is spoken also made it very attractive. A final consideration was the tropical climate and vegetation, which made it seem like home to the many Temple members who came from the American South.

The government of Guyana saw its own advantages in cooperating with Peoples Temple. Race had always played a significant role in Guyana politics. The racial composition of the majority of settlers moving to Jonestown— predominantly African American—corresponded to the composition of the ruling People's National Congress, which comprised Afro-Guyanese. The opposition, the Peoples Progressive Party (PPP), was made up of Indo-Guyanese. The Peoples Temple agricultural project also mirrored other successful economic development projects in the hinterland. This was a goal the government encouraged for its own people. Finally, Jonestown's location in the Northwest District of Guyana, an area in dispute with Venezuela, made the community useful in regional geopolitics. "Whether they knew it or not, then, the Jonestown *communeros* became an element in the attempted solution of all those problems. If they used Guyana, Guyana also used them," according to Lewis.

After the rise of Fidel Castro in Cuba in the early 1960s, Guyana became an unofficial front in the U.S. war against Communism in the Western Hemisphere. The United States clandestinely supported an Afro-Guyanese government against explicitly Marxist political parties. The Central Intelligence Agency funneled money through American trade unions to foment labor violence and destabilize the Marxist-leaning government of Cheddi Jagan, an Indo-Guyanese political leader. In 1964 the British rigged the colony's national elections to ensure Jagan's defeat, and gave Guyana its independence two years later. In 1968 the CIA provided a voter registration system guaranteed to keep Jagan's successor, Forbes Burnham, in power. A referendum passed in 1978 allowed the parliament to amend the constitution without electoral consent. A new constitution made Burnham "president for life" in 1980, where he remained in office until his death in 1985.

A wave of political assassinations occurred in the tiny nation throughout the 1970s. They included the fatal stabbing of Father Bernard Darke, a political activist, in the presence of the police; the shooting death of the Minister of Education; the murder of two opposition party members; and the disappearance of Guyana's Security Chief. The violence culminated in the murder of postcolonial intellectual Walter Rodney in 1980, killed by a bomb explosion in his car. Rodney had been organizing a transracial party, the Working People's Alliance, in an effort to unite dissidents of all ethnicities. Following Rodney's assassination, fear of widespread torture and death squads quelled dissent in Guyana. The deaths of more than 900 Americans in 1978 therefore made Jonestown a part of Guyana's violent past and present, as well as part of the broader story of colonialism in the New World. Jones's close ties to the Burnham government turned Peoples Temple into uncritical, if not unaware, participants in repressive measures backed by U.S. interests.

The Temple maintained close relations with a variety of government ministers. Notes and memos recovered from Jonestown, and an extensive guestbook maintained at the project, indicate frequent visits from officials in education, health, foreign affairs, agriculture, and other departments. Edith Roller, the Temple diarist, documented visits from PNC officials, as well as trips to other areas of the Northwest District by Jonestown residents to attend PNC meetings. In Georgetown, Jonestown musicians and dancers entertained government officials in lively public performances. The Jonestown community had clearly aligned itself with the ruling party and felt indebted to it and dependent upon it for its survival. Cordial and even intimate relationships were encouraged.

THE EARLY PIONEERS

Although Peoples Temple did not sign a formal lease with the Government of Guyana until 25 February 1976, a small group of settlers from California began clearing land in the Northwest District of the country in April 1974. The lease required Peoples Temple to "cultivate and beneficially occupy" at least one-fifth of the 3,852 acres within the first two years and to submit a written report every five years.[2] The early years were difficult, but the pioneers worked long and hard, then voted to work longer and harder from dawn until dusk. The first contingent of settlers lived in government housing near Port Kaituma for eight to ten months while the road was built and the first clearing was made. Almost a year after the project began, the U.S. Ambassador to Guyana, Maxwell Krebs, paid a visit to the Peoples Temple Agricultural Project on 13 March 1975 where he found two buildings constructed and about fifteen to twenty young men.

> The atmosphere was quite relaxed and informal. We talked freely with several of the "pioneers" about their living conditions (uncomfortable), work (tough), aspirations (high), etc. My impression was of a highly motivated, mainly self-disciplined group, and of an operation which had a good chance of at least initial success.[3]

The next official visitor from the embassy was Wade Matthews, the Deputy Chief of Mission, who dropped in unannounced in May 1976. Matthews's report showed the progress made during the year since the ambassador's trip. "I found what appeared to be a frontier-type, active, new agricultural settlement with perhaps half a dozen rustic buildings and metal-roofed open-sides sheds." Matthews noted that perhaps 100 acres or more had been cleared and planted, and that the project had several tractors and other agricultural equipment.

> The people talked as though they were enthusiastic about their work, and, from outward appearances, seemed happy enough. The group at that time was about 2/3 white and 1/3 black (I vaguely recall a couple of apparent Orientals). There were a number of children who acted normally and who accompanied my own children down to a large and well-built cage to see their chimpanzee which had been brought from California.[4]

The first public reference to Guyana by Peoples Temple was an ad in an October 1976 issue of *Peoples Forum*, which solicited donations for an agricultural project, without mentioning where it was. But an April 1977 issue had a front-page story detailing the ways criminal offenders were being rehabilitated in Jonestown.[5] That same month the 40 residents who had been living in Jonestown—including Jim Jones—were joined by almost 400 more. This raised some concerns on the part of the government of Guyana, but U.S. Embassy personnel apparently allayed those fears. Another 500 settlers had arrived by the end of 1977, however, which put great stress on the nascent settlement. The pioneers had constructed fifty houses to accommodate four persons each. But soon each cabin was crowded with eight, sixteen, and twenty people. Those who had been in Jonestown from the beginning wanted to limit immigration until immediate problems had been solved, but the flow of people continued, sometimes as many as fifty a day.

Despite the hardships, a spirit of hope and optimism existed in 1975 and 1976. As Don Beck described his life in Jonestown in the early days:

> At that point with fewer people and less paranoia, the Mission project was almost a paradise. Peaceful, beautiful, a place of equality and mutual respect and support. Building to provide what we defined as necessary. And no meetings with outsiders—so no need to put on performances. Just working for yourself and community. A good feeling. Safe. Safer in the tropical jungle than the urban jungle.[6]

A NOTE ON SOURCES

The sources available for understanding life in Jonestown are problematic. There are apostate accounts that described the jungle community as a concentration camp. Although these stories prompted Congressman Leo Ryan to travel to Jonestown in November 1978 to investigate conditions, they exaggerated some problems. (I will discuss the negative aspects of life in Jonestown in Chapter Five, and Leo Ryan's visit in Chapter Six.) There are letters and papers from Jonestown that depicted the project in idyllic terms, but since mail was censored, these too are difficult to accept at face value. Nevertheless, some facts can be gleaned from letters: while they do not include any criticisms of Jonestown, they do provide some useful information about day-to-day life. Books and articles written by or about survivors present conflicting evidence. The trouble with survivor accounts is that they were all written looking backward, through the prism of the deaths in Jonestown. The event altered memories and reflections so that people saw things in a different light.

The voices of those who died in Jonestown were silenced by the tragedy, so it is hard to know what they really thought and felt. We do have numerous audiotapes of community meetings held in Jonestown that allow some voices to be heard. We have notes, memos, and letters that also give voice to those who died, although these, too, are not unbiased sources. We are most fortunate, however, to have the journals of Edith Roller who was 62 when she died in Jonestown. A former college professor, she had worked at Bechtel Corporation in the San Francisco Bay Area before she moved to Jonestown in January 1978. She kept an extensive and detailed journal, running several thousand pages in total, during her Temple years.

We are able to gain great knowledge about ordinary life in Jonestown from Dr. Roller's diaries. She described what people ate, what kinds of meetings they had, what kinds of entertainment they enjoyed, what visitors came to the project. She wrote about her living conditions, including her physical ailments, in revealing detail. Most importantly, she presented Jonestown without benefit of hindsight: her descriptions are in the moment, and are not shaped by the deaths in Jonestown. She wrote dispassionately and factually.

Her diaries, as well as some of the other sources noted above, help paint a picture of daily life in Jonestown.

STARTING FROM SCRATCH

It is helpful to think of Jonestown as a small town of a thousand people. It had all of the things any ordinary farming community would have: a school, a library, a health clinic, businesses—including a sewing factory, a soap factory, a brick factory, and a small but serviceable sawmill—and "public utilities" to coordinate safety, sidewalks and roads, sanitation, sewage and drains, and water. A generator supplied electricity for the town, which supported street lights, interior lighting, and other amenities. As an agricultural project it produced such crops as cassava, rice, sweet potato, eddo, pineapple, peanuts, and bananas. There were groves for varieties of citrus trees; smaller gardens for vegetables and herbs; barns and facilities for chickens, dairy cows, and pigs; a small animal veterinary facility; provisions for insecticides and chemicals; processing of raw foods (a cassava mill and a rice mill); and a safety steward. Because it was a communal town, it also had a central kitchen, bakery, and herb kitchen, as well as warehouses for storage and laundry facilities. Housing consisted of cabins painted in pastel colors, small huts called "troolies" made of palm leaves, and large, thatch-covered dormitories. A "police force" existed in the form of a security department, which included a "search and apprehend team" (SAT) and housemothers in charge of behavior in various cabins and dorms. A communications center—the radio tower—served as the hub for radio transmissions between Jonestown and Georgetown, and between Jonestown and San Francisco. It also functioned as the center for announcements and dispatches made by Jim Jones over a public address system that ran throughout the village. Finally, since no community should be without entertainment, there were teams for basketball and karate, a dance troupe, and several musical groups, including the Jonestown Express.

Many skilled individuals would be needed to support a community of 1,000 souls: teachers, engineers, mechanics, nurses, cooks, child care workers, carpenters, electricians, farmers, seamstresses, counselors, and others. For some who moved to Jonestown, their job status improved as they took on oversight responsibilities they had never had in the city. "A man from an urban area is in charge of the piggery," wrote John Moore after a visit in May 1978. "Another man with no experience is in charge of the chickery. In both instances they have been successful and are learning."[7] For others, relocation meant doing more or less the same thing: cooking, cleaning, baking, maintaining equipment. For still others, the transfer was a step down the career ladder, with professionals becoming farmhands or carpenters.

About one-third of the residents living in Jonestown were under the age of twenty, and half of all residents were under age thirty, making the community rather youthful in orientation and outlook. There was also a sizeable population of senior citizens, with about one-fourth being age fifty or older. This resulted in a rather large nonproductive force in the community, although senior citizens did make dolls and other crafts to sell in Georgetown. They also did most of the cooking, with the oldest residents washing and prepping greens and other food for meals. Everyone had a way to contribute to life in Jonestown, depending upon their ability. Perhaps most importantly, seniors living in Jonestown provided a monthly income of about $36,000 by donating their Social Security payments to the Temple. This subsidized the enormous expenses incurred by various purchases—such as farm implements, a boat for transporting people to and from Jonestown, and construction equipment to build a sawmill—and by procuring food, since the community was not self-sufficient.

The abundance or scarcity of food has been the subject of conflicting reports. Hyacinth Thrash, who slept in her cabin in Jonestown as the deaths were occurring, said that food was scarce; Odell Rhodes, another Jonestown survivor who fled into the jungle, said that food was plentiful, at least through the end of 1977. Lisa Layton, who died of cancer in Jonestown in October 1978, told her daughter Deborah Layton that seniors ate first in Jonestown.[8] After Deborah left Jonestown in May 1978, she wrote that:

> The food was woefully inadequate. There was rice for breakfast, rice water soup for lunch, and rice and beans for dinner. On Sunday, we each received an egg and a cookie. Two or three times a week we had vegetables. Some very weak and elderly members received one egg per day. However, the food did improve markedly on the few occasions when there were outside visitors.[9]

The more regular reports of Edith Roller showed that the community had meat once or twice a week, that they frequently ate vegetables, and that they did enjoy fish. Her 1978 journal from Jonestown covering 210 days described the meals she ate on 74 days, the treats she had on 15 days, and the guests that visited on 30 different days. For example, on her first day in Georgetown, Guyana, on 20 January 1978, she ate roast meat, cucumber salad, vegetables, and green papaya pie for dinner. Three days later (23 Jan.) she ate liver, mixed vegetables (squash, okra, onions, tomatoes), oranges, coconut. The next day she had shrimp curry. Food in Jonestown was not as plentiful: she wrote of having "bits of pork, veggies, rice gravy" in her first week. Rice was clearly a staple in the community. Larger feasts coincided with visits from government officials or other dignitaries. On the day that Roller wrote that she ate a quarter of a chicken, she also described a musical program for visitors. Food also improved after White Nights, according to Laura Johnston Kohl. After a night of staying awake, protecting Jonestown with rakes and shovels, residents were treated to banquets that included fried chicken and bountiful food.

It is evident that life in the Jonestown community required hard work, long hours, short rations, and intense commitment. But it wasn't all work all the time. Every Sunday night featured movie screenings, ranging from political films like *The Parallax View* to lighter entertainment such as *Far From the Madding Crowd*, and audiotapes of *Sesame Street* for children. The political thriller *Z*—which depicted a political assassination in Greece in 1963—was shown and discussed many times. At the end of the summer of 1978, Sunday afternoons began to be free, the first time residents did not work a seven-day week. Roller described music and dance programs for the visitors who frequented the project. Although work sped up the day before visits in order to make the community neat and tidy, the rules and the schedule were relaxed during the visits themselves.

Like other small towns where everybody knows everybody else—and everybody's business—minor conflicts arose. In addition, petty theft was common. People stole food, but they also stole other people's belongings, or they mislaid scarce commodities, which then were lost. Because people living in Jonestown were trying to learn an unselfish and cooperative way of life, problems that hurt the welfare and survival of the project were identified and brought up at the Peoples Rallies, weekly town meetings held in Jonestown. One journal entry noted:

> Tom Grubbs reported on expensive items he finds in trash cans... Edith Cordell makes a complaint about young people in the cottage who don't help in the cottage and leave everything dirty.
>
>   Marie mentioned teenagers sitting while seniors stand in the dining area. She will be watching and so will police it until we gain sensitivity beforehand. Jack Beam says also tables and chairs are to be returned from where they were taken so that we have a place to sit to eat.[10]

The punishment for violating community rules and norms generally was assignment to the Learning Crew, which was later called the New Brigade. The Learning Crew isolated offenders and made them work extra hours, either in agricultural labor or around the facilities, cleaning and maintaining latrines and walkways, or completing other tasks that needed attention. Usually ten people plus one supervisor comprised the Learning Crew. Offenders had to run from job to job; and they had to request permission to complete ordinary tasks like visiting the bathroom or drinking water, much as in the military. Roller discussed another infraction—a young woman named Daniele (probably Danielle Gardfrey Mitchell) who said she

wanted to return to Texas—and her "trial" and punishment before the
community:

> Her dad Guy Mitchell and sister speak of what Texas was like. Jury
> finds Daniele guilty, gave her a week on PSU [public service unit], must
> speak to 20 seniors a day and smile.[11]

On yet another occasion, Jones called upon people who were either up for
discipline, or had completed their two- or three-day stints on the Learning
Crew and were ready to be released, to perform a dance and pretend to
be overcome by the Holy Spirit. "Get in there, girl, that's good, come on,"
he exhorted Lawanda Mitchell, laughing. "All right, all right, all right. She
just danced her way off the Learning Crew."[12] The Learning Crew/New
Brigade was not a permanent assignment: "People on New Brigade one,
two and three times can get off at any time with good work attitude," said
instructions from Jones, dated 17 March 1978. But on 4 April he added,
"Remember people who are on the New Brigade one day at a time . . . if you
give any shit, you will be on for a long time."[13] There were still more severe
punishments, however, which will be addressed in Chapter Five.

The Peoples Rallies brought together the entire community to set goals and
to make suggestions. They also served as forums for marking the progress
that the project was making toward its goal of self-sufficiency and for identifying problems that were impeding its way. At a rally on 9 June 1978, Phil
Blakey reported that he was working on the compost pit, Mary Wother-
spoon anticipated a visit from a government expert on cassava that month,
Jack Beam noted that a bigger brick kiln was being built, and Jim Jones
broached the possibility of manufacturing charcoal for export that could be
produced under a government contract. At the next week's rally (13 June)
Russ Moton suggested experimenting with high protein corn to distribute
in Guyana.

Agricultural production was an urgent concern in the community, so it
was a major setback when rains washed seeds away from the senior vegetable gardens, thus eliminating a major source of food. The group discussed
reasons for the deaths of 500 chickens, and it was reported that a male duck
was attacking other animals and might have to be locked up, since the female
had been sitting on eggs for three weeks. Notes and tapes from many Peoples
Rallies and an abundance of minutes from "Farm Analysts Meetings" attest
to the consuming interest in food production. Most of the "analysts" had
little or no agricultural experience, so much of the community's farming
occurred on a trial-and-error basis. An agenda for the meeting of Tuesday,
29 August 1978, included discussion of plans for intensive farming, developments at the piggery and the chickery, banana cultivation, a report

on the orchards, and a farm manager report. Despite the frequency of discussion and the primacy of concern, the community had not mastered the basics of agricultural production, and food seemed to remain scarce. The group purchased food in Georgetown and shipped it to Jonestown, and the community was at least two years away from being self-sufficient, according to some estimates.

A TOURIST DESTINATION?

Even in its isolation Jonestown had many visitors. Located about thirty miles from the border with Venezuela, it was accessible only by air and tractor ride, or by boat ride along the coast and up the Kaituma River. People moving to Jonestown from the United States, or traveling between Georgetown and Jonestown, usually rode the *Cudjoe*, a large boat used for fishing as well as transportation. They would arrive in Port Kaituma and then take a bumpy tractor-trailer ride: three miles to the perimeter of the community, and another three miles into the heart of Jonestown. Government visitors to the settlement generally flew into Matthews Ridge, a former bauxite mining settlement about thirty miles from Jonestown. They would then travel twenty-seven miles in a four-wheel-drive vehicle on an unpaved road toward Port Kaituma, before turning into the Jonestown gate.

Quite a few Guyanese visitors made the arduous trek to the project. Guests included Guyana's Minister of Foreign Affairs Fred Wills, the Minister of Education Vincent Teekah, the Northwest Regional Development Director, the Northwest Regional Minister, the British High Commissioner, the Chancellor of the University of Guyana, the Guyana Permanent Secretary of the Ministry of Public Works, the Assistant Director-General of National Service, and Guyana's Chief Medical Officer. Dentists, optometrists, and the government veterinarian were among the visitors who provided services to the community.[14] Local Guyanese also visited the project, comprising Amerindian workers (especially in the beginning), staff members from the nearby Burnham Agricultural Institute, and others.

U.S. Embassy officials made trips to Jonestown to verify the welfare and whereabouts of Social Security recipients. While the embassy, acting under the auspices of the U.S. Department of State, had no legal authority in Guyana, it did have a responsibility to ascertain that American citizens living abroad were welltreated. In addition to the early visits of Ambassador Krebs and Deputy Chief of Mission Wade Matthews, embassy staff traveled to Jonestown on at least five different occasions in 1977 and 1978, prior to the trip of Congressman Ryan in November 1978. Richard McCoy, the Consul for the embassy, interviewed a total of 75 Jonestown residents on three separate occasions between August 1977 and May 1978. Two embassy staff members, Doug Ellice and Dennis Reece, reported after their 7 November 1978 visit that they "shared the same general impressions as follows: the members they met appeared to be in good health, mentally alert (considering the advanced age of some of them), and generally happy to be at Jonestown. They all seemed to be absorbed in their various duties such as shop work, teaching or gardening."[15]

The community was beautified and residents were prepped for visitor questions, whether they were government officials, personnel from either the U.S. or Soviet embassies, or news reporters. Several documents recovered from Jonestown showed how Jones coached people in what to say, and what not to say, to visitors. "Family's a word I wouldn't use," some notes quoted him as saying:

> Because they stuck that with the Moonie-ites. It's a good word but they use it, the Manson Family. They kind of make the word look dirty because in America they only want people to confine themselves to their blood relatives, that way, greater groups can't get together, so I'd say community. I would say our community.[16]

Several audiotapes showed the coaching that occurred prior to visits that included reporters. On one, amid much laughter and kidding, Jones said he would take on the role of a reporter. He asked what kind of food they have to eat.

Woman: We make our own bread. We have rice. We have—
Jones: For Christ's sake. [Crowd laughter] Don't name rice first, please, 'cause that damn woman said we never eat anything, Debbie [Layton] said we never eat anything here but rice. [Laughter] So I'd just forget the rice for the time being. Can't you think of something else?

The woman went on to list pork, beef, chicken, and fish. Jones admonished her, in a friendly tone, to list meat first. Later on in the practice interviews, another faux pas created amusement in the crowd.

Jones: Tell me, how many hours you work, sir, and what do you work at?
Man: I work eight hours a day, and I'm a heavy equipment operator.
Jones: What's your shift, what's your hours?
Man: Seven to six. [Crowd laughter]
Jones: Seven to six means—by last count, eleven. [Crowd laughter] You gotta watch it with reporters. They'll trip your ass.[17]

On other occasions, time off was delayed until after a delegation of visitors came through. People spent extra hours cleaning latrines so they did not smell, clearing walkways, and generally improving the appearance of

Jonestown. Sometimes this backfired, however. A memo to Jim Jones from Harriet Tropp—one of the key leaders in Jonestown—bemoaned the "uglification of Jonestown" and expressed her dissatisfaction with the way decisions were made. The community had attempted to improve its walkways prior to a 1978 visit from Don Freed, an American writer and filmmaker. It is worth quoting Tropp at length because of the issues her memo highlighted, especially her criticism of the way people deferred to Jones against their own better judgment.

> Before we started on the fiasco of beautifying Jonestown for upcoming guests, advice was given on several different occasions, advice that was the product of several meetings and consultations with people who have lived here for several years as well as Guyanese, to the effect that any attempt to fix the road or haul pines in for the paths would only result in a worsening of the situation if done during the rainy season.
>
> Notwithstanding this advice, we decided to go ahead (and I certainly participated in that decision) and try it anyway because "Dad wants it done" and "there must be a way." Well, there wasn't a way. If you look at the road now, it is worse looking than when we started...
>
> I think the above just serves to highlight a problem we have in decision-making. That is, if you say you want something done, we ignored any advice we've been given and we go against our own judgment, and go ahead...
>
> I think the essence of the problem, or at least one aspect of it, is that no one is willing to oppose your opinion in certain matters, and I frankly think that sometimes you are wrong, and no one is willing to say so. I realize this is quite a volatile statement, but I think it is one factor in the dynamics of how this organization functions that gets us in trouble.[18]

It may be difficult to imagine people coming and going at Jonestown, given its great isolation and the effort it took to get there. Nevertheless, the Roller journal and the Jonestown guest book show that there were frequent visitors. In addition, members came and went, traveling to Georgetown and even Venezuela for specialized health care, dentistry, and eyewear. They always had incentive to return, though, given the fact that Jonestown policy required that some family members remain behind.

A SOCIALIST EDUCATION

Because children made up a large portion of the Jonestown population, schools and education consumed much of the town's energy. The town had a school office, two school pavilions, a library, and programs for elementary school, high school, apprenticeships, research projects, adult classes, and a self-described "socialism library." A 1977 Progress Report from the "Peoples Temple Agricultural Project" detailed the various education programs. The report boasted of the learning tools in the preschool, such as manipulative toys, puzzles, individual chalkboards, and a well-equipped playground. At the time of the report, the elementary school only provided grades 1 through 7, though high school was planned for fall 1977. Work-study programs also incorporated practical learning and skills for teenagers and young adults. Classes were not organized by grade or age, but rather according to ability, so that children could progress as rapidly, or slowly, as they wanted. In 1977 the two ability groups were (1) prereading, elementary reading skills, and moderate competency and (2) moderate to well-developed reading skills. The schools focused on Guyanese history and culture, in part to fulfill requirements of Guyana's Ministry of Education, and in March 1978, the Jonestown community celebrated when it received government accreditation for its elementary and high schools.

After November 18, a news report described the "desolate scene" encountered in the community's schools. "Guyana Exercise Books," specially printed by the government, dozens of copies of *New Mathematics for the Caribbean* and *Success in Spelling*, posters, toys, musical instruments, records and tapes, crayons, as well as child-sized tables and chairs and a Snoopy notebook were strewn throughout in one open-air, roofed school room.[19] The reporter listed some of the slogans posted around the structure: "Look, Listen, Learn"; "Be good to those around you;" "Your Attitude Is So Loud I Can't Hear What You're Saying"; and "Black Is Beautiful."

Education was not just for kids, however. Edith Roller reported on weekly classes in socialism, some of which she herself led. Jones devised tests on political news developments and socialist theories that community members of all ages took. If they did not pass, they would have to review basic concepts. Roller's diary entry for 13 June stated that "Jim read names of those who failed socialism test, have to attend socialism class 6 hours. 3 one night and 3 the next. There were 218 excellent and near excellent."[20] Carolyn Layton wrote that the group was "studying everything from Third World politics, Caribbean politics and socialist concepts, general theory, plus socialist economic concepts which are of course very applicable to the farm."[21] A current events quiz asked questions about where Mauritania was, what religion Malcolm X belonged to, who the Rosenbergs were, what Andrew Young said that embarrassed President Carter, and "what did Dad say we must do here in Jonestown before talking about fighting guerilla wars (in Africa)?"[22]

Education in socialist principles occurred at all age levels. Jones read news from Tass, the Soviet news agency, over the loudspeaker system almost every day. News and current events were discussed in school classes and in nightly forums, and residents studied for quizzes and exams on various concepts. Martin Amos, who was almost ten years old, asked a question about African underdevelopment at one of the Peoples Rallies:

> When we was in socialism class, Darren said that in Algeria they have a lot of petroleum. But when I was reading in one of those encyclopedias, it said that after the revolution, it left their economy weak, and I wanna know how it could be weak when they have all this petro-leum?[23]

News discussions focused on events occurring in Africa and in the Soviet bloc. The group identified itself as socialist, and members attempted to inculcate a socialist mentality at all levels—from production planning, to political education, to shared housing. Some even changed their names to Ché (Guevara), Stalin, and Lenin, though Jones cautioned them to give their birth names when asked by reporters.

In autobiographical reflections Jones made sometime in 1977, he claimed to be a Communist as early as Indianapolis. He remarked that he felt sympathy for the Soviet heroes who turned back the Nazis at Stalingrad. He met a Communist organizer in Indianapolis who persuaded Jones to consider Marxism. Jones said he hooked up with other old-style Communists, seeking inspiration from them. He could not accept the inequities of capitalism, nor the desire to accumulate wealth. After considering several possibilities, Jones said that he decided to infiltrate the church in order to practice his Marxism.

As was the case with his theology, though, Jones's definition of Marxism was amorphous and situational, unique to him, as he acknowledged. "I shall call myself a Marxist," he said, "because certainly no one taught me my brand of Marxism."[24] One analysis described him as "an obscure socialist thinker, blending elements of atheism, Christianity, Marxism, Leninism, Maoism, and Third World revolutionary rhetoric into a complicated brew of political sentiments."[25]

If Jones's thinking was disorganized, that of his leaders—the socialism teachers especially—was not, and once in Guyana, key Temple members met with representatives from North Korea, Yugoslavia, Cuba, and the Soviet Union at their respective embassies. The North Koreans were polite and the Cubans were skeptical, wondering about the group's focus on Jim Jones rather than on the collective good. Officials from the Soviet embassy were the most welcoming, and the Temple maintained the greatest contact with them, with frequent visits to the embassy in Georgetown, and a visit of a delegation from the embassy to Jonestown in October 1978. From youngest to oldest, everyone in Jonestown studied Russian in anticipation of a possible move there. And on the so-called death tape made the last day, 18 November, the single voice of dissent asked about moving to Russia rather than killing the children.

An absence of religious language and practice corresponded to the emphasis on socialism and Communist indoctrination that occurred in Jonestown. Jones gave no sermons in Jonestown, but instead interpreted international news, directed the Jonestown economy, and gave monologues—or harangues—at Peoples Rallies. When religion did come up, it was to criticize it. For example, when Jones exhorted residents to pretend to be "in" the Holy Spirit, he was mocking the Pentecostal roots of the movement. He called Jesus an oppressor of black people. Peoples Temple was no longer a religious organization, at least not in Guyana, but was instead a socialistic utopian experiment. Nevertheless, some residents, particularly the elderly, retained their familiar faith, and a few even smuggled Bibles into Jonestown. Moreover, some survivors of Jonestown, as well as members who had stayed behind in California, eventually returned to Christianity.

The deification of Jim Jones also subsided somewhat in Jonestown. Although Jones remained a central figure, as audiotapes made abundantly clear, in the absence of religious rhetoric, he himself lost some of his divinity. No faith healings occurred in the Jonestown pavilion, but residents still spoke about miracles, and Jones continued to take credit for saving the lives of people who went to the health clinic. And when natural deaths did occur—as happened a half dozen times in Jonestown before 18 November— the leadership attributed the death to a lack of faith in Jim Jones. When an elderly resident named Plickards C. Norris died, Jonestown doctor Larry Schacht blamed his death on the fact that he called on Jesus, rather than Jim Jones, with his last breaths. "Owning that power, the power that's in Dad, could've saved him . . . You have to call on Dad, you have to call on the power and the light that's in him."[26]

In general, though, instead of the miraculous, a well-equipped and well-staffed health clinic served the needs of the community, and a single doctor, Larry Schacht, was able to deal with most emergencies. Medical staff delivered babies and treated industrial-type accidents and wounds. The community's major problems were pandemics of athlete's foot and ringworm, with a strong and resistant fungus plaguing most residents, and constipation afflicting the elderly. Nurses checked the seniors once a week, taking their vital signs and reviewing recommended exercise, nutrition, and medication. Several times a year at evening meetings in Jonestown, Jones would ask all of the nurses and those in nursing training to perform breast examinations at the back of the pavilion. If they found any lumps, women would be treated in Georgetown or Venezuela.

A half-dozen staff were also in charge of a special unit in which dissidents and behaviorally disturbed residents were kept sedated, although seriously ill persons stayed in the unit as well. On one occasion in October 1978, Dr. Schacht reminded people that:

> those who look back to Babylon and don't accept Dad as their savior and don't accept his power, think they have their own life to live, like two we have now in the Special Care Unit, lying deathly ill, we have to arouse them *every hour*, just to be sure that they haven't passed, these two have been looking back to Babylon, *repeatedly* write notes about going back to the U.S.A., the U.S.A. where they would be thrown in prison, the concentration camps, and tortured.[27]

Most residents in Jonestown, though not all, did not believe they had anything much to return to in the United States. They had left everything behind—friends, family, financial security—in their commitment to a new life. In addition, Jones drew a bleak picture of life in the United States, telling residents that African Americans had been rounded up in concentration camps, that there were food shortages, and that a fascist dictatorship was imminent. Ironically, a number of relatives, journalists, and government officials back in the United States believed that the threats of a concentration camp, food shortages, and dictatorship were real in Jonestown. Their concerns led to actions which ultimately prompted Congressman Leo Ryan to visit Jonestown.

For Further Reading

For more information about the significance of Guyana, see Gordon K. Lewis, *"Gather with the Saints at the River"*: *The Jonestown Guyana Holocaust 1978*; and Duchess Harris and Adam John Waterman, "To Die for the Peoples Temple: Religion and Revolution after Black Power" in *Peoples Temple and Black Religion in America*. Several survivors' describe life in Jonestown: Hyacinth Thrash's *The Onliest One Alive*; Ethan Feinsod, *Awake in a Nightmare* which provides Odell Rhodes' narrative of a young African American who escaped; and Deborah Layton, *Seductive Poison*, an apostate account. The most revealing glimpses of life inside Jonestown come from Dr. Edith Roller's journals, http://jonestown.sdsu.edu/AboutJonestown/JTResearch/eRollerJournals/index.htm, and from audiotapes made by Peoples Temple and recovered by the FBI in Jonestown: http://jonestown.sdsu.edu/AboutJonestown/Tapes/tapes2.htm. Relations between Peoples Temple and the U.S. State Department and its embassy in Guyana are described in *The Assassination of Representative Leo J. Ryan and the Jonestown, Guyana Tragedy.*

CHAPTER 4

Fighting Monsters

Whoever fights monsters should see to it that in the process he does
not become a monster...
—Friedrich Nietzsche, *Beyond Good and Evil**

Peoples Temple did not operate in a vacuum, isolated from its friends or foes.
Even after the mass migration to Jonestown in 1977, which put a distance
of 4,500 miles and dense jungle between the group and California, external
forces continued to shape internal dynamics. Sociologists argue that we can
understand new religions, such as Peoples Temple, as operating in a dynamic
relationship with the world outside the group. To consider internal factors
apart from external factors does not tell the whole story of a new religion.
The interaction between members and outsiders helps to determine group
attitudes and behavior, just as the interaction between members and their
leader shapes beliefs and actions. In the case of Peoples Temple, negative
publicity and specific threats directed against the group had as much of an
impact as Jim Jones' deteriorating mental health and the use of corporal
punishment.

John R. Hall identified three external groups that influenced decisions
made by Temple leaders and affected events in Jonestown: (1) relatives and
former members; (2) the news media; and (3) government agencies and
officials.[1] This "network of opponents" dominated the concerns of people living in Jonestown. Fear for their very survival, which they believed
was threatened by a conspiracy of enemies, overshadowed all other worries
Jonestown residents may have had. Although nothing so organized as a conspiracy existed, a loose coalition of "cultural opponents," as Hall described
them, believed the worst about alternative communal groups in general, and

feared the worst about Peoples Temple in particular. Drawing upon cultural prejudices against new religions—or cults, in popular terminology—these opponents were able to mount a formidable campaign against Peoples Temple.

This chapter takes a critical look at the Temple's opponents and their campaign, while the next chapter takes a critical look at what was happening within Jonestown.

THE CONCERNED RELATIVES

Although thousands of people stepped through the doors of Peoples Temple in its California heyday, membership seemed to solidify between 2,000 and 3,000 persons. This means that the vast majority of people who visited the Temple did not join, and of those who joined, many left. The Rev. Ross Case, for example, who had been a Temple leader in Indianapolis, quit the church shortly after the move to California, disgusted by the growing adulation and deification of Jim Jones, but other more significant defections followed.

A few of the individuals who left between 1973 and 1977 formed the nucleus of the Concerned Relatives, a group which developed in opposition to Peoples Temple. Jim Cobb Jr., Mickey Touchette, and Wayne Pietila were all part of the Gang of Eight who defected in 1973. Elmer and Deanna Mertle left in December 1975 when they had the opportunity to operate a rest home in Berkeley owned by Elmer's mother. (Because they legally changed their names to Al and Jeannie Mills, due to fears of reprisal after they left Peoples Temple, I will use those names henceforward, since those are the names they chose to use.) The Millses had signed ownership title to nineteen houses over to the Temple, and were dismayed with both their loss of property and their treatment within the Temple. Neva Sly departed secretly in February 1976 after she had been beaten with a rubber hose during a catharsis session. The manager of KFRC radio helped her find housing after observing the welts on Neva's legs. Grace Stoen, the head counselor for the Temple, escaped with Walter Jones in July 1976. They were frightened and exhausted by relentless demands and endless work. Grace's husband Tim Stoen, the most powerful man in the Temple next to Jim Jones, abandoned the group in June 1977. All of these defectors left behind relatives: children, spouses, siblings, parents. While many truly felt in fear for their lives, they also believed that their relatives would not come to any harm by remaining with the Temple, at least at first.

Ex-members met informally between 1976 and 1977. The Millses organized a reunion of "traitors" in 1976, which included the Purifoy family, Joyce Shaw, and Grace Stoen. They reviewed "the years of terror" and found the experience cleansing but painful.[2] They discussed the brutal beating of a member who had molested a young boy. According to a story confirmed by several independent sources, the Planning Commission oversaw the punishment: the accused was stripped and hit repeatedly with a board; his penis was struck until it drained blood. This beating prompted the defection of others.

On 15 January 1977, the Millses and other ex-members met with George Klineman, a freelance reporter, and David Conn, a former elder in a Disciples of Christ congregation who was a friend of Al Mills. Klineman put the defectors in touch with an agent from the U.S. Treasury Department. They told him that weapons and money were being smuggled into Guyana. The Treasury agent informed Klineman in late February 1977 that "there would be a full-scale government investigation involving federal, state, and local law-enforcement agencies."[3] These early discussions that former members had with reporters and federal agents, and amongst themselves, were ad hoc and informal.

Three factors aligned in mid-1977 that led to the formation of more organized opposition: the Millses' informal network of former members who met to discuss their experiences; a news media investigation of Jim Jones; and most important, the arrival of Tim Stoen. A news story about an article planned by *New West* magazine brought together several former members who were willing to speak publicly about their experiences. Marshall Kilduff and Phil Tracy included first-person accounts by Al and Jeannie Mills; Grace Stoen and Walter Jones; Birdie Marable, who left after a three-week cross-country trip packed into a Temple bus; Laura Cornelious, an older African American woman who left after another older woman was threatened with a live snake; and four from the Gang of Eight: Mickey Touchette, Wayne Pietila and his wife Terri Cobb, as well as Terri's brother Jim Cobb. The defectors described fake faith healings, public disciplinary sessions, questionable property transfers, and a nonstop round of meetings. The reporters summarized the accounts by saying that "life inside Peoples Temple was a mixture of Spartan regimentation, fear and self-imposed humiliation."[4]

Going public with their concerns liberated former members from their fears of reprisal for leaving the Temple. They had the backing of a sympathetic media, and the summer of 1977 saw a wave of negative news stories, including some at the national level, that detailed abuses in Peoples Temple. But media coverage, in and of itself, was insufficient to unite Temple defectors hostile to Jim Jones. Although the Millses had many contacts within the community of defectors, it took the legal genius of Tim Stoen to help the Concerned Relatives organize the amorphous fear and anger of ex-members into a group that could mount an intensive and successful campaign against Jones and the Temple. The goal of the organization, according to Hall, was not only to rescue family members: "The Concerned Relatives demanded nothing less than that Jonestown cease to exist as a bounded communal society."[5] In other words, reparations and repatriation eventually became insufficient for the relatives.

The Concerned Relatives developed a three-pronged strategy to accomplish their goal. The first element was legal and financial. By filing lawsuits—either to regain property donated to the Temple or to regain custody of minor children—they could drain Temple resources. The second element consisted of creating media interest in Jonestown. The relatives called the project a "concentration camp" in which people were held against their will. Negative coverage kept the Temple on the defensive. The third element was to lobby government officials to investigate and intervene in Temple activities. Although many relatives were concerned about the welfare of family members in Jonestown, the driving force behind the strategy outlined here was a single custody case that involved a six-year-old boy.

TIM AND GRACE STOEN

Tim Stoen, a Stanford law school graduate, was a middle-class and upwardly mobile young lawyer when he joined Peoples Temple in Redwood Valley. He first met Jim Jones, who served on the board of the Legal Services Foundation of Mendocino, when Stoen applied for, and obtained, the job as director. Stoen was also a deeply religious man who had attended Wheaton College, a conservative evangelical school in the Midwest. He found in Peoples Temple what he believed was the chance to live out his desire to help humanity in his capacity as an attorney. Throughout his years in Peoples Temple, Stoen held a number of positions in public life, including Assistant District Attorney for both Mendocino County and San Francisco County. He also oversaw a complex system within the Temple in which affidavits, property transfers, and other legal documents and measures were used to control members.

In addition, Stoen planned a number of dirty tricks against former members or perceived enemies. These included having members make menacing phone calls to ex-members and intimidate opponents by threatening or actually filing lawsuits. The lawyer for the Temple also suggested illegal activities. In one such incident in 1975, Lester Kinsolving—a reporter who had published critical articles in 1972—inadvertently left his briefcase in the home of John Moore. Stoen suggested throwing the briefcase off the San Francisco–Oakland Bay Bridge and denying that Moore had ever seen it. While Stoen and others met with Moore in San Francisco, urging him to give them the briefcase so it could disappear, two Temple members actually broke into Moore's Berkeley home and photocopied the documents inside the briefcase.[6]

Grace Grech married Tim Stoen, twelve years her senior, when she was nineteen. Although she later said she never felt comfortable in Peoples Temple, she rose rapidly to the position of Head Counselor. In this role she served as mediator, or gatekeeper, for people who sought advice from Jim Jones about personal problems. When Grace Stoen fled the Temple in 1976, she left her four-year-old son John Victor in the custody of Tim and several other members in the group. Perhaps emboldened by publicity about the *New West* article or encouraged by Al and Jeannie Mills, she had a change of heart, and in summer 1977 applied for a divorce from Tim and custody of John Victor. Jim Jones challenged Grace, however, and claimed custody himself. He had already taken the child to Guyana, where Maria Katsaris cared for him in Jones's cabin.

The custody issue became not merely a clash between two parents but turned upon the paternity of the child himself. Two weeks after John Victor was born, Tim Stoen, his putative father, signed an affidavit that stated that Jim Jones had fathered the child. The affidavit declared that Stoen was unable to sire a child himself, and that he had asked Jones to impregnate Grace Stoen. "My reason for requesting James W. Jones to do this," read the affidavit, "is that I wanted my child to be fathered, if not by me, by the most compassionate, honest, and courageous human being the world contains."[7] Marceline Jones, Jim Jones's wife, witnessed the declaration, and according to Tim Reiterman and John Jacobs, fully believed that Grace had made sexual demands upon Jones, as had other women. Regardless of whether the affidavit was true or not, most Temple members believed that Jones was the father of John Victor Stoen. The boy became a symbol for the community, and attempts to wrest him away from his Jonestown family were understood as part of a larger plot to break up other families and the community itself.

The Stoen custody case bounced between the courts in California and those in Guyana. In September 1977, Grace Stoen's lawyer, Jeffrey Haas, traveled to Guyana and Jonestown in an effort to serve a California court order on Jim Jones. He returned without success. On 18 November 1977—a year to the day before the mass deaths—a California court awarded physical custody to Grace, and joint custody to both Grace and Tim, although they were legally separated.[8] Armed with the custody order, the Stoens returned to Guyana in January 1978 to seek legal remedy there. The custody order meant that Jones could face arrest if he returned to California without John Victor.

The Stoen case became a major, if not the overriding, concern of the U.S. Embassy in Georgetown, Guyana. Hundreds of cables flew between Georgetown and Washington, D.C., and between Guyana's capital city and San Francisco. State Department records released under the Freedom of Information Act (FOIA) documented phone calls, letters, and meetings with the Stoens and their attorney, both in Washington and in Georgetown. When they were in Guyana, the Stoens complained that Guyanese officials were harassing them, and that the judge assigned to the case in Guyana had been compromised, or threatened, by Temple members. A somewhat weary Embassy Consul wrote in January 1978:

Frankly, at this point I feel like a tennis ball who keeps being hit from one side to the other. Obviously, no matter what we do one side will complain of favoritism. However, I do believe it is important that we keep in touch since I'm afraid the Stoen case and People's Temple problems will be with us for awhile.[9]

Richard A. McCoy's prediction turned out to be quite accurate. Thanks to Stoen's efforts, almost 100 members of Congress had contacted the State Department about the custody case by the end of January 1978.

THE FIRST PRONG: LEGAL ACTION

The legal challenges to Peoples Temple began in an ad hoc way, although eventually legal action emerged as a conscious strategy. In fall 1977 Grace and Tim Stoen and Beverly and Howard Oliver filed custody suits against the Temple; Al and Jeannie Mills sought to recover property they donated to the Temple while they were members. In spring 1978, three more suits were filed: Steven Katsaris, the father of Maria Katsaris, a Temple leader, alleged slander and libel since his daughter claimed he had molested her; Jim Cobb, a former member, also filed a libel suit; and Wade and Mabel Medlock sued to recover their property. The attorney of record in all three cases was Tim Stoen.

The Stoens could pursue legal remedies because John Victor was a minor. Other parents could not, however, because their children were adults. Although Howard and Beverly Oliver petitioned the California court to have their teenage son William returned to them from Jonestown, he was able to remain with his older brother Bruce until he turned eighteen. Steven Katsaris attempted several times to visit his twenty-four-year-old daughter Maria, only to have a cold and bitter meeting with her in the presence of U.S. and Guyanese officials at the end of 1977. Maria had earlier claimed that her father had sexually molested her, but she refused to discuss it at his meeting with her. He attempted a rescue—planning to kidnap her in Georgetown and to fly her out of Guyana—but the plot failed.

Most of the lawsuits could be classified as nuisances rather than real threats, especially since a foreign court would be unlikely to award custody to relatives living in America. Moreover, Tim Stoen had a conflict of interest: he had been an attorney for Peoples Temple, advising Temple membership on the very issues he now challenged, so he could not legally or ethically represent plaintiffs against it. Charles Garry, the Temple's legal advisor in San Francisco, tried to reassure the leadership with these facts, and filed a countersuit against Stoen. Nevertheless, Temple members and leaders viewed these suits as evidence of a conspiracy against it, organized and led by one of its own: Tim Stoen.

THE SECOND PRONG: NEWS COVERAGE

Peoples Temple had always had a complex relationship with the press. While some reporters and columnists extolled its virtues, others emphasized its vices. As early as 1972 Lester Kinsolving had written up charges against the Temple, which subsequent reporters continued to repeat. In 1977 Marshall Kilduff and Phil Tracy reiterated many of the same themes that appeared in Kinsolving's series of articles. But *San Francisco Chronicle* columnist Herb Caen came to the Temple's defense, as did Dr. Carlton Goodlett, publisher of the San Francisco *Sun-Reporter*, the city's African American newspaper. Two reporters in particular, however, contributed to the fear of the media that grew in 1978: Kathy Hunter, wife of the executive editor for the Ukiah *Daily Journal*, and Gordon Lindsay, an English reporter for the *National Enquirer*.

Hunter traveled to Guyana in early May, planning to visit Jonestown. But her ties to another local paper, the *Santa Rosa Press Democrat*, which had published negative stories about Peoples Temple, led the Jonestown leadership to decide to keep her out of the community. Hunter claimed that Temple members interrogated and threatened her in Georgetown. She also said Guyanese police posted a guard outside her hotel room. Hunter fled the country in terror, returning "to the glare of television lights" where she was greeted by Tim Stoen. This merely confirmed Temple suspicions about her actual motives.[10] Several months after Hunter's return to Ukiah, Mark Lane—the Temple's newlyhired celebrity attorney—publicly mocked her for asserting that Guyana had a pro-Chinese government. Reading from her article at a press conference designed to show media bias against Peoples Temple, Lane quoted:

And what did I see staring at me from the wall on the right hand side of the Prime Minister of Guyana? A near life-size oil of China's Mao Tse-Tung. Looks like it's down the road to Peking for Guyana, if [Prime Minister Forbes] Burnham's referendum passes, and it looks like it will.[11]

The picture actually depicted Arthur Chung, the president of Guyana. Hunter's story was picked up by other news outlets, however, including some in San Francisco.

Hunter received threatening letters and phone calls after her return, and said she was attacked by two men in her home who forced her to drink alcohol. Peoples Temple ran an ad in the *Press Democrat*, offering to pay a reward of $5,000 for any information leading to the arrest of those who attacked the journalist. There were no takers. Undaunted, Hunter continued to write critical articles. Although Charles Garry wrote a letter requesting a retraction for an article published in July, the paper failed to make one, and instead published an article that described new issues confronting the Temple. The last in a series Hunter wrote focused on legal problems Jim Jones was facing. She reported in an article dated 10 August 1978 that the Los Angeles District Attorney was considering filing criminal complaints against Jones, charging grand theft and extortion. The article went on to state that, "There are many people in Ukiah now who, while licking their wounds of pride and frustration and parrying the taunts of those who say I told you so, wish they had listened more carefully to those who repeatedly brought their charges of charlatanism, fraud, and behind-the-scenes manipulations of human lives to their attention."[12]

Its dealings with Kathy Hunter proved to the Temple that it could not get a fair deal from the media, and this seemed to be confirmed by a major exposé planned by the *National Enquirer* at the instigation of Tim Stoen. Gordon Lindsay, a freelance reporter, flew over Jonestown in June, without notifying the Jonestown leadership or, apparently, the government of Guyana. Charles Garry wrote to Vibert Mingo, Guyana's Minister of Home Affairs, to complain about the unauthorized reconnaissance. Lindsay attempted to enlist the aid of John and Barbara Moore, who spoke with him by telephone for an hour and a half. John wrote that Lindsay referred to Jones's "concubines," and said that the reporter repeatedly tried to put words into his mouth.[13] Tim Stoen called the Moores around the same time and urged them to speak out against Jim Jones.

Notes by a Temple member who read the Lindsay article called it "explosive."[14] The exposé claimed Jones was a mixture of "Moon and Manson," a reference to the Rev. Sun Myung Moon, leader of the Unification Church, and to Charles Manson, leader of the Manson Family, which brutally murdered at least nine people. The article included salacious details about the Temple, including the fact that Temple leader Paula Adams was having an affair with Guyana Ambassador Laurence Mann, Carolyn Layton's son Kimo was fathered by Jim Jones, and Jones slept with many women in Peoples Temple. It relied primarily on critical remarks that Deborah Layton made following her recent defection in May 1978, although it also turned to twelve former members, including Tim Stoen, for information. The Temple paid Mark Lane to quash the story, and he succeeded. According to Reiterman and Jacobs, a Temple member gave $7,500 to Lane, and he procured the article.[15] This is confirmed by a note in Temple files that stated, "It is explosive. The article and the means of getting it. It was 7½ rather than 10, but the guy who gave it to Mark made him swear it would never leave his hands. Mark has the copy and will keep it, though told to destroy it." The figure "7½" refers to the $7,500 paid to retrieve the article. Lane did not recount this incident in his own book, *The Strongest Poison*.

THE COURT OF PUBLIC OPINION

On 11 April 1978, in their first official appearance as the "Concerned Relatives," about fifty family members and friends mounted a public offensive by delivering an "Accusation of Human Rights Violations by Rev. James Warren Jones Against Our Children and Relatives at the Peoples Temple Jungle Encampment in Guyana, South America" to Temple members at the San Francisco headquarters.[16] The document was carefully directed at Jones, rather than at Peoples Temple or any individual members, and began "We hereby accuse you, Jim Jones, of the following acts violating the human rights of our family members." The text went on to list three main categories of grievances. The first concerned a suicide threat made in a letter by Pam Moton, in which she wrote that, "I can say without hesitation that we are devoted to a decision that it is better even to die than to be constantly harassed from one continent to the next." The second charged Jones with "mind programming" and intimidation, which provided as evidence Steven Katsaris's accounts of his discouraging and frightening visits with his daughter Maria in Guyana. The "Accusation" referred to Katsaris's affidavit that "reveals the terrifying effect of your mind-programming on his daughter, a bright 24-year-old, which has caused her to deny belief in God, to renounce family ties, and to manifest symptoms of sleep-deprivation and a serious personality change." The third grievance cited provisions in the U.N.'s Universal Declaration of Human Rights, the U.S. Constitution, and the Constitution of Guyana to allege that relatives were denied basic human liberties such as freedom of speech, freedom of movement, and freedom to send and receive mail without censorship. Presenting various affidavits in support, the document alleged that Jonestown relatives were forced to break off contact with any relatives who criticized Peoples Temple. It noted that passports and money were confiscated, family visits limited or prohibited, and the ability to leave Jonestown curtailed.

The final category, under the heading "Relief," asked for specific remedies for the grievances and began by addressing the suicide threat:

We hereby demand that you, Jim Jones, immediately cease and desist from the aforesaid conduct and that you do the following additional acts immediately:
1. Publicly answer our questions regarding your threat of a collective "decision...to die," and publicly promise U.S. Secretary of State Cyrus Vance and Guyana Prime Minister Forbes Burnham that you will never encourage or solicit the death of any person at Jonestown, whether individually or collectively, for any reason whatsoever...[ellipses in original]

The "Accusation" included more than a dozen appendices, including an affidavit by Yolanda Crawford, who had lived in Jonestown for three months. Among other charges, she asserted that Jones said that the United States is the "most evil" nation in the world, calling its political and industrial leaders "capitalistic pigs," and that Jones ordered residents to report on each other to prevent treason. Jones also directed harsh punishments when people broke the rules, Crawford said. "The punishments included food-deprivation, sleep-deprivation, hard labor, and eating South American hot peppers." She remarked several times that Jones said he was ready to die for the cause and asked others to commit to it as well.

By targeting Jim Jones, the relatives attempted to disconnect the leader from his people. They were not criticizing their own family members, the document seemed to say, but rather were trying to protect them from the machinations of an evil dictator. This kind of divorce was bound to fail, however, because members of Peoples Temple felt a deep loyalty to Jones as well as to the movement. In addition, they identified with Jones: what happened to him would happen to them.

A break for the Concerned Relatives came with a very high profile defection in May 1978. Deborah Layton, a financial officer and part of the inner circle that handled Temple funds, fled Guyana using a plane ticket her sister had left for her at the U.S. Embassy in Georgetown. Richard McCoy, the U.S. Embassy Consul, flew with Layton back to the United States and listened to her account of life in Jonestown with concern. He advised her to report her charges to various government agencies and officials and warned against going to the media. But Layton went instead to Al and Jeannie Mills, and with the help of Tim Stoen prepared an affidavit. Heading her declaration "Re: the Threat and Possibility of Mass Suicide by Members of the People's Temple," Layton held a press conference in June.[17]

Layton had lived in Jonestown for about four months, caring for her mother Lisa Layton, who had cancer. Her declaration described austere living conditions and depicted Jones as becoming more mentally unstable. "There was constant talk of death," she reported. "In the early days of the People's Temple, general rhetoric about dying for principles was sometimes heard. In Jonestown, the concept of mass suicide for socialism arose." The wire services picked up the story, and news accounts appeared around the country, successfully supporting the Concerned Relatives' effort to present Jonestown as an armed camp facing the potential of mass suicide. With press conferences, investigative reporters, and ongoing negative exposure of Peoples Temple, the second prong of the Concerned Relatives' strategy was working.

THE THIRD PRONG: THE GOVERNMENT

The final element of the Concerned Relatives' offensive against Jim Jones and Peoples Temple, namely, lobbying government officials to investigate the movement, was perhaps the most successful part of their effort. Unfortunately, the relatives did not consider the effect these actions might have upon residents of Jonestown. As outsiders, they were legitimately concerned about family members living in Guyana, and were willing to do anything to get them out, including kidnapping them. But the view from inside was quite different. People in Jonestown lived under a cloud of fear: they were afraid their relationship with Guyanese officials would deteriorate; they were afraid they would lose children and adults if they left the country; they were afraid Jim Jones would be arrested; and they were afraid of invasions by hostile relatives, the Guyana Defense Force, or the CIA. They lived in what they believed was a constant state of siege—a belief only somewhat manufactured, for they *were* besieged and harassed in a number of ways by several agencies in the U.S. government

Media accounts of the departure of Temple members throughout 1977 alerted the Social Security Administration that many beneficiaries had left the country. SSA asked the U.S. Postal Service to notify it of any address changes marked Guyana, but Postal Service officials went a step further. They directed that all U.S. Treasury checks forwarded to Guyana be returned to the government instead, in violation of federal law. It was only because of the intervention of Congressman Phillip Burton that the problem was resolved, and Temple members received the benefits to which they were entitled.

Several ex-members met with a U.S. Treasury agent early in 1977 to discuss firearms violations and smuggling. This conversation led to a U.S. Customs Service search of Temple cargo bound for Guyana from ports in the southeastern United States. Although the search found nothing illegal, the Customs report was forwarded to the U.S. State Department and to the European police agency INTERPOL. Jonestown leaders found out about the INTERPOL report from their friends in the government of Guyana. While they laughed at what they thought were outrageous charges, they feared the report would damage their relationship with government officials.[18] After the Jonestown deaths, the Guyana police found only thirty-five weapons in the community; the Bureau of Alcohol, Tobacco and Firearms traced most of them to a gun shop in Ukiah.[19] Although the weapons had indeed been smuggled into the country, FBI records also show that several residents in Jonestown had filed applications for legal permits with the Guyana government.

The Concerned Relatives also monitored shortwave radio communication that occurred between San Francisco and Guyana and encouraged other ham radio operators to listen in as well. The Temple used shortwave to pass messages back and forth from the United States to Guyana and from Georgetown to Jonestown. They went "out of band" to do this: that is, they shifted to an unauthorized frequency to conduct Temple business. Not only did the Federal Communications Commission not allow this type of shift, it also prohibited conducting business on the amateur airwaves. Prompted by complaints from shortwave listeners (who were encouraged by the Concerned Relatives), the FCC began to monitor Temple radio traffic. They issued warnings and threatened to revoke the licenses of Temple operators in the United States But the FCC's concern went beyond merely monitoring unauthorized uses of the airwaves. Transcripts of conversations between FCC engineers indicate a less than impartial attitude toward Peoples Temple, which they likened to Scientology. They stated that they really wanted to "shut them down" and "cross these guys on a pin head if we would." They notified the Guyana Telephone Company of its investigation into one of the licensees living in Jonestown. And they made tape recordings of Temple radio traffic for the agency and possibly for the FBI. Altogether, the agency turned over twenty-six audiocassettes and four reel-to-reel tapes to the FBI after 18 November.[20]

FOIA documents received from the CIA as part of the decision in the lawsuit filed by Fielding McGehee III (*McGehee v. Central Intelligence Agency*) revealed that the CIA had also been monitoring activities in Jonestown. It is likely that several embassy staff members—including Ambassador John Burke, Deputy Chief of Mission Richard Dwyer, and possibly Consul Richard McCoy—were CIA operatives.[21] McCoy personally told me that the embassy knew of the visits Jonestown leaders had made to Communist embassies, including those of Cuba, North Korea, and the Soviet Union. CIA records clearly show that the agency was keenly aware of events in Jonestown. And the State Department in Washington, D.C., as well as the U.S. Embassy in Georgetown, were barraged with letters from family members seeking the welfare of their relatives living in Jonestown. U.S. State Department cables demonstrate that the Stoen custody case, in particular, took up an enormous amount of time for embassy personnel.

Perhaps more terrifying to the leadership in Jonestown than the CIA was the threat posed by the Internal Revenue Service. The IRS began investigating the Temple's unrelated business income in the spring of 1977. This was the income generated by care facilities, nursing homes, property rentals, and other revenue sources that did not directly come from parishioners and did not directly support the mission and activities of the Temple. If certain proceeds could be taxed, it would greatly reduce the amount of money the group had to spend, especially on its support of the community in Jonestown.

No single entity, no one agency, posed a lethal threat. Moreover, the Concerned Relatives could not take credit for prompting all of the investigations, although their successful publicity campaigns did make government officials sharply aware of Peoples Temple. But taken together, all of these instances of government interest in, and investigation of, Jonestown and Peoples Temple jeopardized the survival of the project. Without financial resources, especially the income from seniors, the community could not exist. Without radio traffic, Jonestown could not communicate with the Temple in San Francisco or Georgetown, in those pre-Internet days. Without goods—not weapons, but durable medical goods, food, clothing, heavy equipment—the community could not even begin to become self-sufficient. If we consider how the situation looked from inside Jonestown, we can begin to imagine how precarious the future appeared to residents. In their minds, the existence of an organized opposition that had poisoned public opinion about the Temple and was attempting to dismantle the community in Jonestown was nothing less than a full-blown conspiracy.

The Concerned Relatives didn't see it that way. Indeed, they seemed to have no idea of the impact their pressure was having within Jonestown. Thus, when Congressman Leo J. Ryan announced his intent to visit Jonestown, the relatives felt that, at last, someone at the highest levels of government was taking up their cause! The view from inside Jonestown was rather different, where Ryan was seen as a potential nemesis: the last straw in the culmination of a yearlong series of problems caused by the Concerned Relatives.

For Further Reading

Several first-person accounts give glimpses into the activities of the Concerned Relatives. They include Jeannie Mills' book *Six Years with God* and Deborah Layton's *Seductive Poison*. In addition, some journalistic accounts detail activities of the Concerned Relatives. George Klineman and Sherman Butler wrote *The Cult That Died* with David Conn, a book that describes their own contacts with Al and Jeannie Mills and the Concerned Relatives. *Raven: The Untold Story of the Rev. Jim Jones and His People*, by Tim Reiterman with John Jacobs presents the story of the Concerned Relatives very sympathetically. A more balanced assessment of the relatives comes from John R. Hall in *Gone from the Promised Land*, while a more critical look at the Millses comes from Lowell Streiker in "Reflections on the Human Freedom Center," an essay that appears in *The Need for a Second Look at Jonestown*.

CHAPTER 5

The Abyss

...And when you look long into an abyss, the abyss also looks into you.

—Friedrich Nietzsche, *Beyond Good and Evil**

In many respects the Concerned Relatives' strategy was extremely successful. They staged media events that kept Peoples Temple in the spotlight. Their lawsuits, even though they were little more than nuisances, cost the Temple money, time, and energy. The government investigations that they instigated threatened the very future of Jonestown, and still more investigations were in the works. The primary goal of their strategy seemed to be working—they were winning in the court of public opinion—and it helped to create an atmosphere of fear and desperation in Jonestown.

Internal forces were fracturing the community as well, however. Spartan conditions grew more severe as the community's attempt to become self-sufficient failed. Control of dissent—as opposed to punishment for breaking the rules—increased, as did testing of loyalty. Jim Jones's mental and physical health deteriorated markedly throughout 1978, so much so that most residents in Jonestown were aware of his decline. Finally, White Nights, Jonestown's description of its emergency preparedness drills, coupled with suicide rehearsals occurred with more intensity and frequency.

When my parents, John and Barbara Moore, visited Jonestown in May 1978, they found a productive community in which people seemed relatively wellnourished, happy to be there, and actively farming. "We came away from the Peoples Temple Agricultural Project with a feeling for its energy and enthusiasm, its creative, wholesome ways (imagine no television—but weekly movies for all), and an understanding of the fascination and high sense of adventure it holds for its residents."[1] Although audiocassettes indicate that this was, in part, the public face Jonestown put on for visitors, it is also evident that the reality was not completely at odds with the façade. A number of developments occurred between September 1977 and November 1978 that combined to bring Jonestown to the brink of the abyss.

THE DECISION TO RELOCATE

One factor that seemed to play a role in the deterioration of Jonestown was the implicit decision to relocate to a Communist country, thereby abandoning operations in Guyana. Although Jonestown leaders investigated several alternatives, it appeared that the Soviet Union was the first-choice destination. Everyone in Jonestown was learning Russian, from oldest to youngest. Charles Garry, the Temple's San Francisco attorney, reported on hearing seniors practicing Russian. Vocabulary worksheets recovered from Jonestown, as well as notes by Edith Roller, demonstrated the strength of commitment to learning the Russian language. An internal document, dated 25 October 1978, discussed various parts of the Soviet Union that might be appealing for Temple members: the areas with a Mediterranean climate, such as the Black Sea or near the Caspian Sea, were top choices, ahead of places with a "southern" climate or a "northern" climate, "not unlike Minneapolis, Minn. Or colder."[2] The memo indicated a desire for a warm climate, although it also recommended that a delegation from Jonestown visit the less desirable areas in winter to evaluate conditions and to judge their suitability for a mass migration.

Part of the impetus for the move was the community's ongoing failure to achieve self-sufficiency. Eugene Chaikin, a member of the Temple who served as its legal advisor, listed the potential problems caused by the lawsuits filed by Steven Katsaris and Wade and Mabel Medlock, especially if the courts found against the Temple:

> This leaves us in a severe predicament here. The predicament will increase as our population increases. We do not feel that as the community is now structured it can ever be financially self-sufficient (we have put 20 times more effort into band and karate in the last six months than into the construction of a sawmill) and we see that historically small, self-contained communities have always failed.[3]

Chaikin wrote that the financial reserves of Peoples Temple were insufficient to continue operations in the long run. He pointed out that more efforts were spent on public relations—presumably fighting the efforts of the Concerned Relatives—than on creating a solid financial foundation upon which to support the community. He gloomily concluded that:

So long as we have to cover our ass, so long as P.R. has priority over production, so long as we are not free to invest and use our money in [George]town, we will not make it here. Unfortunately, time is very much against us now.

Internal documents from Jonestown indicated that discussions were occurring about whether to let people return to the United States Chaikin believed that the group's financial problems might be solved if the dissidents left the community: there would be more resources and fewer troublemakers. Carolyn Layton disagreed, noting that seniors were the primary financial base of the community. "Though a good number would I think stay," she wrote, "the breakdown in structure would have terrible consequences for the discipline of the group as a whole. This does not include possible PR and legal problems," she added.[4]

THE OBSESSION WITH LOYALTY

Chaikin's and Layton's memos to Jones suggest another factor that contributed to the deterioration of life in Jonestown: the continued defection of leaders. In Jonestown this became manifested in increasing demands for loyalty coupled with increasing suppression of dissent. Tim Stoen, the group's highest leader and second only to Jim Jones, had deserted the movement in summer 1977. Not only had he joined the opposition in an attempt to recover his son, his legal and organizational skills gave the Concerned Relatives an effective structure and strategy. It soon became clear that Stoen was spearheading most of the group's efforts: he was representing relatives in lawsuits filed against the Temple; he sent letters to heads of state and to members of Congress charging human rights violations in Jonestown; and he solicited other relatives to join the organization.

Then Deborah Layton defected in May 1978. She had been one of those responsible for Temple finances, entrusted with large sums of cash to deposit in various international banks. When she left, Jonestown leaders had to scramble to change bank accounts. Like Stoen, she joined the opposition. And, like Stoen, she was a traitor in the eyes of Jonestown residents.

It should not be surprising, then, that an obsession with loyalty and a hatred of defectors—real or potential—developed in Jonestown. If two committed leaders could not only leave, but also turn against the movement, who could be trusted? Criticism of life in Jonestown was considered treason; residents were required to report such talk, both in written comments and evaluations of each other, and at weekly Peoples Rallies. According to Deborah Layton, "No one had any confidence in himself or anyone else, not even family."[5] She described an incident in which an eleven-year-old boy reported that his father had told him "that he'd figured a way out." The father was assigned to the Learning Crew, and the son was moved into better quarters.

Anyone who expressed a desire to return to the United States was considered subversive, undermining the cause by a desire for bourgeois material comforts or, worse, giving aid and comfort to the enemy, namely the Concerned Relatives. Instead of tolerating freedom of movement and of access, Jones and the leadership feared every departure as a form of betrayal. Thus, people were kept under strict supervision. In the fall of 1978, when Monica Bagby said to Vernon Gosney, "Let's get the fuck out of this place," his initial reaction was to think it was a trap. But he decided to trust Monica, and they made a pact to do whatever it took to leave Jonestown together. Their mutual encouragement gave them the strength to approach Congressman Ryan on 18 November, and though both were wounded during the shootings at the Port Kaituma airstrip, they survived.[6]

In addition, public avowals of loyalty to the cause—and hatred of one's family—were routinely required. In a form of "witnessing," Jonestown residents would stand up and denounce their relatives, describing the tortures they would inflict upon them. At a community meeting on 13 April 1978, Jones asked, "What the hell do you think ought to be [done]—just tell us, right quick, one line, what do you think should be done with your relatives?"[7] The responses ranged from beating them up to blowing them up. One young woman said:

Dad, I'd personally like to grab my father and string him up by his nuts and have a hot poker, sticking it in some coals and sticking it up his ass, and burning the hell out of him, for doing the things he's doing, because he knows that you saved my sister's life and he knows all the good things you did for us both, and he knew that we wanted to come over here and live peacefully, and this is why he's causing all this hell—

Jones: [High laugh]. I'm sure when you have him tied up by his balls and a hot poker goes up his ass, he would realize something. [High laugh] It's too much, these people. [Laughs]

Young Woman: —just to get him to realize that he's trying to ruin our freedom and trying to take away my daughter's freedom. And I'd like to thank you, Dad.

Jones: Thank you. [Conclusively] He'd realize something, I'd say. [Crowd laughter.]

No one in Jonestown took these statements seriously: they understood them to be a form of testifying to the cause, of demonstrating one's loyalty, especially if one's family members were among the Concerned Relatives who were causing all of the trouble. The more visible the opposition of relatives, the more vociferous and violent the forms of revenge articulated.

Nevertheless, the audio statements of children, teenagers, and others describing the ways they plan to kill family members were chilling.

THE INTENSIFICATION OF PUNISHMENT

Punishments for infractions also seemed to escalate in intensity as people tried to escape what became an increasingly intolerable situation. Keith Wade was severely beaten for running off. When Tommy Bogue and another teenager ran away, they were returned in shackles, their heads were shaved, and they were forced to chop wood until Stephan Jones intervened.[8] A woman with a phobia about snakes suffered intensely when a snake was set on her body and crawled upon it. People were berated for crimes ranging from expressing a critical opinion, to having unauthorized sex, to running away. Children were terrorized by being left in the jungle and told there were tigers nearby.

A new form of social control was introduced: a sensory deprivation chamber. Designed by Tom Grubbs to be a humane form of behavior modification, it was a six-by-four-foot cubicle in which dissidents or those who were emotionally unstable were kept for as long as a week. Though not completely dark—victims could see daylight—it was extremely small. Victims would receive mash and water each day of confinement. When Marceline Jones learned of the box, she insisted that nurses check the vital signs of those confined to it at least every few hours.[9]

Finally, the most intractable problem people were handled in the Extended Care Unit where they were kept under sedation. These were residents who had mental problems or who desperately wanted to leave. Charles Garry suspected that Eugene Chaikin was kept there because of his dissident opinions, when he was unable to meet with the lawyer on Garry's last visit to Jonestown in November 1978; this was confirmed by Mark Lane. Vernon Gosney reported that "he watched Shanda James, Fairie [Fairy] Norwood, and Temple attorney Eugene Chaikin sedated and transformed into shells of their former personalities."[10] In addition, Christine Lucientes, Vincent Lopez, and Patsy Johnson were put into Extended Care.[11] Jones would threaten miscreants with Extended Care if they did not change their attitudes, but it was also used to control people who were mentally ill. Instructions for the medical staff stated, for instance: "Barb Walker is to be kept in 'No Capacity.' She has threatened to kill everyone that kept her away from Steven. Keep her under control in the infirmary."[12] While minor infractions led to assignment on the Learning Crew, Extended Care was reserved for the most serious troublemakers.

THE DETERIORATION OF JIM JONES

An autopsy of Jim Jones found toxic levels of pentobarbital in his body. U.S. Embassy Consul Richard McCoy told me that "by May 1978 it was clear he was on drugs." When U.S. Embassy officials visited Jonestown on 7 November, they described his speech as slurred, his behavior erratic, and his mentation confused. Jones's instructions for 16 October 1978 advised residents to beware of the full moon:

> It's full moon and the sixteenth. Most people it affects positively. We are 98% water and we rise like the tide. Most people it affects positively and some it affects negatively. So we have to be more aware for dangers to our life or crippling disorders or diseases around the sixteenth and the full moon.[13]

John Jacobs, co-author of *Raven*, found a note in Jonestown written by Annie Moore, my sister, in which she said, "I just wanted for you to know that I do not mind being your nurse and there is nothing more I would rather be." The note expressed her frustration with her inability to solve Jones's health problems, especially her failure to be able to give him drugs to help him sleep.

Jones had a history of mental exhaustion. His work on the Indianapolis Human Rights Commission led to his hospitalization at Methodist Hospital. This led to his departure from Indianapolis to Hawaii in 1961 to take a leave of absence, on doctor's orders. Jones collapsed at a Housing Authority meeting in San Francisco in March 1977, and left for Guyana a few days afterward. But Jones had physical symptoms as well. When Dr. Carlton Goodlett, Jones's physician, examined him in August 1978, the physician diagnosed several serious health problems, including an extremely high fever and a fungal disease in his lungs. After the deaths in Jonestown, the *New York Times* reported that Dr. Goodlett believed that Jones would have died by the end of 1978.[14]

Jones's mental and physical decline affected morale in the community. He had expressed a desire to die on numerous occasions. Now his yearning was shared by those who seemed to have given up the fight as well. Had he communicated hope and enthusiasm, his followers would have adopted a different attitude, but his own despair and resignation seeped into all discourse. After Deborah Layton's defection, residents were asked to describe "Dad's Worst Pain." Rita Dennis, age fifteen, wrote that, "He said that he died on May 13 when Debby turned traitor, at least a part of him died. Also he said he is moral because he stayed alive when he don't want to, also he does everything for us, gives us all we need."[15]

WHITE NIGHTS

"White Nights" signified a severe crisis within Jonestown and the possibility of mass death during, or as a result of, an invasion. Jones coined the term, differentiating it from "Black Night" because he was concerned about the racial connotation of that terminology.[16] White Nights had occurred in

Ukiah and San Francisco, but they lacked the intensity of the emergencies in Jonestown, where the entire community assembled to resist an attack. The first one in Jonestown most likely occurred in September 1977, when the Stoens's attorney, Jeff Haas, was in Guyana. Haas had traveled to Jonestown to serve Guyana court papers upon Jones; when community members ripped down the summonses, he persuaded a Guyana court to issue an arrest warrant for Jones. Jonestown leadership believed the community was in danger; they precipitated a state of siege in which residents believed that they were under attack by the Guyana Defense Force. Men, women, and children armed themselves with farm implements, and stood on the perimeter of Jonestown for days, expecting an armed assault. Carolyn Layton wrote that they feared that a government marshal might come at any moment to arrest Jones, and so:

> we had decided that we would die if that were required and it seemed to us that it was. We had received at that time no concrete assurances of anything. No one who has not faced death would fully understand it. A line of people with cutlasses just waiting.[17]

Deborah Layton wrote that she experienced a White Night a few weeks after her arrival with her mother Lisa Layton, probably in January 1978. She heard gunfire from the jungle as everyone raced to the central pavilion that night. Jones announced that they were under attack by the Concerned Relatives and the CIA. "The United States Government does not want us to survive," she reported Jones as saying. "They threaten to surround, attack, torture, and imprison us. We don't want that, do we?"[18] After the community lined up to take poison in order to prevent the torture of babies and children, Jones called off the White Night saying that the crisis was over.

How many White Nights were there in Jonestown? The answer really depends upon how a White Night is defined. I am differentiating between Peoples Rallies, at which residents were called up, criticized, and punished before the community; routine alerts during which residents gathered—frequently in the middle of the night—to ward off danger; and White Nights during which residents truly thought they were in grave peril and faced certain death. While there were frequent meetings that were called White Nights, not every alert carried the possibility of revolutionary suicide; that is, the act of killing oneself to make a political statement. For the purposes of this discussion, I am defining a White Night as an event at which people believed they were threatened, at which they declared their willingness to die for the cause—that very night if necessary—and at which they were prepared to take poison. They were interactive, with Jones probing the beliefs of the assembly and participants raising their own questions. Audiotapes made throughout 1978 revealed a sense of impending doom in discussions about ways to escape, ways to fight, and ways to die. By these criteria, there were about a half dozen full-fledged White Nights. This number is supported by evidence found in audiotapes, Edith Roller's journal, and reports given by survivors.

Usually White Nights corresponded to perceived threats, such as the September 1977 incident that followed Jeff Haas's visit. In 1978 there were at least five White Nights: January 1978, described by Deborah Layton, probably coinciding with the trip of Tim and Grace Stoen to Georgetown, Guyana; February 1978, resulting from the failure of the community doctor to receive an official government license to practice medicine; April 1978 in response to the Concerned Relatives' news conference and media coverage relating to their "Accusation;" May 1978, the night Layton defected; and October 1978, while key leaders of Guyana, including Prime Minister Forbes Burnham, were out of the country.

The White Night of 16 February 1978—the date provided in Edith Roller's journal and confirmed by audiotapes made during the crisis— occurred when the government of Guyana issued Larry Schacht, the project's doctor, a temporary, rather than permanent, license to practice medicine. Jones also announced a power struggle in the Guyana Cabinet, resulting in a friend of Jonestown being ousted by a critic, suggesting that the two events were linked. Supporting the view that White Nights were unusual occurrences, Jones remarked that "We went several months without a goddamn White Night... We're in a wartime emergency... It may not have any meaning at all, but we need to find out where the hell people's heads are."[19] He asserted that the United States was exerting strong pressure in the matter.

It is clear from the tapes made that this February White Night was a test of the community. Various options for resistance were outlined that included moving to the Soviet Union; charging a task force with taking care of the group's enemies in the United States; sending volunteer troops to help in African liberation struggles; going into the jungle as a group and adopting a militant stand; or taking "a potion and we *go*, all of us go." Jones felt that the black-on-black violence that could result from resistance would send the wrong message to the world. Some in the community recommended going on a hunger strike. Jones seized upon this and suggested that some could go to Washington, D.C., and immolate themselves in an act of protest. Others proposed various means of escape.

But the tide turned when several began to say that they felt like dying that night. One woman mirrored the sentiments of many when she said:

> I don't mind dying for the cause, because I *believe* in it. And I do feel that there's need for some people to pave their way through the jungles for refuge or whatever, so that the only true form of socialism can continue to exist... If the enemy came through the jungle, everyone should be willing to die. Fight.

Some expressed concern about the children: what would happen to them if people were fighting? One man said he would not want his daughter to fall into the hands of the fascists. "As much as I wouldn't like it, there's only one way to go. She would have to be put to sleep." When someone suggested committing suicide, Jones stated that personal, individual suicide was an immoral act. "Only revolutionary suicide is justified, when you consider that . . . there's no way to make any moral sense out of further fighting."

The press conference convened by the Concerned Relatives in San Francisco, coupled with the absence of Jonestown's staunchest supporters in the Guyana government (who were out of the country), precipitated the April 1978 White Night, which began on the twelfth and lasted off and on for two days. The first part of the event was devoted to berating Stanley Clayton and his girlfriend Janice Johnson, as Jones expounded on the ways in which sex interfered with the revolution. In times of crisis, he said, "You people won't even rise above your vaginas and your dicks."[20] Eventually, the discussion turned to escape and resistance, revolutionary suicide, and protecting the children from fascists by killing the children. Jones invited people to leave, but then added that "they'll make your life more miserable when you get in the United States."[21] One man challenged another, asking him what he would do if his daughter's life was threatened by the fascists. Since the girl was eleven, Jones said she could fight until she was dead, "unless it came to an overwhelming invasion, and then we would gently put them to sleep." He again asserted that any suicide for selfish reasons—which he claimed were always hostile reasons—was immoral, and would result in being reincarnated in a lower life, form. But revolutionary suicide was honorable. It was during this White Night that residents fantasized about the various ways they would torture their relatives, if they only got the chance.

SUICIDE DRILLS

As early as 1973, when the Gang of Eight defected, Jones proposed a "translation," or a suicide of the leadership, according to Jeannie Mills.[22] A number of former members reported an actual suicide drill that occurred during a Planning Commission meeting in San Francisco. This incident probably occurred in 1976 when Jones asked his inner circle to drink some wine, and then informed them that they had drunk poison that would kill them within forty-five minutes. No one rebelled or questioned his decision, and some expressed concern that their children were not participating along with them. Jones then announced that there was no poison; it had merely been a test. "The thought of dying had raised expressions of loyalty, and sacrifice, even of the lives of their children," Reiterman and Jacobs observed. "For some, incredibly, it was a beautiful sight to behold."[23]

Edith Roller's journal for the 16 February 1978 White Night—which began at 6:00 in the morning and ended at 10:30 that evening—described a suicide drill.[24] After discussing the range of options, Jones declared there was no other choice but revolutionary suicide:

> All would be given a potion [Roller wrote], juice combined with a potent poison. After taking it, we would die painlessly in about 45 minutes . . . The seniors were allowed to be seated and be served first. At the beginning those who had reservations were allowed to express them, but those who did were required to be first. As far as I could see once the procession started, very, very few made any protest. A few questions were asked, such as an inquiry about those in the nursery. Jim said they had already been taken care of.

Roller reported on her thoughts as she waited in line to receive the poison, musing on her impending death. She didn't think that the immediate problem warranted such a drastic solution. In fact, she doubted that they were actually receiving poison. She thought about others who had died bravely— Nathan Hale and Charles II—and then wondered why she didn't think about political martyrs like Victor Jara and Salvador Allende. She thought about her sisters, and about the poetry she wouldn't be able to read. "I had to die sometime," she wrote, but admitted, "I must say I didn't look forward to it with joy." As she got closer to the vat of poison, she tried to check the time:

> I was annoyed that I did not have my watch. Then I was amused at myself. When one is about to die, what difference does it make what time it is? I couldn't very well write in my journal: "I died at 5:30 p.m. on the 16th of February 1978."

When Jones announced that they weren't drinking poison, some were disappointed, including Roller. She regretted that she was not going to be relieved of her extra chores on the Learning Crew.

Statements Jonestown residents made to outsiders repeated the rhetoric heard in the suicide drills. On 14 March 1978, Pam Moton wrote a letter to all members of the U.S. Congress, in which she complained of the harassment from U.S. government agencies that Peoples Temple and Jonestown were receiving. It is evident, she stated, "That people cannot forever be continually harassed and beleaguered by such tactics without seeking alternatives that have been presented. I can say without hesitation that we are devoted to a decision that it is better even to die than to be constantly harassed from one continent to the next." She concluded by writing, "I hope you can look into this matter and protect the right of over 1,000 people from the U.S. to live in peace."[25] This declaration of her willingness to die alarmed the Concerned Relatives, who included Moton's letter as an appendix to their "Accusation."

A month later Harriett Tropp reiterated Moton's avowal of suicide as an option if the relatives' badgering did not cease. In response to the Concerned Relatives' "Accusation," she read a prepared statement over the shortwave radio in which she cited Martin Luther King's affirmation of ultimate commitment to the cause when he said, "We must develop the quiet courage of dying for a cause."[26] She went on to say that the people in Jonestown would resist, actively, "putting our lives on the line if it comes to that." She compared the community to the Jews who resisted in the Warsaw Ghetto, and to Patrick Henry:

> If people cannot appreciate that willingness to die if necessary, rather than to compromise the right to exist, free from harassment, and the kind of indignities we have been subjected to, then they will never understand the integrity, the honesty, and the bravery of Peoples Temple nor the depth of commitment of Jim Jones to the principles he has struggled for all his life.

She concluded that, "It is not our purpose to die . . . but under these outrageous attacks, we have decided to defend the integrity of our community and our pledge to do this. We are confident that people of conscience and principle will understand our position. We make no apologies for it."

In handwritten notes directed to Jim Jones, others affirmed a willingness to kill their relatives before killing themselves. One man wrote that he knew how to use a handgun from his security job and was willing to use it. Another wrote that, "I would go back and get [Temple defector] Liz Foreman and [reporter] Lester Kinsolving. [Jim] McElvane agreed with me one time that I would be capable of assassination and maybe get by with it. After it was done I would commit self-immolation at an appropriate location." An African American woman wrote a note suggesting she go to Washington, D.C., and set herself on fire to make their demands known. After the community had viewed the film *Day of the Jackal*, several alluded to the torture methods they had seen. One writer said, "I could do like *Day of the Jackal* only to kill Tim Stone [*sic*] and then commit revolutionary suicide." Others pledged to blow themselves up at the Pentagon, or in other buildings and on bridges for maximum destruction.[27]

THE CONSPIRATORS UNMASKED

Overwhelmed by the success of the Concerned Relatives' publicity initiatives, Peoples Temple members wanted to develop a countervailing strategy that would tell their side of the story. They sought a writer or filmmaker who would show Jonestown as it truly was: a glorious socialist experiment. To that end they approached filmmaker Paul Jarrico, who turned them down, and Don Freed, a screenwriter, who did not. Freed had written *The*

Killing of JFK and *Code Name Zorro*, and co-authored *Executive Action* with Mark Lane, who asserted that a conspiracy had existed to assassinate John F. Kennedy. In 1978, the two were part of the Citizens Commission of Inquiry, which was investigating the Martin Luther King Jr. assassination. Freed and Lane charged that convicted assassin James Earl Ray had not killed King, but rather government conspirators had set up Ray as a fallguy. Freed traveled to Jonestown in late August 1978 and discussed the King-Ray case. The community impressed him greatly, as did its fears of various intrigues against them. And Freed impressed the community, as Carolyn Layton wrote: "He was thrilled with this place—just couldn't stop talking about it. He envisions people from all over the world coming to see and write about it—from major universities."[28]

Although Freed had considered writing about Jonestown, he decided that a book might take too long to develop, given the urgency of the Temple's cause. An aggressive public relations program was what was needed. It is clear that the community saw Freed as a potential savior, since he seemed to believe in the possibility of a real conspiracy. And Freed brought concrete hope to the group: first, by enlisting Mark Lane, a high-profile personage in conspiracy circles, in the counteroffensive; and second, by identifying an actual conspirator, Joe Mazor.

Joe Mazor was a colorful character. An ex-convict, he nevertheless obtained a California private investigator's license. He claimed to have investigated Jim Jones in 1976; and in August 1977 he turned over an audiotape to local law enforcement that purported to have Tim Stoen threatening Marvin Swinney into signing over the deed to his house in Redwood Valley.[29] After damaging news articles hammered the Temple throughout that same summer, Mazor rounded up more than a dozen clients from relatives who wanted to get their children out of Jonestown. He alleged that he was involved in a plot to kidnap the children, a scheme which supposedly coincided with the September 1977 six-day siege in Jonestown. But, he said, the plan was abandoned when the strike force failed to find barbed wire in Jonestown and he observed how happy children seemed to be. He did locate two of the children who had been in the Millses' care, although Charles Garry pointed out that they happened to be living in San Francisco with their birth mother.[30]

Peoples Temple sent Carol McCoy to Mazor, pretending to be a parent who wanted to get her four children out of Jonestown.[31] The only date cue in the document is Mazor's reference to a parent who went to Guyana and jeopardized the possibility of ever getting his daughter back. He may have been alluding to Steven Katsaris's unsuccessful trip in September 1977 to visit his daughter Maria, or to Katsaris's disastrous encounter two months later in which Maria said her father had molested her. Mazor told Carol McCoy that he had already recovered some children but did not say who. He said Jim Jones was a very smart con man, who was able to outwit the relatives. He also said Peoples Temple was selling the passports of Jonestown residents and that they had already appeared on the black market. (This was not the case, since a trunk full of all the residents' passports was found in Jonestown.) Mazor's main motivation was financial: "I'm not going to encourage you or discourage you," he said to Carol McCoy, "but it's going to cost and there's always a chance you may not get [your children]."

On 5 September 1978, Don Freed, Joe Mazor, and Mark Lane converged in a San Francisco hotel suite for an interview that included Pat Richartz, an aide to Charles Garry. A conspiracy existed, but it excluded Mazor at that point: the other three pretended to be discussing a film project with the private eye as a way to probe what he actually knew and how he had been involved with the Concerned Relatives. "The principal investor in this area," Freed told Mazor, "likes the idea of a controversy in a real-life story, in a real foreign country, and a real large group of people."[32] The interview was wideranging, although much of it focused on Tim Stoen, who Mazor asserted had worked for the CIA and had a record with INTERPOL. The private detective believed Stoen guilty of committing fraud while he was both a Temple member and employed as an officer of the court in the district attorneys' offices in Mendocino County and San Francisco County. "I have never talked to Tim Stoen," Mazor said, "because as far as I was concerned, Tim Stoen was always as dirty as Jones was." Freed added, "And maybe a lot worse."

When Jim Jones heard of Mazor's assertion that Stoen worked for the CIA, he broke into tears, according to Mark Lane. "He began to sob, unable to control his weeping," wrote Lane in his own account of the events at Jonestown. "A stunned audience sat quietly, wondering what Jones had learned that had affected him so profoundly...He said hoarsely into the microphone, 'I have been waiting for this day all my life. We now have proof—real proof—that Stoen is working for the CIA.'" The audience began to cry when they heard these words, believing that the intolerable pressure under which they had been living might be coming to an end now that the truth had come out.[33] Lane's book asserted that Mazor never said any such thing about Stoen, even though a transcript of the 5 September interview clearly stated that Stoen was linked to INTERPOL; that he had "intelligence connections" and ties to the CIA; and that he criticized Communism publicly while standing in front of the Berlin Wall. "If you have this guy going back to the Berlin Wall in the fifties [sixties], associated as he is with the American intelligence at that time," asked Lane at the interview, "and then the idea later on is to destroy the Temple, is it possible he is in deep cover, setting up a whole series of things which even the Temple didn't know about at the time?" Moreover, a summary of the discussion prepared by Freed and sent to Jones and Garry stated that: "Included in the conspiracy are...Tim Stoen, with the knowledge and connivance of both the FBI and the CIA."[34] Freed added, "Bring Mazor to Jonestown at once."

Less than a week after the interview, Joe Mazor and Charles Garry were in Guyana, where Mazor revealed his role with the Concerned Relatives and expressed support for those living in Jonestown. They were primed with an assessment Sharon Amos had done on Mazor's "sociopathic" personality. His conversations showed "that he feels he can out-con people . . . If we act very impressed with his abilities, it might soften him so he can be a big hero." But, she added, "It looks like he'll sell out to the highest bidder."[35]

Nevertheless, the leadership took much of what Mazor asserted at face value, unable to separate the wheat from the chaff. Again the conversation focused on Tim Stoen, his ties to the CIA in the early 1960s, and the criminal charges the attorney might be facing. This was good news for the Temple since Garry was in the middle of a legal offensive against the former Temple legal advisor. Mazor also said that the Temple had been infiltrated three years earlier by an FBI agent, who had since left.[36] Notes from the conversation were a mishmash of allegations, some of which were true, some of which were false, and most of which were impossible to verify one way or another. But this did not stop the group from attempting to hire Mazor for their own purposes and from trumpeting him as a conspirator who, having realized that the Concerned Relatives were lying and Peoples Temple was telling the truth, had switched sides.

In his own book *The Strongest Poison*, Mark Lane went to great lengths to discredit Mazor. He detailed the contradictions in the investigator's accounts, as well as the improbability of many of his claims. Regardless of whether the detective or Lane were telling the truth, Jim Jones and the people in Jonestown believed that they had found what they were looking for. CIA spies—even though Mazor refused to name them—were working in Jonestown. The U.S. Embassy had sent an assassination squad to kill Jones.[37] Stoen must have embezzled millions while working for the Temple. And so, Joe Mazor went from pariah to partner.

Lane arrived in Guyana as Mazor and Garry were leaving, and reached Jonestown on 15 September 1978, just ten days after the fateful fake movie interview. The lawyer drew parallels between the conspiracy to kill Dr. King and the conspiracy against Jones. On his way out of Guyana, he held a press conference at Lamaha Gardens, the Temple's headquarters in Georgetown, and announced that a "massive conspiracy to destroy Peoples Temple" existed. He repeated the charges at a formal press conference in San Francisco on 3 October, but not before outlining a detailed proposal for a "counteroffensive" the Temple should undertake against Tim Stoen, the Concerned Relatives, and, most importantly, government agencies.

In a document dated 27 September 1978, Lane asserted that, "Even a cursory examination reveals that there has been a coordinated campaign to destroy the People's Temple and to impugn the reputation of its leader Bishop Jim Jones."[38] He identified the CIA, the FBI, the IRS, the FCC, and the U.S. Postal Service as players in the intrigue and asserted that members

as the means, ordering the drugs. Dr. Schacht tested potassium cyanide on one of the pigs to see how quickly the poison took effect, and to determine whether death were painful. A survivor interviewed by FBI agents in December 1978 reported seeing two bags of cyanide delivered to Jonestown via the group's boat the *Cudjoe*.[44]

It is clear that for almost a year residents of Jonestown had been conditioned to think and talk about, and to make plans for, the possibility of mass suicide. Ordinary suicide would be selfish, but revolutionary suicide would send a message to the rest of the world. The declaration of one's willingness to die indicated one's commitment to Jim Jones and to the community. It was proof that one was not a traitor.

Temple members' reflections on, and discussions of, their own deaths, constituted a highly ritualized activity. Suicide was simulated and a narrative of martyrdom was repeated, practiced, and rehearsed again and again. These rehearsals undoubtedly made the final White Night a success, for without them the last act would have been unthinkable.

For Further Reading

Deborah Layton describes the conditions of desperation, tension, and anxiety under which Jonestown residents lived in her book *Seductive Poison*. Tim Reiterman and John Jacobs also provide firsthand accounts of persons they interviewed in *Raven*.

Notes Jonestown residents wrote to Jim Jones and audiotaped testimonials in Peoples Rallies show how residents felt about their opponents. They also provide ample evidence of ongoing indoctrination into the concept of revolutionary suicide and the possibility of dying for socialism. In addition, audiotapes made during White Nights dramatically depict what happened during the manufactured sieges that occurred in Jonestown with increasing intensity throughout 1978. Several tapes are noted by "Q" number in the endnotes.

CHAPTER 6

Preserving the Ultimate Concern

It's been a pleasure walking with all of you in this revolutionary struggle. No other way I would rather go to give up my life for socialism,
communism, and I thank Dad very much.
    —Woman about to take poison, *Jonestown Audiotape**

The decision to die did not occur suddenly or surprisingly. It was discussed
and rehearsed for months. In addition, the activities of cultural opponents
continued to threaten the existence of Jonestown. These activities escalated
over the course of 1978, and culminated in the visit of Leo Ryan. Violence
erupted because Jonestown residents believed that Ryan jeopardized their
ultimate concern, which was to be in solidarity with all oppressed peoples,
but especially with African Americans. He represented the power of the state
and its ability to destroy the community.

Historians and religious studies scholars use the term "millennialism" to
describe any group that is working toward a radically new future: it could
describe nineteenth-century Marxists who predicted a type of secular utopia,
or twenty-first century Christian fundamentalists who believe the battle of
Armageddon will be fought in Israel in the near future. Catherine Wessinger,
a professor of Religious Studies at Loyola University, New Orleans, called
groups that expect far-reaching changes to come after a major catastrophe or
a series of disasters "catastrophic millennialists." She identified groups that
anticipate gradual change and expect improvements to arrive step-by-step
over a long period of time, "progressive millennialists."[1]

People joined Peoples Temple and moved to Jonestown because they believed they could bring about a new society based on liberty, justice, and
racial equality. In that sense, they were progressive millennialists. Just as

they viewed Jonestown as an ideal society, they also believed that the United States was corrupt, a fascist dictatorship was at hand, and African Americans and their sympathizers could expect to be arrested, imprisoned, tortured, and killed. They saw the world dualistically, with good guys (themselves) and bad guys (those who opposed them). In that sense, they were catastrophic millennialists. What happened then, when their dream of fundamental change was deferred or thwarted?

According to Wessinger, Peoples Temple was a "fragile" millennial group, in that the movement felt harassed and "perceive[d] their millennial goal (their ultimate concern) as failing."[2] Internal as well as external pressures caused the residents of Jonestown to turn to violence in order to protest and to resist the injustices they believed were occurring. As Wessinger wrote:

> If members of a catastrophic millennial group perceive themselves as being persecuted by outside cultural opponents, and furthermore, perceive that they are failing to achieve their ultimate concern, this will be a group that is likely to commit violent acts in order to preserve its ultimate concern.[3]

The residents of Jonestown found themselves in this exact situation by November 1978. They believed that the commitment to racial unity embodied in their community was in mortal danger.

A VISIT IS ANNOUNCED

Congressman Leo Ryan, a Democratic congressman from San Mateo, grew interested in Peoples Temple in late 1977 after reading a news article about the death of Bob Houston, a Temple member and the son of Sam Houston, a friend and constituent of the congressman. Sam and his wife Nadyne were convinced that Bob had been murdered by Temple members. Bob was a Southern Pacific trainman who had been crushed by a train in the railroad yards. An official investigation reported it an accident. Ryan met with the Houstons, and in short order became involved with the Concerned Relatives, due in part to letters from other constituents. Ryan also had an interest in cults because one of his daughters belonged to a new religion.

Many saw Ryan as a crusader willing to take risks to enact meaningful change and important legislation, such as sponsoring the Hughes-Ryan Act which required the president to report covert operations to Congress. Others considered him reckless and foolhardy, a grandstander who sought publicity by going undercover in Folsom Prison and then writing a play about his experience, and by taking on those who hunted baby seals.

Although he had notified the State Department in September that he planned to visit Jonestown sometime after 10 November, Ryan did not inform Jim Jones of the trip until 1 November, when he sent a letter declaring his intent. He did not request an invitation, but announced that he would be meeting with Guyana government officials as well as traveling to Jonestown. Though initially receptive, the leaders of Peoples Temple changed their minds when they learned he was bringing reporters and relatives with him. They felt that Ryan showed a lack of impartiality by including enemies of the Temple in his delegation. A cable from John Burke, the U.S. Ambassador to Guyana, told the Secretary of State that:

> PT seemed convinced that Codel [Congressional Delegation] was hostile, would be arriving with well-developed prejudices against PT and merely wanted an on-the-spot visit to enable Codel to return to U.S. and reiterate prejudiced view of People's Temple community with more authority than before. PT officials had apparently cited to [Guyana Ambassador Laurence] Mann coincident visit by NBC camera team as proof-positive of Codel's bad faith.[4]

Jim Jones announced the congressman's visit to the community with an alert: "Attention, attention. Every member of the community must come to the pavilion immediately . . . We may have the invasion, not with guns, but with hostile racists."[5] Jones told the assembly that relatives were "planning some kind of violent action against us, an entry into our project by force." He asked those present to come up with a list of any relatives they thought might be hostile to the project, with the idea that they might persuade Guyanese officials to prevent the entry of anyone on the list into the country. Pages and pages of the names of relatives to be denied admittance were gathered. But the list was so extensive and far-reaching and included so many people who had never shown hostility or animosity to the group, that it could be—and maybe should be—read as a catalogue of farewells.

Although Jones claimed that Ryan was a fascist who supported Augusto Pinochet (the congressman had in fact voted to authorize military aid to the Chilean dictator's regime), a fact sheet that the group prepared painted a different picture:

> Congressman Leo Ryan—A Fact Sheet—Eleventh District, Democrat 53 years old, born in Lincoln, Nebraska, career as a high school teacher and principal
>
> Does not list his religion as most other congressmen do
>
> His district is suburban, white collar, white; a generally Republican district, but not very Reagan-like conservatives . . .
>
> He is very tight with Andrew Young, who was the keynote speaker at his big testimonial, which some of us attended in 1976. He is

considered a liberal, and his voting record, with only a few exceptions, is straight liberal

FOR defense spending cuts
FOR Chrome ban on Rhodesia
FOR delay of B-1 bomber
FOR Consumer Protection Agency[6]

Fearing that antagonistic relatives accompanying Ryan would damage their relations with Guyana officials, Temple leaders in Georgetown planned to warn their friends in government by making outrageous allegations: Tim Stoen was a transvestite, Jeannie Mills enjoyed sex by imagining children being tortured, Howard Oliver was a bookie and a drug dealer. They also made, or planned to make, a $500 gift to the People's National Congress with the announcement that their sawmill was operating, and the comments, "and as we prosper we want Guyana to prosper." Government leaders urged Jones and his staff to let Ryan into Jonestown, saying that this would allow the community to make its case before the public. But feelings in Jonestown ran extremely high against both the congressman and his entourage. About two weeks before their arrival, residents agreed that they would kill anyone who attempted to step onto the property, even their own children. Jones believed that his estranged daughter Suzanne was one of those coming, and proclaimed that he would not hesitate "to blow her brains apart like a piece of cabbage." The remark was met with cheers by the community.[7]

Jones put the impending visit within the context of world affairs: terrorist attacks in Italy, Angola's liberation struggle, opposition to the Shah of Iran, and the defeat of African American members of Congress in recent elections, such as Mervyn Dymally for Lieutenant Governor of California, Congressman Charles Diggs of Detroit, and Senator Edward Brooke of Massachusetts. "Remember, we are still in a state of siege," said Jones.[8] He noted that some infiltrators may try to secretly come up via the Kaituma River. "So we must unify and forget what little differences and disagreements and what we may feel are deprivations, and realize that we are under the onslaught of a direct move of a mercenary fascist effort of the United States of America." To resist this effort, more than 800 people signed a "resolution of the community" dated 9 November that stated they did not wish to see Congressman Ryan, the media, or any "members of a group of so-called 'concerned relatives.'"[9]

Despite the siege mentality, the community continued to plan for the future. The basketball team was looking forward to its scheduled match in Georgetown against Guyana's national team. The Jonestown Express, the community's showcase musical group, was rehearsing for an upcoming concert in Georgetown. Radio traffic indicated the day-to-day concerns of running the project, with notations about medicines to procure, debate over the purchase of a dead pig for food, doctor and dentist appointments, and other mundane tasks. In fact, the basketball team was in Georgetown during Ryan's visit. Although Jones had ordered the players to return to Jonestown, they refused the command, saying they wanted to stay and play the game.

Complicating matters for the group was a rift between its two rival attorneys, Mark Lane and Charles Garry. While Garry handled the Temple's legal affairs in San Francisco, managing cases in which the organization was either a defendant or a plaintiff, Lane had been hired to run the high-profile media and legal counteroffensive against the Concerned Relatives. Temple leaders turned to Lane, rather than Garry, to handle Ryan's visit, and Garry first learned of Ryan's trip from the newspapers. Competition and professional jealousy between the two men resulted in conflicting instructions and directions for Temple residents in Guyana. But Lane assumed the role of point man, and initially wrote Ryan asking him to delay the trip until after his own testimony before a House committee regarding the King case was completed. Ryan responded by saying that the schedule would not be changed.

Before the trip, Ryan and his staff members met frequently with State Department officials concerning the visit. On 13 November, Ryan brought along Deborah Layton and other Concerned Relatives to one of the meetings to "review charges of mistreatment of Jonestown residents."[10] The next day the delegation flew to Guyana. It included people who had filed suit against Peoples Temple: Steven Katsaris and his son Anthony; Tim and Grace Stoen; Howard and Beverly Oliver; and Jim Cobb. It also included reporters like Tim Reiterman and Gordon Lindsay who had written critical stories about the Temple, as well as an NBC-TV news team whom Lindsay had contacted. The reporters initially encountered difficulties when they tried to enter the country, gaining entry only after the U.S. Embassy intervened.

Several Concerned Relatives showed up unannounced at Lamaha Gardens in Georgetown and were turned away. But some informal contacts between Jonestown residents and the visitors resulted in friendly conversations. Grace Stoen talked with Stephan Jones about her son John Victor, and cried during the whole conversation. Leo Ryan also dropped in at Lamaha Gardens, and his openness seemed to encourage occupants there to recommend that he be allowed into Jonestown. Nevertheless, Tim Stoen's threat to "liberate at least some of the people who are down here against their will," loomed large in the minds of Jonestown residents.[11]

A day or two before Ryan's arrival in Jonestown, Jones made a number of implicit and explicit threats against the congressman. "I don't know how long he'll stay, and I don't know what necessarily will take place and what kind of sequential arrangement. But I can assure you that if he stays long enough for tea, he's gonna regret it."[12] The crowd applauded, and when he asked if anyone wanted to talk with Ryan, they shouted, "No!" He referred to an encounter Clare Bouquet—one of Ryan's constituents and a Concerned

Relative—had with members of the basketball team in Georgetown, noting that she said she had a change of heart regarding the Jonestown community, and that she thought her son Brian was happy there. After naming some of the other family members who were part of Ryan's delegation, Jones simply said (to applause), "We been debating about dying till, hell, it's easier to die than to talk about it." After a break in the audiotape, Jones directed people over the public address system, "to get some rest, lay down, rest, groom yourself so you look well, dress the very best you can." Clearly, this portion was taped on 17 November, for Jones announced that they should anticipate the appearance of Ryan around five o'clock. He advised them to be pleasant and friendly but to keep to themselves. Toward the end Jones said somewhat prophetically:

> Now one thing before it's finished. I love you, and that love has carried you thus far, and it could carry you on. Be in peace.

Marceline then picked up and praised the community for its success.

> We are family, we are comrades, we've done what has never been done in the history of the world under the leadership of Jim Jones, and we are here and we're proud of it.

The tape ended as she asked the group to sing the Guyana national anthem together.

THE FATAL TRIP TO JONESTOWN

Ryan's party left the Georgetown airport at 2:00 p.m. on Friday, 17 November, with no assurances that they would be able to get into Jonestown. But according to Tim Carter, a Temple member who had posed earlier that month as a defector so that he could infiltrate the Concerned Relatives, it didn't matter to Ryan whether he actually got inside the community.[13] Jim Jones and the people of Jonestown were in a no-win situation, just as Tim Stoen had planned it: either Ryan would be stopped at the gates to Jonestown, so "it would be a big media event, and they would launch a media blitz" or, if Ryan were allowed into Jonestown, the congressional party would get at least one person to defect. Stoen estimated that he could get at least ten people to leave with Ryan. Either way, Stoen said, "We can do a great deal of damage to the Temple," according to Carter: "[Stoen] made it very plain that the Ryan trip was part of a whole campaign to destroy the Temple. This is their whole life. This is their entire commitment."

The plane that arrived at the Port Kaituma airstrip accommodated eighteen people: the official party included Ryan; his aide Jackie Speier; Deputy Chief of Mission at the U.S. Embassy Richard Dwyer; and Neville

Annibourne, an officer from the Guyana Ministry of Information; the Temple's two lawyers, Lane and Garry; eleven reporters; and four representatives of the Concerned Relatives.[14] The people from Jonestown who met the airplanes were relatively uncommunicative. They allowed Ryan, Speier, and Dwyer to come to Jonestown, but kept reporters and relatives at the airstrip. Garry and Lane eventually convinced Jones to allow both groups to visit, although the Temple leader insisted that reporter Gordon Lindsay stay in Port Kaituma. While they waited for the others to come, Ryan and Speier interviewed individuals whose family members had made inquiries.

Dinner in Jonestown that night was barbecued pork, greens, and potatoes. The visitors were entertained by the Jonestown Express, and by vocalist Dianne Wilkinson. Although her job in Jonestown was to take popular songs and rewrite the lyrics for a socialist sensibility, that night she sang "That's the Way of the World" by Earth, Wind, and Fire, unchanged. Marceline welcomed everyone and asked Ryan to speak. He mentioned that he had encountered several former students from his teaching days in San Mateo County at the project. He briefly turned serious and reminded his audience that he was making a congressional inquiry to find out more about the operation.

> But I can tell you right now that from the few conversations I've had with some of the folks here already this evening, that whatever the comments are, there are some people here who believe this is the best thing that ever happened to them in their whole life.[15]

After the crowd cheered for several minutes, he jokingly expressed the regret that they couldn't all register to vote in his district. Some reporters thought that the enthusiasm of the audience, and their appreciation of the music and of Ryan, were staged; but people who were more familiar with Peoples Temple—like Tim Carter and Mark Lane—believed the response was absolutely genuine.

Reporters interviewed Jones afterward, but, over their protests, he sent them back to Port Kaituma for the night. Before then, however, Richard Dwyer had received a note from a resident expressing the desire to leave. Vernon Gosney asked the Deputy Chief of Mission to help him leave that very night. Although Dwyer said that was not possible, he agreed to make arrangements the next day. Gosney also slipped a note to Don Harris, the NBC reporter, explaining that he and Monica Bagby both wanted to leave. The reporters spent the night in Port Kaituma talking with local Guyanese and swapping horror stories about Jim Jones and Peoples Temple.

Ryan and Speier continued to interview residents on the morning of 18 November, and the reporters returned to the project. The journalists chafed at a tour given by Marceline and, deciding they no longer had anything to lose by becoming more aggressive, they began to demand entrance to a dormitory that housed about eighty to one hundred elderly women. They were shocked to find row after row of bunk beds.

Meanwhile, two families—the Parks and the Bogues—expressed a desire to leave with Ryan. These defections seemed to devastate Jones, and he tried to talk them into staying, but they felt he could not be trusted to let them leave once the delegation had gone. They departed with Ryan and the media.

Tim Stoen's estimate of the number of defectors was close: fourteen people left with Ryan, not including Larry Layton, who posed as a defector. Others expressed the desire to leave, but stayed out of loyalty to their family. Al Simon tried to take his children out, but his wife Bonnie vociferously objected, and they remained. Two families and some young adults also left early that morning, saying they were planning to have a picnic. Julius Evans and his wife and children, Leslie Wilson and her son, and Richard Clark and Diane Louie quickly made their way to the railroad tracks that led to Matthews Ridge, about thirty miles away. Two other residents—Johnny Franklin and Robert Paul—met up with them in the jungle, and all eleven arrived on foot late that evening.

Ryan said he would stay in Jonestown to negotiate safe passage for others who wished to leave. But when Don Sly attacked him with a knife, Richard Dwyer expressed concern about the congressman's safety, and persuaded him to head for the airstrip on a Temple truck.

The defectors, the journalists, and Ryan and his aides waited anxiously at Port Kaituma for two planes to take them to Georgetown. When a small Cessna and a twin-engine Otter landed, it was obvious that not everyone would be able to leave that day. Ryan wanted to get the defectors to safety as quickly as possible, and asked the reporters, anxious to file stories in Georgetown, to stay behind. Dwyer reported Sly's attack on Ryan to the local district officer, and asked that the news be radioed to the police in the capital. He then made his way back to the landing strip with Neville Annibourne. A few Guyanese stood along the perimeter nearby. Journalists, who were filming the departure, as well as Ryan and Speier, were on the airstrip as relatives began boarding the airplanes, when shots rang out from a tractor pulling a trailer that had parked at the side of the runway. According to Richard Dwyer:

> The firing continued for several minutes and then there was a short pause before the firing recommenced. It seemed to me that one or more of the assailants with shotguns was proceeding amongst the wounded, firing a blast at each of them... The truck and tractor were heard to drive away and after a few moments those who had not been wounded and the ambulatory wounded began to get to their feet... I went over to the Congressman, who had been badly hit. It was clear that he was dead.[16]

Five people were killed on the airstrip, four of them deliberately targeted: Leo Ryan; Bob Brown, an NBC cameraman; Don Harris, an NBC reporter; and Greg Robinson, a photographer from the *San Francisco Examiner*. Patricia Parks, one of the defectors, was accidentally shot and killed as she attempted to board one of the planes. Jackie Speier was shot at point-blank range, but survived the four bullet wounds she sustained. The Guyanese police who witnessed the shooting had not involved themselves in what appeared to be an incident that involved only Americans.

Once the shooting outside the aircraft started, Larry Layton began to fire inside the Cessna, using a gun he had smuggled onboard. He wounded Monica Bagby and Vernon Gosney before his gun jammed and he was disarmed by Dale Parks. While the Otter was disabled due to gunfire, the Cessna took off with Bagby, leaving Gosney, seriously injured, behind. Layton was turned over to the police.

A number of defectors fled into the surrounding jungle once the shooting started, and did not emerge for hours, or until the next day. Dwyer took charge of those remaining on the airstrip and spent a sleepless night caring for the wounded, which included journalists, defectors, and himself.

THE DEATHS IN JONESTOWN

After Ryan's group left Jonestown, the loudspeaker urged everyone to come to the central pavilion, the scene of the previous evening's entertainment. A tape recording of the event repeats many of the themes and tropes of previous White Nights: the fear of imminent invasion; the desire to protect the children; the need for the community to take action.[17] Jones predicted that someone was going to shoot the pilot of one of the planes, an indication that he knew Larry Layton was only posing as a defector. He said the time had come to be kind to the children and the seniors, and to "step over quietly," in what he claimed was a revolutionary act. He then invited dissent.

Only a single person opposed him, at least according to the audiotape. Christine Miller, a sixty-year-old black woman, asked if it was too late for Russia. Jones responded that Russia would no longer accept the group because of the "stigma" that arose because of the deaths he presumed had occurred.

Miller had defied Jones on previous occasions. According to several sources, Jones threatened her with a gun at an earlier group meeting, saying he could shoot her and get away with it.

> Christine replied, "You can shoot me, but you are going to have to respect me first." Jones repeated his threat with more menace, but Christine wouldn't back down. "You can do that," she said, "but you are going to have to respect me first." A moment later, Jones was

standing before her, holding the gun to her head, shouting his rage at her defiance. She looked him in the eye and said calmly, "You can shoot me, but you will respect me." The standoff ended when Jones—not Christine—backed down.[18]

Miller was respected in Jonestown, and she stood her ground on the final day, throwing Jones's words back at him: "I feel like as long as there's life, there's hope. That's my faith," she said. Jones had said this at a White Night, shortly before she arrived in Jonestown.[19]

Miller continued to argue with Jones, saying that too few people left "for twelve hundred people to give them their lives for those that left." I'm not afraid to die, she declared, and Jones agreed. She went on:

> But I look at the babies and I think they deserve to live, you know? When we destroy ourselves, we're defeated. We let them, the enemies, defeat us.

Jim McElvane, who had arrived just two days earlier, then challenged Miller:

> Just hold on, sister, just hold on. We have made that day. We made a beautiful day, and let's make it a beautiful day. That's what I say.

The crowd applauded McElvane. Miller persisted, but eventually the others shouted her down.

Just as the group had discussed on several prior occasions, the children were given the poison first. Odell Rhodes, one of the few surviving eyewitnesses to the events, reported that two nurses brought out a vat of poison-laced fruit punch. Ruletta Paul, a young mother sitting in the front row with her infant child, stood up and walked to the table without being asked. Rhodes recounted:

> "She just poured it down the baby's throat. And then she took the rest herself. It didn't take them right away. She had time to walk down outside. I watched her go, and then the next woman, Michelle Wilson, she came up with her baby and did the same thing."[20]

As the children were dying, residents of Jonestown stepped forward to announce their commitment to die. McElvane assured people that life on the other side would feel good, "you've never felt so good as how that feels." One woman proclaimed that "This is nothing to cry about. This is something we could all rejoice about." Yet another declared that "I never felt better in my life. Not in San Francisco, but until I came to Jonestown. I had a very good life." Others thanked "Dad," that is, Jones; one man said, "I'd just like to thank Dad for giving us life and also death."

Once the children died, it was time for the adults. Towards the end of the tape, Jones asked:

> Where's the vat, the vat, the vat? Where's the vat with the Green C on it? Bring the vat with the Green C in. Please? Bring it here so the adults can begin.

Their death was agonizing, according to eyewitness accounts, with children and adults going into violent convulsions. Although the medical staff had added tranquilizers and pain relievers to the mixture, they did not anticipate the rapid effectiveness of the potassium cyanide.

Rhodes, a former heroin addict who was a crafts teacher in Jonestown, described the children he watched die. At least one hundred were placed in a field in front of the pavilion. Although he had decided to run away, he admitted:

> There was too much going on; you couldn't ignore all those kids; you couldn't walk out on them while they were dying like that.[21]

Rhodes found a chance to escape when he heard the doctor ask for a stethoscope. He made his way to the medical department, found a group of invalids in wheelchairs, walked out the back door, and hid under the building until nightfall. He fled into the jungle, and made his way to Port Kaituma by midnight, where he told the local police what had happened. He spoke by phone with police in Georgetown, who undoubtedly reported the deaths in Jonestown to Guyana authorities, who then informed U.S. Embassy officials. This probably explains the cable from NOIWON (National Operational Intelligence Watch Officers Network) that came to the White House at 3:29 a.m. on 19 November: "CIA NOIWON reports mass suicides in Jonestown."[22]

Stanley Clayton was another individual who, like Rhodes, decided it was not his time to die. Although Rhodes said that people died more or less willingly, Clayton maintained that events were more chaotic, with more coercion. He told reporters that there was confusion and resistance, with nurses and others forcing children and parents to take the poison.[23] Syringes used to squirt the poison into people's mouths were found around the vat. Moreover, armed guards prevented people from leaving, although in the end, they died by poison as well.

Clayton, who had been publicly humiliated in Jonestown on several occasions, watched his girlfriend and her family die, then told the guards who encircled the pavilion that he wanted to say goodbye to some of his friends who were standing in line on the other side. Clayton ducked under one building and then ran for the jungle. Two elderly Jonestown residents, Catherine Hyacinth Thrash and Grover Davis, also survived: Thrash slept through it all, while Davis, who was hard of hearing and had missed the initial alert, turned around when he saw the children dying and fled, hiding in a dry well until Sunday morning. Finally, three Temple aides—Tim Carter, who had posed as a defector in San Francisco; his brother Mike, one of the radio room operators; and Mike Prokes, who handled public relations—were dispatched by Maria Katsaris with pistols and suitcases full of cash destined for the Soviet Embassy in Georgetown. The three of them witnessed the deaths beginning before they left. They were detained in Port Kaituma and held in custody with Clayton, who was also suspected of being dangerous.

Two others escaped the deaths in Jonestown: Mark Lane and Charles Garry. Jones sent them away from the pavilion with guards as the deaths were beginning. Lane recognized Garry Dartez Johnson, one of their guards, and addressed him by his nickname. "Hello, Poncho," Lane greeted him. Johnson said that they were all going to die. When Lane said that he and Garry would tell the truth about Jonestown, Johnson embraced them and said goodbye. The two lawyers stumbled into the jungle, and spent the night arguing with each other as they struggled to find their way to the road into Port Kaituma. Lane stated that he heard cries and screams Sunday morning. "It seemed that women and children were being pursued, perhaps hunted." He then reported that he heard automatic weapon fire.[24] This story led the Guyana Defense Force to enter Jonestown very cautiously, expecting to be attacked at any moment. Lane's account continues to reverberate in a range of conspiracy theories.

Odell Rhodes, who had not yet fled from Jonestown, said that after darkness fell, he heard an announcement on the P.A. system that everyone with weapons was to assemble in the radio room. He then ran off into the jungle. Stanley Clayton, also still on-site, said he returned to Jonestown in the dark to pick up some things when he heard a gunshot. Although the dogs and the community's pet chimpanzee Mr. Muggs had all been shot, the only human gunshot victims were Jim Jones and my sister Annie Moore. While Jones had wounds that were consistent with suicide, the gun was found several feet from his body. It may have been moved or disturbed by Guyanese who went into Jonestown before the GDF arrived. Annie, however, had clearly committed suicide, and may have been the last to die in Jonestown.

There were four more deaths that day. Messages radioed from Jonestown to Lamaha Gardens used a prearranged code to inform people there that it was time to die. Sharon Amos, a longtime leader in the movement, took her three children—Liane Harris and Martin and Christa Amos—into the bathroom, where she slit the younger children's throats. Then she and Liane apparently mutually slit each others'. Jim Jones also issued the encoded order to die to members at the San Francisco Temple, but his son Stephan, a member of the basketball team staying in Georgetown, sent repeated radio messages urging them not to proceed.

Douglas Ellice, Consul at the U.S. Embassy, was monitoring the ham radio traffic between Jonestown and Georgetown that day.[25] He had spoken with

Amos, who informed him that Ryan's party needed an extra plane because of people leaving; she also facilitated a brief conversation between Ellice and Dwyer, who was connected through the radio transmission. Ellice spoke several times with Ambassador Burke that afternoon and evening, puzzling over a coded message. He probably heard the order that prompted Amos to kill her children: "There's a lot of cryptic traffic going back and forth about having somebody's children go to meet Mr. Fraser," he told Burke, "and the children don't have any vehicles to go do it." Seeing Mr. Fraser meant to die.[26]

REVOLUTIONARY SUICIDE

Jim Jones constructed a narrative of the deaths long before 18 November. The group would be committing an act of "revolutionary suicide," an expression he appropriated from Huey Newton, the Black Panther Party leader. "Take our life from us," Jones said on that last day.

> We laid it down. We got tired. We didn't commit suicide; we committed an act of revolutionary suicide protesting the conditions of an inhumane world.

Three suicide notes found after 18 November repeated the feeling of protest, and even despair, that some in Jonestown believed signified the meaning of their deaths. A brief letter from Tish Leroy, a forty-eight-year-old white woman, was addressed to "Dad" and found in Jones's pocket. She wrote

> Dad
>
> I see no way
> out—I agree
> with your decision—
> I fear only that
> without you the
> world may not make it
> to communism—Tish
>
> For my part—I
> am more than
> tired of this wretched, merciless
> planet & the hell
> it holds for so
> many masses of
> beautiful people—
> Thank you for the *only* life I've known[27]

A letter from Annie Moore appeared to be directed to outsiders and expressed bitterness and regret over the loss of the community.

> I am 24 years of age right now and don't expect to live through the end of this book.
>
> I thought I should at least make some attempt to let the world know what Jim Jones and the Peoples Temple is—OR WAS—all about.
>
> It seems that some people and perhaps the majority of people would like to destroy the best thing that ever happened to the 1,200 or so of us who have followed Jim...
>
> Jim Jones showed us all this—that we could live together with our differences, that we are all the same human beings. Luckily, we are more fortunate than the starving babies of Ethiopia, than the starving babies in the United States.
>
> What a beautiful place this was. The children loved the jungle, learned about animals and plants. There were no cars to run over them; no child-molesters to molest them; nobody to hurt them. They were the freest, most intelligent children I had ever known...

The last line of the note read: "We died because you would not let us live in peace."[28]

A third note, like Annie's, was directed to outsiders in an attempt to interpret the meaning of Jonestown and the lives and deaths of those who lived there. Although it was unsigned, Richard Tropp probably wrote this message, titled "The Last Day of Peoples Temple," and addressed it "To Whomever Finds This Note:"

> Collect all the tapes, all the writing, all the history. The story of this movement, this action, must be examined over and over. It must be understood in all of its incredible dimensions. Words fail. We have pledged our lives to this great cause. We are proud to have something to die for. We do not fear death. We hope that the world will someday realize the ideals of brotherhood, justice and equality that Jim Jones has lived and died for. We have all chosen to die for this cause. We know there is no way that we can avoid misinterpretation. But Jim Jones and this movement were born too soon. The world was not ready to let us live.
>
> I am sorry there is no eloquence as I write these final words. We are resolved, but grieved that we cannot make the truth of our witness clear.
>
> This is the last day of our lives. May the world find a way to a new birth of social justice. If there is any way that our lives and the life of Jim Jones can ever help that take place, we will not have lived in vain.[29]

Tropp was the community historian, and had been drafting the story of the movement. He had asked people to write their autobiographies, and had even written a few chapters for his own book about Peoples Temple. His elegy to Jonestown attempted to describe what people were trying to do.

> *Please try to understand.* Look at *all.* Look at all in perspective. Look at Jonestown, see what we have tried to do. This was a monument to *life,* to the renewal of the human spirit, broken by capitalism, by a system of exploitation & injustice. Look at all that was built by a beleaguered people. We did not want this kind of ending—we wanted to live, to shine, to bring light to a world that is dying for a little bit of love. To those left behind of our loved ones, many of whom will not understand, who never knew this truth, *grieve not,* we are grateful for this opportunity to bear witness—a bitter witness—history has chosen our destiny in spite of our own desire to forge our own. We were at a cross purpose with history. But we are calm in this hour of our collective leave-taking . . .

Tropp's last words: "If nobody understands, it matters not. I am ready to die now. Darkness settles over Jonestown on its last day on earth."

Today we might call the deaths in Jonestown an act of political martyrdom rather than an act of revolutionary suicide, as the term was originally defined. Both actions result in death, and both contain an element of hope that others will take up the cause. But there are differences between the two. In revolutionary suicide, according to Huey Newton, one faced death at the hands of the oppressor when one challenged the power structure in a revolutionary way. "As Newton used it, the term emphasizes revolution over death," wrote Duchess Harris and Adam John Waterman.[30] Jones distorted the original meaning of revolutionary suicide by emphasizing death rather than revolution. Martyrdom, rather than revolution, was Jones' goal.

Nevertheless, the concept of revolutionary suicide provided the people of Jonestown the theoretical, and perhaps theological, justification for taking their dramatic last steps. It allowed residents to preserve their ultimate concern of being in solidarity with their oppressed brothers and sisters by dying rather than succumbing to separation. They perished rather than abandon their commitment. For them the choice was clear: they chose death over betrayal, and loyalty over survival.

For Further Reading

Although there are many accounts of the last days of Jonestown, some are more credible than others. The House Committee Report on *The Assassination of Representative Leo J. Ryan and the Jonestown, Guyana Tragedy* presents a number of government reports and documents that flesh out the story of Leo Ryan's visit, and the investigations conducted in the wake of his murder. There are several first-person accounts. *Awake in a Nightmare*, by Ethan Feinsod, relies on the eyewitness testimony of Odell Rhodes, and seems to be a factual account based on Rhodes's perspective. Mark Lane's *The Strongest Poison* recounts the lawyer's own involvement in the final weeks of the community, and *Raven*, by Tim Reiterman with John Jacobs, provides a glimpse of what happened at the Port Kaituma airstrip by a reporter who was there. An excerpt of Richard Dwyer's account of the airstrip events appears in *Dear People*. In addition, audiotapes released by the FBI shed light on life in Jonestown and reveal the reaction the community had to Leo Ryan's impending visit. No single source is perfect, of course, but through the process of triangulation, it is possible to come up with a realistic and fairly accurate idea of what happened on 18 November 1978.

CHAPTER 7

Dehumanizing the Dead

> Our resting place was designed to provide a peaceful setting for local families. We wish to maintain that status and there is no way the Jonestown dead would be acceptable.
>
> —Cemetery Manager, Marin County*

The deaths of 900 Americans in Jonestown, as well as the assassination of a United States Congressman, put Guyana on the world map. Although many confused the small South American country with Ghana, in Africa, or New Guinea, off the coast of Australia, it was the tiny nation sandwiched between Venezuela and Suriname that immediately drew international attention. The fact that Americans were involved complicated the situation greatly, since it required several U.S. government agencies to work in cooperation with a number of Guyanese government agencies. Although American and Guyanese interests occasionally ran in tandem, such as the mutual concern for identifying and capturing the murderer of Congressman Ryan, they did not coincide on issues such as the disposition of the bodies lying in the jungle. Both governments, however, wanted to deny any association with, or responsibility for, Peoples Temple.

Several competing interest groups jockeyed for control in the initial aftermath. Various government entities, families, religious associations, the news media, and cult experts had concerns that frequently collided. This collision resulted in the dehumanization of those who died in Jonestown.

The families of those who died in Jonestown comprised one interested party. They wanted to learn, and dreaded to know, the fate of their loved ones. This cohort, bound together in grief, had to deal with the problem of recovering the dead, burying their relatives, and mourning their loss. News trickled out slowly, however, with initial reports stating that only 300 to 400 bodies had been found. Where were the others, they wondered? It took eight days to account for all of the bodies, and even longer for the bodies to be identified and relatives notified. For some, grief led to an anger that prompted them to seek financial damages from Peoples Temple and from the official receiver of its assets once the corporation was dissolved. Rather than closing the gap between the living and the dead, however, the attempts to obtain financial settlements—to cover everything from mental anguish to medical expenses—increased the alienation felt by many.

Yet another faction consisted of religious organizations. Individuals and institutions of faith had to decide how to respond to Jonestown as both a religious and a moral event. How should they react to such a disaster, given that a religious group was involved? While some denounced Peoples Temple and Jonestown as satanic and irrelevant to their brand of faith, others attempted to respond with compassion and understanding for both the victims and their families. Efforts to stress the differences between good religion and bad religion were opposed by endeavors that pointed out the commonalities that existed. Yet the voices heard loudest in the media belonged to critics of nontraditional religions.

The media, alarmed over the violent deaths of three journalists and captivated by a news story of tremendous significance, comprised a final interest group. Hundreds of reporters descended on Guyana in the aftermath in search of exclusive interviews, eyewitness accounts, and a fresh angle on an incredibly bizarre event. News coverage focused on the sensationalistic, and it was all sensational: from Jim Jones's sexual habits to life in Jonestown to the final day in which hundreds were murdered or took their own lives. In addition, news outlets turned to cult experts—and only to cult experts—for analysis. These experts knew next to nothing about Peoples Temple, and exaggerated the differences between Temple members and ordinary members of society by claiming that only those who were alienated, lonely, weak, or vulnerable would join a new religious movement.

The media and cult experts contributed to the dehumanization of the people who died in Jonestown, but they were not the only ones. Individuals living in Guyana and the United States, government agencies, and public officials all distanced themselves from what they perceived as the crazy cultists who killed themselves. In addition, the possibility of ethical, if not criminal, liability was present for a number of Guyanese officials with close ties to Jones and his aides, and for American embassy officers who knew the most about the project. Local, state, and federal agencies came under scrutiny and had to explain, and justify, their actions prior to 18 November. The Disciples of Christ, the denomination to which Peoples Temple belonged, had to clarify the nature of the relationship the Temple had to the national denomination, which gave wide latitude to its member congregations. Elected officials in California scrambled to dissociate themselves from the organization that provided volunteers for their campaigns. Jonestown was a political hot potato and could burn anyone it touched.

These efforts to demonize those who died and to move the Jonestown dead to the margins of humanity were part of an overall pattern of "rituals of exclusion" identified by David Chidester.[1] These rituals focused on preventing the bodies of the Jonestown victims from contaminating the wider society. The rituals also emphasized the "otherness" of Peoples Temple, and at the same time helped interested parties defend actions taken before, during, and after 18 November. This chapter looks at the variety of ways the process of isolating and marginalizing the Jonestown dead occurred.

REMOVING THE DECEASED

A major problem immediately confronted Guyana authorities: once the dead and wounded at the Port Kaituma airstrip were attended to, what was to be done with all of the bodies discovered in Jonestown? Because Mark Lane had reported hearing automatic weapon fire, the Guyana Defense Force carefully entered the community on Sunday morning, 19 November, expecting to be attacked. Their initial body count, 383, had a bogus precision to it, but probably sounded more convincing to superior officers than saying "about 400." Guyana police arrived the next day, 20 November, and began to investigate the crime scene. Assisted by Odell Rhodes and some other Jonestown survivors, they identified almost 200 bodies. Rain, however, washed away the names on the tags, and identification became more difficult due to the rapid state of decomposition.

Meanwhile, U.S. troops at Fort Bragg, Fort Lee, Dover Air Force Base, Charleston Air Force Base, and the Panama Canal Zone were put on alert Sunday morning, according to Jeffrey Brailey, a Specialist Six practical nurse stationed with the 601st Medical Company in Panama who was flown to Matthews Ridge.[2] Told that around 400 Americans had taken poison, Brailey's unit began to arrive in Georgetown on 20 November, bringing medical equipment and some types of antidotes with them. More than a dozen Special Forces also arrived from Panama, expecting to comb the jungle for survivors or to protect the medical units from ambush by terrorists. The soldiers found neither.

U.S. Ambassador to Guyana John Burke had assumed that the bodies would be repatriated to the United States, and this explains the rapid response of U.S. military forces. On Tuesday, 21 November, however, Secretary of State Cyrus Vance proposed burying the victims in a mass grave in Guyana. When officials in Guyana balked at the proposal, it became clear that American soldiers would bag the remains and ship them to Dover Air Force Base in Delaware for processing. A team from U.S. Army Graves Registration began to work on Wednesday, 22 November. Five days later their work was complete. The advanced state of decomposition, coupled with the fact that bodies were piled on top of one another, created an initial discrepancy in the body count, which stood at 410 for almost a week. The final count for the deaths in Jonestown was reported at 909.

Once the bodies were repatriated to the U.S., Guyana then had to adjudicate who was guilty for their deaths. A coroner's jury of four men and one woman met in Matthews Ridge in December 1978 to consider the testimony of several witnesses. Dr. Leslie Mootoo, Guyana's Chief Pathologist, did rough autopsies in the field on at least seventy persons, and found injection marks in their shoulders. He also observed numerous syringes without needles, indicating that poison had been squirted into people's mouths. He concluded from this that 700 had died unwillingly, which meant that only 200 people had died voluntarily. Nevertheless, the jury's initial verdict was that all 909 had committed suicide. But when the presiding magistrate remonstrated, the jurors changed the verdict and determined that all but three people—Ann Moore, Maria Katsaris and Don Sly—were murdered.

It was impossible to ascertain the extent of coercion that occurred during the mass deaths, however, since only seven formal autopsies were performed. The U.S. government sought the autopsy of Jim Jones. Families requested autopsies of Lawrence Schacht, the Jonestown doctor; Maria Katsaris; and my sisters, Carolyn Layton and Ann Moore. Only two decedents, Richard Castillo and Violet Dillard, were chosen at random from the remaining 904 victims. Even more unfortunately—at least in terms of learning how people had actually died in Jonestown—bodies were routinely embalmed at Dover Air Force Base, and the potential for any meaningful toxicological or physiological evidence was destroyed. Clearly Jim Jones and Annie Moore had been shot, and their deaths were consistent with suicide. But the findings for the others listed the cause of death as "probably" cyanide poisoning and manner of death as "undetermined."

Various officials asserted that no U.S. entity was responsible for conducting autopsies on American citizens who had died abroad, but this had not been the case when more than 300 citizens died in an airplane crash the year before at Tenerife in the Canary Islands. After that particular disaster, bodies had been shipped to Dover, where autopsies and identification proceedings were conducted. Indeed, it was Dover's experience handling the Tenerife victims that contributed to the decision to ship the Jonestown bodies there rather than to the morgue at Oakland Army Base, which would have been much closer to family members. Writing thirty years after the events in Guyana, Dr. Cyril Wecht, Past President of the American College of Forensic Sciences, analyzed the reasons for the lack of appropriate medicolegal examinations at Dover. He concluded that the deaths in Jonestown "failed to arouse the sensitive interests and pragmatic concerns of the people in charge because the victims were perceived as 'cultists.' The unspoken attitude was something like: 'what did you expect from such lunatics?' 'they got what they deserved'."[3]

Another reason that might account for the failure to perform meaningful autopsies was the jurisdictional labyrinth that various players had to navigate. Multiple entities, including agencies in Guyana, were involved throughout the entire process. Dr. Mootoo reportedly took samples of fluids and tissue, and turned these over to U.S. Embassy personnel. But American pathologists never received the samples.[4] On the U.S. side, a Joint Humanitarian Task Force consisted of several federal agencies, all of which had separate responsibilities: the State Department notified families and released bodies; the Defense Department handled the logistics of body removal, clean-up, and storage; the Justice Department investigated Leo Ryan's death, and the FBI worked on identification; and the Office of Management and Budget monitored costs.[5] This was just the beginning of numerous investigations that would occur in the year following the deaths.

THE SEARCH FOR THE GUILTY PARTIES

In addition to the problem of removal of the bodies and the question of culpability for the deaths in Jonestown, responsibility for the deaths at the airstrip and in Georgetown had to be addressed. Larry Layton was immediately arrested at Port Kaituma and held for the murder of Leo Ryan. Charles Beikman, a longtime Temple member from Indianapolis, was arrested at Lamaha Gardens and held for the murder of Sharon Amos and her three children. At a preliminary hearing held in Georgetown, Stephan Jones declared to an astonished courtroom that he was guilty of the deaths at Lamaha Gardens. Although Stephan was speaking in solidarity with Beikman, and may have been expressing his own feelings of guilt for not stopping all of the deaths that had occurred, the prosecutor took him seriously. He spent three months in jail before he was released for lack of evidence. Beikman accepted a plea bargain arrangement in 1980, pleading guilty to the charge of attempted murder in exchange for dismissal of the murder charges. Although he had already served eighteen months in jail, the judge sentenced him to an additional five years at hard labor. Two years later, Beikman was released and returned to his native Indiana.

Larry Layton went to trial in Guyana in May 1980, also on charges of attempted murder. Although the jury acquitted him after a few hours of deliberation, he was returned to custody and was extradited to the United States in October to face charges on four counts, including conspiracy to kill a United States Congressman. By July 1981, when jury selection for his trial in the United States began, Layton had been imprisoned for almost three years. The American jury was deadlocked after eight days of deliberations, and on 26 September 1981, Judge Robert Peckham declared a mistrial. Layton was released on bond until federal prosecutors retried him on the same charges five years later. At the second trial, the jury found Layton guilty on all four counts. Some jurors said that if the defense team had offered an explanation for Layton's participation at the airstrip, they would have been able to acquit him. But the defense did not present a single witness, because they felt that the prosecution had amply made their own case for Layton: namely, that he was severely depressed over the death of his mother in October 1978, that he was in no way the leader of a conspiracy, that he had not actually killed anyone, and that he was under the control of Jim Jones.

In an unexpected development, some of the people Layton had injured in the shooting, as well as jurors at his trial, wrote to Judge Peckham asking for leniency in sentencing. The court received more than sixty letters in support of clemency. One letter said that "in my mind [Layton] is no different than any other victim of Jim Jones. I cannot separate him from those who were found dead in the jungle."[6] A fifty-page presentencing report prepared by Loren Buddress, a senior probation officer, presented results of interviews he conducted with people who had been at the Port Kaituma airstrip. Vernon Gosney, whom Layton had shot three times in the stomach, told Buddress that:

> It was a closed community and [Layton] was extremely needy of Jones's approval. I see him as a totally basically destroyed person . . . I don't feel he is a threat to anyone.

Others echoed Gosney's assessment, and both prosecution and defense psychological evaluations argued that mitigating circumstances be taken into consideration. Judge Peckham did indeed consider a range of factors when, on 3 March 1987, he sentenced Layton on the four different counts, one of which was a life sentence, but with eligibility for parole fixed at five years.

Layton served four years at the federal prison on Terminal Island near Long Beach, California, before his first parole hearing in 1991. After a two-day review, the Parole Commission decided to extend Layton's sentence to fifteen years before the next opportunity for a parole hearing; this was later extended to twenty years by the chair of the United States Parole Commission. Members of the commission erroneously believed that Layton had actually killed two people, and felt that a sentence requiring more than forty-eight months above the minimum "is warranted because there were multiple victims who were murdered and there were attempted murders of others." Judge Peckham wrote the commission to object, restating the facts of the case and reiterating the justice of his recommendation for parole eligibility at five years, but the new and longer sentence stood. A midsentence parole hearing in 1993 might have resolved the issue, but Judge Robert Peckham died in February, his voice in support of compassion silenced.

Layton was transferred to a medium-security facility at Lompoc, California, where he worked in the library and tutored inmates in literacy. In 1997 Larry Layton's family mounted a campaign before the Federal Pardon Attorney in the hope that President Bill Clinton might commute Layton's sentence before he left office. Working with the Rev. Philip Wogaman, the president's pastor at Foundry United Methodist Church in Washington, D.C., the Layton family assembled a report hundreds of pages long that documented all of the steps in the sentencing process. The leading letter came from Thelton E. Henderson, Chief Judge for the United States District Court in Northern California, and the successor to Judge Peckham on the court. When the list of those pardoned by President Clinton was released in January 2001, however, Layton's name was not there.

Undaunted, the family petitioned the Parole Commission for a hearing, and was granted one in September 2001, ten years after the first hearing. This time three witnesses testified on behalf of Layton: Vernon Gosney, who was now a police officer; Loren Buddress, the federal probation officer who had prepared the initial report for Layton's sentencing; and Frank Bell, Layton's attorney. It is not clear whether it was the absence of victims' objections to parole or the presence of two law enforcement officers speaking on Layton's behalf that persuaded the hearing officer to grant him parole. Layton was released in April 2002, after serving nineteen years in prison in Guyana and the United States. This was a long time, considering that he was "a small cog in all of this," in Richard Dwyer's words.

STILL MORE INVESTIGATIONS

A federal statute making it a crime to murder a member of Congress anywhere in the world enabled the Justice Department to look into Ryan's death. FBI agents interviewed repatriated Jonestown survivors in an attempt to find out if there was a conspiracy to kill the congressman, and if more crimes were planned. Rumors of Temple hit squads circulated within days of the mass deaths, fueled by fears expressed by former members. The assassinations of George Moscone and Harvey Milk—the mayor and a city supervisor of San Francisco, respectively—on 27 November 1978 by Dan White, a former city supervisor, also fed anxieties about death squads. A federal grand jury was convened in San Francisco on 8 December to consider the possibility of more Jonestown-related violence but found no evidence of any hit squads.

In addition to the Justice Department investigation, Congress held an inquiry into the death of one of its members. The Chair of the House Committee on Foreign Affairs, Clement J. Zablocki, authorized a congressional investigation into Leo Ryan's death since he had died on government business. The findings made by a staff investigative group were published and released at a one-day hearing on 15 May 1979. Their conclusions were summarized in thirty-seven pages, with 700 pages of appendices which included reproductions of State Department cables, correspondence between the committee and various government agencies, reprints of newspaper articles, and copies of official rules and regulations governing the FOIA, the Privacy Act, and the Central Intelligence Agency. Much of the report was classified, including sections that discussed whether that a conspiracy existed against Peoples Temple. In 1998, on the twentieth anniversary of the Jonestown deaths, a group of scholars held a press conference in Washington, D.C., to ask that the complete report be released; as of this writing, however, the classified portions remain unavailable for public inspection.

While congressional investigators praised U.S. Embassy staff for their exemplary crisis management on 18 November and in the aftermath of the tragedy, they harshly criticized the performance of the State Department for not acting aggressively in light of "highly irregular and illegal activities in Jonestown," and for failing to adequately warn the congressman about the extent of the risks of his trip to Jonestown. The State Department's actions came under so much fire that the department commissioned two retired foreign service officers to scrutinize its handling of Peoples Temple and Jonestown. John Hugh Crimmins and Stanley S. Carpenter examined two main areas of State Department involvement: first, its relationship with the Concerned Relatives, especially its handling of the Stoen custody case; and second, its relationship with Leo Ryan. The "Crimmins Report" found that representatives of the State Department had thoroughly briefed Ryan, who had had as much information, and possibly more, as they did. The report did fault embassy officials, however, for narrowly interpreting the Privacy Act and not attempting to look beneath surface appearances in Jonestown. It particularly blamed Ambassador John Burke for not taking steps to intervene in some way. The ambassador had in fact sent a cable in June 1978 asking for authorization to approach the Guyana government about Jonestown. He also telephoned the Guyana desk officer in Washington, D.C., to call his attention to it. But the Office of Special Consular Service responded by telling Burke that any approach to the Guyana government might be construed as American interference in domestic affairs. The ambassador sent a second cable in September when he learned of Ryan's visit, but this too was apparently ignored.[7]

Other government agencies came under examination. The Bureau of Alcohol, Tobacco and Firearms and the U.S. Customs Service were called on to account for the presence of weapons in Jonestown. Although the media reported thousands of arms in Jonestown, Guyana police found only thirty-five weapons, which BATF traced primarily to a gun shop in Ukiah, California. The Customs Service had conducted an investigation in 1977 but had not been able to document any violations, although it was clear that both cash and weapons had indeed been smuggled out of the country. Initial news reports also claimed that more than 150 children in foster care died in Jonestown, prompting U.S. Senator Alan Cranston (D-Calif.) to ask for an investigation by the General Accounting Office (GAO). The GAO found that "no children, while in foster care, died in Guyana. However," the report continued, "a few of the victims of the tragedy were wards of Peoples

Temple members and were taken to Guyana without court approval."[8] The federal Department of Health, Education, and Welfare (now the Department of Health and Human Services) was asked to demonstrate, and did so successfully, that welfare fraud did not occur. California state welfare officials concurred, and a state investigative report observed that, "neither the initial state review nor the local investigations could find any evidence to support early allegations of large scale support of the People's Temple operation through the improper use of welfare funds."[9] In other words, Peoples Temple did not engage in systematic welfare fraud. The San Francisco District Attorney attempted to determine whether voter fraud had occurred in the 1975 election of Mayor George Moscone, because Peoples Temple was credited with the mayor's win. Since election returns had been routinely destroyed, results of the investigation were inconclusive.

THE MONEY TRAIL

It was difficult for investigators as well as the public to reach a sense of closure, perhaps because they could not punish anyone. Apart from the assassination of Congressman Ryan and the attempted murder of Deputy Chief of Mission Richard Dwyer, investigators could not find evidence of any crimes that could be prosecuted in the United States. Moreover the majority of Peoples Temple members were dead, including the perpetrators of the murders in Guyana. Those who were alive, primarily the ones living in San Francisco, were not guilty of anything other than belonging to Peoples Temple. With their leader dead and their utopian experiment ended, they filed for dissolution of the nonprofit corporation in December 1978, and in January 1979, California Superior Court Judge Ira Brown Jr. ordered the church dissolved and its assets distributed by a court-appointed receiver. He also ruled that people had four months in which to file claims upon the assets. There were plenty of claimants: the government of Guyana wanted to recover the cost of damages incurred on the two planes at Port Kaituma; U.S. officials initially claimed that the bodylift operation cost $12 million; individuals who were wounded at the Port Kaituma airstrip sought reimbursement for medical expenses; and relatives and former members asked for damages and return or recompense for property and funds donated to the Temple.

Rumors of millions of dollars in assets circulated, though only members of Jones's inner circle had access to the accounts and account numbers, and knew the full extent of the Temple's holdings. These included Deborah Layton and Terri Buford—whose defections in 1978 caused consternation within the leadership—Tim Stoen, Maria Katsaris, Eugene Chaikin, and my sister Carolyn Layton. By the end of 1978, most of the Temple's known financial resources had been identified: they totaled about $8.5 million in cash in various bank accounts in Panama and Switzerland. Robert Fabian, the court-appointed receiver, then followed a complicated trail of dummy corporations, numbered accounts, cash deposits, and individual signatories to recover additional funds. He regained Social Security funds in exchange for settling the suit *United States v. Peoples Temple*, in which the Justice Department and the IRS accepted $1.4 million for their claims. Fabian sold the Temple's Geary Boulevard headquarters and the Redwood Valley property, and auctioned off other properties and furnishings. He also wisely invested the Temple's assets under his control, so that they were earning about $3,000 per day at the time he proposed a settlement to the claims.[10] As receiver, he and his law firm were paid at the rate of $100 per hour; Fabian projected his expenses to be $1.5 million over a three-year period.

In May 1980, Fabian proposed to settle the $1.8 billion in claims against Peoples Temple by issuing "Receiver's Certificates"—prorated shares of Temple funds—to plaintiffs in wrongful death suits. In addition, he offered certificates to people who had been injured at Port Kaituma and to those who could document that they had donated property to the Temple. But he disallowed any claims for defamation, false imprisonment, emotional distress, federal civil rights violations, and attorneys' fees.

While more than 400 claimants accepted the offer, 200 refused to settle, among them 110 elderly individuals who rejected the receiver's offer of 3% of the claimed value of their life-care contracts with the Temple. Those who had been seriously injured at the airstrip also refused Fabian's proposal. These cases went to arbitration, and the majority were successfully resolved, with the exception of those wounded at Port Kaituma and the heirs of those killed there, who continued to resist a settlement. Two years after his initial proposal, Fabian offered $1.575 million to the airstrip claimants, one-tenth of the total Peoples Temple pie. The judge overseeing arbitration accepted the offer, and in August 1982, Judge Brown gave final approval for the dispersal of Peoples Temple assets. With so many claims, and a limited amount of funds, each Receiver's Certificate came to about sixty-four cents on the dollar.

A few days before the fifth anniversary of the Jonestown deaths, Judge Brown formally terminated Peoples Temple as a nonprofit corporation. The court had paid out more than $9 million in claims that totaled $2 billion. The bulk of the funds did not go to members of Peoples Temple, but to "everyone *but* the ones who helped build the Temple," according to a woman who complained to Judge Brown.[11] Another wrote:

> I beg you to please consider the total picture . . . The injustice of now having our hard-earned assets go to people who cared nothing for us when we were alive.

Temple assets first went to the government, then to those hurt at the airstrip or the heirs of those who were killed, to seniors who had life-care contracts with the Temple, and finally to family members or others who could make wrongful death claims.

BURYING THE DEAD

One of the first decisions Judge Brown made was to ask a religious organization to present a plan for transporting unclaimed and unidentified bodies from Delaware to California so that Temple assets could be used for their interment. An interfaith religious organization, the Guyana Emergency Relief Committee (ERC), was created in San Francisco within ten days of the deaths. The ERC set as its top priority the securing of funds from Peoples Temple assets to bury the Jonestown victims, with a second priority being to assist survivors of the tragedy, including providing counseling and financial aid. In early December, ERC formed a number of subcommittees to deal with legal affairs, relatives, finances, the media, and actual burial. "It had become obvious that neither state, federal, nor local government, by itself, was able to effectively cope with the problem of properly seeing to the interment of the dead bodies," said background notes to a press conference held in January 1979. The notes remarked on the slow-moving, cumbersome, and insensitive levels of bureaucracy.[12] The ERC was the only group that went to court on behalf of the Jonestown victims. The driving force behind the ERC, Donneter Lane—executive director of the San Francisco Council of Churches—remembered how the religious community in the Bay Area mobilized around a single concern: burying the victims.

> Politics got in there to the extent that people weren't really concerned with burying the dead. All they were concerned about was how much money they were going to sue for, and who was going to get the bodies... There were people who were just waiting to capitalize on this whole scene. The religious community moved in and did just the opposite.[13]

Composed of representatives of the Northern California Board of Rabbis, the Roman Catholic Archdiocese of San Francisco, and the San Francisco Council of Churches, the ERC received standing as a friend of the court to participate in judicial proceedings addressing the Temple's financial affairs. Other claimants, including the children of Congressman Ryan, opposed their request for funding.

ERC received calls and letters from hundreds of relatives seeking assistance in burying more than 500 loved ones, according to committee records. Members of the group discussed cremation as an option, especially in light of the cost of transportation and burial, but decided that cremation would only "add to [the] despair and create an anger that could explode." The ERC got bids from trucking companies, funeral homes, and cemeteries for the costs of transportation and burial, and in February 1979 presented a comprehensive plan to the court for interring 599 Jonestown victims, at a total cost of $302,786. The figure was scaled back when the committee learned that only 561 bodies remained at Dover Air Force Base: 308 had been identified but were not claimed, though 286 kin had been contacted; an additional 253 remained unidentified. The Armed Forces Institute of Pathology had the names of these decedents—primarily children—but they were unable to match names to the bodies, although they did notify next of kin for approximately 227 of these dead.[14]

In April and May 1979, Larmore Moving Company, a Delaware firm, brought 251 bodies to Oakland Army Base and 46 bodies to Fort MacArthur in Los Angeles, for relatives to claim. Public officials in Delaware were present for the send-off, relieved to see the bodies depart because they feared a mass grave in their state. The Temple receiver had allowed $540 to reimburse families who had already paid for interment, and to cover costs for those who had not yet recovered their loved ones. Relatives claimed at least forty bodies in Oakland, and six in Los Angeles. Larmore transported an additional 248 unidentified remains, primarily children, to Evergreen Cemetery in Oakland. Several other cemeteries had initially offered to bury the bodies, and then backed down due to community pressure. Eventually, all the unclaimed and unidentified bodies were buried at Evergreen on a hillside overlooking San Francisco Bay.

OTHER RELIGIOUS RESPONSES

The ERC represented one end of a spectrum of religious reactions to the deaths in Jonestown, which ranged from compassion and concern, to outrage and condemnation. Religious institutions in the San Francisco Bay Area, where people personally knew those who died in Jonestown, responded with prayer services and public condolences. The Berkeley Area Interfaith Council issued a "Statement in Response to Jonestown Tragedy" on Thanksgiving Day, 23 November. "We join in sorrow with those who mourn . . . In trying to do good, we can become evil," the statement read, in recognition of the idealism of those who died.[15] A letter from the Northern California Conference of the United Church of Christ said, "We confess our own responsibility for the tragedy at Jonestown insofar as we failed to reach those disinherited who misguidedly traveled to Guyana in search of liberation." Other ministers and religious leaders made similar observations about the failure of institutional religion, as well as of American society, to meet the needs of the people who followed Jim Jones. Muhammed Isaiah Kenyatta wrote in 1979:

We who are of the same body and blood of Jesus Christ, who was crucified anew nine hundred times on one afternoon in the jungle, must confess that we, too, have found America. And we are it. We are its sustainers and sufferers, its victims and executioners.

We must repent of what America has become.[16]

Other religious responses followed a more traditional critique of false prophets and underscored the warnings the Bible gives about them. David Preus, President of the American Lutheran Church, wrote that "As with all false Christs, Jones demanded absolute personal trust and allegiance. Jesus invites the same personal trust and loyalty. What a world of difference between trusting James Jones and trusting Jesus Christ." An article by Mark Albrecht and Brooks Alexander in the *Spiritual Counterfeits Project Newsletter*—a Christian countercult publication—argued that "As long as the secular analysts ignore God's consistent proclamation that humanity is fallen and living in alienation from God and is in need of reconciliation through the only reigning Lord, Jesus Christ, they will continue to put Band-Aids on broken arms." The Vatican newspaper *L'Osservatore Romano* called the deaths in Jonestown "a manifestation of a pseudo-mysticism which betrays the cause of Christ."

The sharpest distancing from Jonestown and Peoples Temple came from African American church leaders. In late December, national representatives of the Southern Christian Leadership Conference, the National Conference of Black Churchmen, the Progressive National Baptist Church, and African American pastors from around the country discussed and planned a coordinated response to the tragedy. "The people are at a low point and don't want to admit they were made fools of," said one participant in the discussions. "It's an opportunity for us to lift them."[17] Church leaders attending the "Consultation on the Implications of Jonestown for the Black Church and the Nation," co-sponsored by SCLC and NCBC and held in San Francisco in February 1979, blamed the tragedy "perpetrated upon the Black masses [on] unscrupulous and unprincipled White leadership." Dr. Kelly Miller Smith's opening statement made it clear from the outset that:

> In no way is People's Temple being thought of as a "Black Church." Rather, the concern of Black church persons with this catastrophe is rooted in the fact that the *real* Black church is life-affirming and is, therefore, concerned with *anything* which causes the deaths of the masses of Blacks.

The President of the National Conference of Black Churchmen concluded his address by stating that "wherever Black life is disrespected, Jonestown is there."

Twenty-five years after the consultation, one of the participants, Dr. J. Alfred Smith, pastor of Allen Temple Baptist Church in Oakland, California, reflected on the role black churches played during the rise of Peoples

Temple in the Bay Area, and upon its demise in Jonestown. "We as the San Francisco Bay Area Christian community must shoulder a portion of the blame for Jim Jones' success," he wrote. "If my African American pastor peers had met the needs of the people, instead of just preaching about them, Jim Jones would not have flourished in San Francisco."[18] Alfred Smith's self-reflexivity was absent from the consultation held in 1979, as two-hundred African American pastors and church leaders rushed to separate themselves from Jim Jones's demonic ministry. They failed "to question what it was within the Black Church that Jim Jones addressed and that we didn't," according to Smith.

Leaders of the Disciples of Christ (Christian Church) also tried to distance themselves from Jonestown. Peoples Temple had been a member of the denomination since 1960, and Jones was ordained by the Disciples in 1964. A statement made to the press by Dr. Kenneth L. Teegarden, president of the church, described the church polity of the Christian Church, which allowed congregations to withdraw, but which did not have a policy for removing congregations. "Because of this awesome tragedy," he said, "we will initiate, at the earliest possible moment, a proposal to determine whether this denomination . . . wants to develop a procedure . . . for removing congregations from fellowship."[19] But a process of "disfellowshipping" a congregation was never implemented, according to Karen Stroup. Instead, requirements for ordaining Disciples ministers "became formalized and gained at least some accountability."[20] Denominational seminaries now keep a close eye on seminarians who are planning to enter the ordained ministry.

Karl Irvin Jr., president of the Northern California-Nevada region and the Disciple with the most contact with Peoples Temple in San Francisco, came under the heaviest fire for failing to review, to investigate, or to discipline the church. He reflected on the questions people asked him—"Do you feel blood on your hands? Do you feel responsibility?"—by saying that "my ministry was never able to touch the leaders and the pastors of the People's Temple in such a manner that the massive self-destruction could have been avoided." He cautioned against limiting freedom, though, and warned of the dangers inherent in "a larger control over congregational life and movement, a ban on the organization of 'non-mainline' groups and cults." News interviews, however, quoted Irvin and other Disciples leaders as saying that Temple leaders "hoodwinked" them and gave them a "snow job." A recently published *Encyclopedia of the Stone-Campbell Movement*, which encompasses the Disciples of Christ, carries no entry for Jonestown, Peoples Temple, or Guyana. It devotes fewer than 100 words to an entry on "Jones, Jim."[21]

RITUALS OF EXCLUSION

In his reflections, Irvin alluded to the general fear of cults and the resulting attempts to contain them. Cult experts and psychiatrists exacerbated cultural anxieties about new religions, and published numerous articles that decried brainwashing and coercive practices utilized by some groups—such as cold showers and sleep deprivation—and denounced strange rituals, weird beliefs, and unusual behaviors. Dr. Hardat Sukhdeo, a New Jersey psychiatrist of Guyanese descent, said that "American cults might be more of a threat to society than to themselves."[22] Richard Delgado, a UCLA law professor, claimed that "everybody is vulnerable. You and I could be Hare Krishnas if they approached us at the right time."[23] Ronald Enroth, a sociologist and cult expert, said "that a typical cult member is 18 to 22 years old, white, middle or upper-middle class, and has at least some college education and a nominally religious upbringing."[24] In other words, almost any young person was at risk. Yet Peoples Temple did not fit the profile of a typical cult, since more than two-thirds of the people who died in Jonestown were African American, and almost a third were under the age of twenty. The important point for cult experts, however—several of whom testified at a one-day hearing that U.S. Senator Robert Dole (R-Kansas) held in February 1979—was that all cults were dangerous and Jonestown proved it.

In *Salvation and Suicide*, religious studies scholar David Chidester analyzed the various ways the Jonestown victims were excluded from public sympathy by the media, by the government, and by religious institutions and leaders.[25] He cited news accounts that emphasized the "defilement, impurity, and contagion" of the Jonestown bodies being processed in Delaware, and the hurdles that government agencies raised to getting death certificates. He noted the apparent fear that "any burial of the Jonestown dead in Delaware soil would present a spiritual danger." This fear existed in California as well, where cemeteries that had initially been contracted to handle the bodies backed out at the last minute, fearing the grave would become a pilgrimage site. The Jonestown dead "tended to be perceived as a dangerous invasion of threatening, foreign influences that, by their mere presence, disrupted the sense of order."

In addition, Chidester identified the presence of "cult madness" as a theme in popular culture, where people involved in new religions are characterized as criminal, violent, mentally ill, irrational, and strange. Parents used this otherness to justify the kidnappings and deprogrammings of their adult children involved in new religions in the 1970s and 1980s. The events of Jonestown supported the opinion that cults were dangerous and would inevitably lead to death or destruction. In 1993, cult experts used the threat of mass suicide to persuade federal officials, including Attorney General Janet Reno, that children of the Branch Davidians were in imminent danger at Mount Carmel, Texas. This fear led to the deadly standoff that resulted in the deaths of more than eighty Branch Davidians and four government agents. As recently as 2008, cult experts raised the specter of mass suicide or violence in arguing for the necessity of quick action to save the children who were part of the Fundamentalist Church of Jesus Christ, Latter-day Saints in San

Angelo, Texas. Four hundred and forty children were removed to foster care before a court ordered their return to their mothers.

In death, as in life, Peoples Temple members were pushed to the margins of society. The strangeness of their deaths was emphasized. The uniqueness of their lives was decried. Their commitments, both good and bad, were condemned. And society was reassured by scholars, journalists, and pastors that Jonestown had nothing to do with the rest of us.

For Further Reading

Jeffrey Brailey's eyewitness account, *The Ghosts of November*, describes his experiences as a member of the 193rd Infantry Brigade stationed in Panama and dispatched to assist with the bodylift from Jonestown. Several chapters excerpted from *A Sympathetic History of Jonestown*, by this author, describe the aftermath and appear on the website http:// jonestown.sdsu.edu: "Last Rights," "Closing the Books," and "Residual Suspicion." These are the main sources for learning about autopsies, Peoples Temple finances, and U.S. government investigations. *The Assassination of Representative Leo J. Ryan and the Jonestown, Guyana Tragedy: Report of a Staff Investigative Group to the Committee on Foreign Affairs, U.S. House of Representatives* (a.k.a. *House Committee Report*) provides additional information about U.S. government activities both before and after 18 November. In *Salvation and Suicide*, David Chidester provides many examples of the way the media, the government, and the public distanced themselves from Jonestown and Peoples Temple in the aftermath of the deaths.

CHAPTER 8

Jonestown Re-enters American Culture

In all due respect to my colleagues, they're drinking the Kool-Aid that somehow I have changed positions on the issues...
—Senator John McCain*

Within a few years after the deaths in Jonestown, public figures used Kool-Aid as a metaphor for murder. Lane Kirkland, President of the AFL-CIO, denounced President Ronald Reagan's policies in 1982 as "Jonestown economics," which featured a budget that administered "Kool-Aid to the poor, the deprived and the unemployed."[1] Today, however, "drinking the Kool-Aid" may mean anything from enthusiastic support to blind obedience. It gained momentum during the 1990s in computer industry jargon, and continues among programmers. "Did I drink Microsoft Kool-Aid?" asked computer analyst Joe Wilcox. "Sadly, yes."[2] The rock music critic Touré titled his book of reviews *Never Drank the Kool-Aid* to signify his independence from group-think regarding popular music artists. Touré explained the origin of the expression and wrote that it means "buying into what someone else tells you."[3] An article from a June 2008 issue of *The Nation* said, "You do not have to binge-drink the Obama Kool-Aid to see the possibilities here."[4] A *Washington Times* sports writer admitted that, "Texas Tech and Clemson Kool-Aid sure tastes good."[5] Kool-Aid is everywhere we look.

It is unlikely that many people who use the expression know of its origins in Jonestown, however. If they do, they have dissociated the deaths of more than 900 people from their thinking. Or they have consciously or unconsciously repressed the events so that they can talk about Kool-Aid without evoking memories of Jonestown. It is as difficult to believe that people would knowingly joke about mass deaths in Guyana as they would joke about the Holocaust, although undoubtedly people do both. "As a surviving former member of Peoples Temple, when I first heard someone speaking about 'drinking the Kool-Aid,' I was deeply offended," wrote Mike Carter.

> I thought, "How can these people trivialize such a horrific event such as the mass suicide/murder of over 900 people?" I thought it, but I didn't say it. Over the past 25 years, I have learned it is much easier to keep quiet.[6]

Drinking the Kool-Aid (even though it was a British imitation—Fla-Vor-Aid—that was used in Jonestown) is the most visible way in which Jonestown has re-entered American culture. The last chapter described the ways in which Peoples Temple was excluded from mainstream America, either through the dehumanizing ways the bodies were treated, the condemnation of the group by many religious leaders, or the implication raised by the number of government investigations that Peoples Temple must have been a criminal organization. This chapter describes the ways in which the Temple and Jonestown have been integrated and incorporated into American life. Although three decades have elapsed since the deaths occurred, a generation of artists, writers, musicians, and others who were not even alive in 1978 is finding meaning and significance in Jonestown. They are interpreting Jonestown in surprising new ways that transcend and transform the original narrative of "what happened" in Jonestown.

THE POPULAR CANON

Interpretations of Jonestown were initially limited to the interested parties: survivors, the news media, cult experts, and scholars of new religions. The first three groups swiftly established the norms by which Peoples Temple would be discussed and understood. Within two weeks of 18 November, reporters who had been to Jonestown published two quickie paperbacks. Within a few years, former members and relatives had written more than a dozen books. These accounts reiterated the narrative about Peoples Temple created prior to 18 November, and repeated by the media afterward. I call these works a "popular canon"—that is, a catalog of writings that tell the story of Jonestown and Peoples Temple in a familiar way, the way most people think about them—and summarized that narrative in the Introduction.

The popular canon focuses on the most dramatic and sensational elements of the history of Peoples Temple. These are the elements that also appear in analyses made by cult experts who considered Jonestown not just emblematic of dangerous cults, but rather typical of all cults. These experts suggested that any new religion might lead its followers to commit violent acts or suicide, and bolstered their beliefs with numerous accounts of ex-cult members who said they were ready to kill for the cause.[7] Thus, the life and death of Peoples Temple became a cautionary tale in the popular canon, a morality play which pitted the forces of good (the Concerned Relatives, the congressman, the journalists) against the forces of evil (Jim Jones and his brainwashed followers). This popular canon exists today, and can be seen in television documentaries on cable networks, in exploitative online videos, and in Jonestown anniversary coverage in the mass media.

THE SCHOLARLY CANON

But over the past three decades a scholarly canon has emerged to challenge both the facts of the basic narrative as well as the interpretation of their meaning. In 1989, Thomas Robbins wrote an article that described two waves of scholarly literature. The first wave primarily comprised a handful of articles, one short book, and a collection of essays that considered Peoples Temple from a number of different perspectives: organizational structure, ideology, patterns of resocialization, general worldview, and ritual behavior.[8] Robbins excluded the large body of psychiatric and psychological analyses that emerged in the decade after Jonestown, concentrating instead on the fields of history and sociology. (I have included some of these psychological analyses in the listing of "Resources" at the end of this book, however.)

The second wave of literature that Robbins identified included two books that I have relied on in this current volume: David Chidester's *Salvation and Suicide* and John R. Hall's *Gone from the Promised Land*. In addition to documenting the ways society excluded Peoples Temple members after Jonestown, Chidester helped readers to understand the theology of Jim Jones and Peoples Temple, and to humanize both. He articulated the ways in which mass suicide might be the logical, and even rational, outcome of a commitment to the apostolic socialism found in the New Testament book of Acts (2:44-45, 4:34-35). "Socialism was regarded as the demonstration of divine love," he wrote, "the mathematics of Principle, the workings of God in action."[9] Socialism was love, divine love, and it was the principle by which Peoples Temple members were to live.

> His claims to have been Jesus, Moses, and Lenin have often been cited to illustrate Jones's belief in reincarnation, his delusions of grandeur, or his false claims to ancient authority. But these were the three models for his revolutionary salvation.[10]

Jones was Jesus when he assumed power over traditional religious mythology; he was Moses when he led an oppressed people out of bondage; he was Lenin when he led a revolution to create a new socialist order in which people could become truly human. Published ten years after Jonestown, Chidester's analysis transcended the caricatures of pop analyses by seriously considering the religious beliefs and commitments of Jones and his followers.

John R. Hall's book, appearing in 1987, was a meticulouslyresearched account of Peoples Temple as a movement that reflected American social, cultural, and religious history.[11] He related each moment of the Temple's life—from Jim Jones's childhood to the group's relationship with Guyana officials—to parallels in U.S. history. In this way, Hall demonstrated how completely American the Peoples Temple phenomenon was: from its ties to Pentecostalism to previous Social Gospel movements to radical revolutionary parties, Peoples Temple could not be understood apart from its place in American life. Like Chidester, Hall moved Jonestown from the periphery to the center of American thought and life. *Gone from the Promised Land* showed how well Peoples Temple fit into American culture, and clarified when it did not fit. Hall also identified the role that cultural opponents played in contributing to the internal dynamics of Jonestown.

When scholars started comparing Peoples Temple with other new religions and looking at gender and race, a third wave in new religions studies could be identified. These analyses placed different aspects of the group in sharp relief. Mary Maaga examined the role of women in *Hearing the Voices of Jonestown*.[12] Against much feminist literature and cult analyses, she argued that women in the Temple gained power by having sex with the leader. Women rose to positions of power and authority much faster than they could have outside the Temple. They essentially ran Jonestown, according to Maaga. This is a very different understanding of the role that members play from traditional descriptions of cult life.

A number of scholars, including C. Eric Lincoln and Lawrence Mamiya, Archie Smith Jr., and Mary R. Sawyer examined the role African Americans played in Peoples Temple. They related the similarities and differences between Father Divine's Peace Mission and Jim Jones's Peoples Temple. Smith pointed out the problem of "audience corruption," the process by which both the group leader and the followers construct—and distort—a social reality together. "Jones could not have orchestrated the idea of his deification without the support of his followers. Jones, too, was a victim of his ego deification process."[13] Sawyer identified a black church that operated within the Temple, even in Jonestown.

The most unique scholarly depiction of Peoples Temple came from an archivist at the California Historical Society, the repository of thousands of pages relating to the group and its members. Denice Stephenson compiled scores of primary source documents culled from the CHS collection to put together *Dear People: Remembering Jonestown*.[14] Stephenson provided historical background to frame the texts so that readers could follow the story of Peoples Temple as it unfolded in letters, diaries, news reports, brochures, instructions, autobiographies, and other primary sources. *Dear People* was the first anthology of writings by and about Peoples Temple members. It included many items from people who died in Jonestown, and gave one of the first book-length glimpses into their hearts and minds.

All of these scholarly perspectives supplied new lenses through which to view Peoples Temple and Jonestown. What were the religious beliefs of the members? What role did women and African Americans play? How was Peoples Temple similar to other new religions, and how was it different? The discussion of these questions showed how thin and inaccurate the popular canon was. It revealed that Peoples Temple raised deeper and more complex issues than simply a mad cult leader and his brainwashed followers.

VOICES FROM JONESTOWN

A significant development in the scholarly writings that can be traced through Hall, Chidester, and Stephenson was the use of audiotapes and texts generated by the Temple itself to gain an understanding of the organization. The FBI recovered almost a thousand audiotapes—both reel-to-reel and cassette—from Jonestown. While the majority of the material on the tapes came from the 1970s, a few sermons from the 1960s and even from Indianapolis were found as well. About 350 of these tapes were either blank or contained only music; the remaining 613 tapes were each reviewed, summarized, and catalogued into one of five categories by the FBI. It is evident that some tapes were used and reused, with a sermon from San Francisco abruptly ending, and a sermon from Indianapolis picked up in midsentence. An audio analysis of the tape made on the last day (Q 042), for instance, revealed that the events were recorded over an old tape, which explained the sounds of what some previously believed was an organ playing in the background as people were dying.[15]

James Reston Jr., author of *Our Father Who Art in Hell*, can be credited with helping to make the tapes public. His appeal to U.S. Attorney General Benjamin Civiletti in January 1980 to release the FBI's collection drew the support of three Members of Congress as well as two legal counsels to President Jimmy Carter. The request prevailed, and Reston went on to write his book, which served as the basis for a National Public Radio documentary titled *Father Cares: The Last of Jonestown* that aired in 1981. Reston selected the most lurid and horrifying tapes for the program, and an instructional pamphlet that accompanied the two-cassette boxed set included several warnings about the content:

IMPORTANT

Certain segments of the original Jonestown tapes included in this program are shocking and unpleasant, due in some cases to offensive language and in others to the psychological impact or disturbing content of the passages. Because the program may cause psychological stress in some listeners, it is recommended that the entire program be carefully screened before it is played for students. It is also suggested that intended audiences be fully apprised of the content of the tape.

The radio program reflected the style of Reston's book, which he called "a novel in reality." In the book, characters voiced inner thoughts and motivations as they were about to die. Although he relied on the tapes for much of the dialogue, Reston was also willing to create his own. Yet all subsequent historians who have used the FBI tapes must appreciate Reston's persistence in obtaining access to them.

The audiotapes have attracted a new generation of listeners in the first decade of the twenty-first century. Thanks in part to Reston, the Jonestown Institute (an organization that consists of my husband Fielding McGehee and myself) received all 971 tapes from the FBI, including more than 50 that had been initially withheld from disclosure. Transcripts, summaries, and MP3 files of more than 200 tapes appear on the *Alternative Considerations of Jonestown and Peoples Temple* website as part of the Jonestown Audiotape Project.[16]

People who request copies of tapes give different reasons for their interest in Jonestown. One young man found himself drawn to a religious group that seemed to have cultlike overtones; he encountered comparisons with Peoples Temple. "Call it a morbid fascination or perhaps just a need to know the truth, but I felt a need to read all I could on Jonestown," wrote Paul Schmatzok.

> This is the reason that I volunteered to help transcribe some of the audiotapes among the 500 yet to be done. Although I've only gotten started with the work, it is already obvious to me that those around Jim Jones were completely devoted to him for reasons only they can explain.[17]

A woman who was eight at the time of the deaths initially thought that Jim Jones was a typical guru who preyed upon gullible people. A documentary challenged her beliefs about Temple members and prompted her to listen to some audiotapes. "I wanted to hear what it was truly like in Jonestown on a daily basis and hear them in their most ordinary, mundane circumstances," wrote Tina Columbus.[18] She found laughter and normal conversations on many, though even the happy discussions were tempered by the undercurrent of revolutionary suicide.

Dean Coughlan was twelve at the time of Jonestown; a documentary also triggered his interest and he ordered some tapes.

> Ironically, the more I heard, the deeper the mystery became. The answers I was searching for seemed to be drifting further away. Six

months later, having consumed many thousands of words on the subject, the mystery remains unsolved. My initial expectations of uncovering sinister and clandestine wrongdoings in the middle of the jungle were not realized. Perhaps in that respect maybe there never was a mystery, at least not the one I had expected.[19]

Voices from Jonestown have become an integral part of considerations of Peoples Temple today. Before the twenty-first century only critical voices had been heard; now, more nuanced and varied perspectives are available and accessible. A major reason for this dramatic shift is the willingness of many more Temple survivors to tell their story. It has taken years for people who belonged to Peoples Temple at the time of the deaths to gain the courage, fortitude, and support to come out of the closet of fear, shame, and guilt to tell their stories. Their voices altered the way Jonestown appeared in two important documentaries in 2005 and 2007.

The People's Temple, a play written by Leigh Fondakowski with Greg Pierotti, Stephen Wangh, and Margo Hall, debuted at the Berkeley Repertory Theatre in April 2005.[20] Because so many people in the San Francisco Bay Area knew about the Temple or knew Temple members, the play generated tremendous interest and excitement. The playwrights—some of whom had authored *The Laramie Project*, a documentary-style play about the murder of Matthew Shepard—interviewed dozens of individuals, including news reporters, members of the Concerned Relatives, family members, and Temple survivors. They incorporated these interviews, along with dialogue from audiotapes, letters, news articles, and songs recorded by Temple members, into a three-hour production that covered the sweep of the Temple's history.

Yet the writers of *The People's Temple* would be among the first to admit the difficulty of getting at "the truth" of Peoples Temple. Greg Pierotti expressed it by saying, "I no longer believe that the tragedy of Peoples Temple is something that I can get to the bottom of. I have come to respect this story as far more vast than the span of my individual understanding."[21] The playwrights were faced with the task of imagining a world much better than this one, in the words of Temple survivor Bryan Kravitz. "You can't fathom it because you've never had it. You lived in this society. We, they, these people you've talked to, had an opportunity to see something else."[22]

The People's Temple marked a distinct departure from earlier dramatizations. *Guyana: Crime of the Century* (also known as *Guyana: Cult of the Damned*) starred Stuart Whitman in a film that varied so dramatically from the facts that the lead character was called James Johnson, rather than Jim Jones; Leo Ryan became Lee O'Brien. An amazon.com reviewer rated it as "utter tripe" and gave it one star: "John Ireland, Stuart Whitman, Gene Barry, and Yvonne De Carlo should also have known better than to appear in this movie." Another, more widelyknown dramatization, was *Guyana Tragedy*, which was also called *Jonestown Tragedy: The Story of Jim Jones* (and occasionally, *The Mad Messiah*). This 1980 TV mini-series earned Powers Boothe an Emmy for his portrayal of Jones. *Guyana Tragedy* showed how Jones might have started out with good intentions in Indianapolis, but how power and his ideals corrupted him. At the same time, however, it departed from the facts in its depiction of Jonestown in many ways (for example, it showed Leo Ryan driving up to Jonestown in a late-model car, and a character modeled after Tim Stoen being shot down in broad daylight by automatic weapon fire). Both films relied on the popular narrative, rather than on the voices from Jonestown, and focused on Jones as their subject.

Thus, Fondakowski's dramatization of Peoples Temple signified a major shift in understanding Jonestown, one that attempted to capture the ambiguity and multiplicity of viewpoints inherent in the story. Rather than presenting a morality play, *The People's Temple* revealed how complicated the movement really was. "American culture prefers simple stories, with obvious villains and heroes," wrote Fondakowski eighteen months into the writing process. "So our struggle as writers is to allow all the different perspectives to live together on stage—and to help audiences tolerate the contradictions which challenge American attempts to simplify."[23]

Jonestown: The Life and Death of Peoples Temple also demonstrated the complexity of the Temple's history and members. Award-winning filmmakers Stanley Nelson, Marcia Smith, and Noland Walker produced the ninety-minute documentary for PBS's *American Experience* series. It aired in April 2007, although screenings at film festivals around the country throughout 2006 garnered a number of awards for the film. The filmmakers became intrigued by the subject when they heard survivors talking about Peoples Temple on the twenty-fifth anniversary of the deaths. "They still spoke of Peoples Temple with a great degree of fondness," said Stanley Nelson, "as one of the greatest times of their lives. They hated Jim Jones, but they loved Peoples Temple."[24] The Nelson film captured this paradox, clarifying for the first time on film why people might have wanted to join the Temple.

Previous documentaries tended to appear at specific anniversaries, and usually contributed to the popular canon, with two notable exceptions. Jim Hougan, an investigative reporter, produced *Jonestown: Mystery of a Massacre* for the A&E cable television network in 1998. Packaged in Bill Kurtis's *Investigative Reports*, the program was based on Hougan's extensive research into Jim Jones's alleged CIA connections and raised the possibility of CIA involvement in the Jonestown deaths. Another documentary that A&E aired on the twentieth anniversary also departed from the norm. *Jim Jones: Journey into Madness*, produced by Ron Steinman and packaged in the *Biography* series, offered a less two-dimensional portrait of Jones than other programs. These two television programs contrasted noticeably with most TV presentations; other documentaries re-enacted the death scene, told the story with "good guys and bad guys," as one scriptwriter explained to me, or focused on the most shocking aspects of Peoples Temple. It was more comfortable to retell the popular story than to go against the grain, despite all of the evidence and material that lent itself to new and interesting interpretations.

THE CANON OF CONSPIRACY THEORIES

Another interpretive category that challenged the popular canon was a body of conspiracy theories that arose within weeks of 18 November 1978. The shifting body count, the presence of drugs found in Jonestown, the idea that "black folks do not commit suicide,"[25] the presence of a CIA official at the scene, and other incongruities helped to created a "conspiratorial canon" that persists to this day. Enough credible references to the Central Intelligence Agency appeared early on to raise questions among the most skeptical people. For example, the *House Committee Report* on Ryan's assassination asserted that "no conclusive evidence is available to indicate that the CIA was acquiring information on Mr. Jones or People's Temple."[26] But information released as a result of the FOIA lawsuit *McGehee v. CIA* indicated that the CIA was indeed "monitoring" Jonestown,[27] and the earliest report of the deaths came from CIA intelligence.

Allegations of CIA involvement began with Jones himself during his years in Brazil. Some theories held that he was working for the CIA and with Dan Mitrione in particular. Mitrione had been a police officer in Richmond, Indiana, when Jones was a teenager, and some believe he was recruited to spy on local Communists there.[28] The two supposedly reconnected when both Jones and Mitrione lived in Brazil. The former police officer gained notoriety for teaching South American police how to torture political prisoners. In 1970 he was kidnapped and assassinated by the Tupamaros, a Uruguayan guerilla group. Other stories that emerged after 18 November about Jones's foray into Brazil continued to fuel conspiracy theories.

There seem to be three broad categories of speculators: professional conspiracists, Internet conspiracists, and nonprofesional conspiracists.[29] I define professional conspiracists as those writers who find conspiracies everywhere they look. John Judge, who established the Coalition on Political Assassinations (COPA) and has identified conspiracies in the John Kennedy and Martin Luther King deaths, also found sinister forces at play in Guyana. His twenty-five-page essay, "The Black Hole of Guyana," presented a well-documented and well-developed conspiracy theory concerning Jonestown, with 291 footnotes.[30] Judge looked skeptically at the body count and at the presence of American Green Berets, and asserted that British troops murdered 700 Jonestown residents who were living a miserable existence as part of a CIA-sponsored mind-control experiment. Judge put the tragedy at Jonestown into the context of his larger concern, namely, the threat to democracy posed by U.S. intelligence agencies.

Like the professional conspiracists, Internet conspiracists find conspiracies everywhere, but they are a bit more playful, and it is difficult to tell when they are being serious and when they are satirizing society and themselves. Matthew Farrell's *World Domination Update* was one site that questioned the competence of the conspirators: "You'd think if Jones killed himself, it'd be known anti-Jones propaganda. Likewise, if the whole thing was framed to *look* like a group suicide, why would 'they' be so sloppy about details: just shoot Jones and put the gun in his hand—that's a *no-brainer*."[31] Other sites demonstrated their dependence on print materials like Judge's essay, on conspiracy articles published by the Church of Scientology, or on a well-researched article by Jim Hougan. The Internet conspiracists seem more interested in conspiracy for the sake of conspiracy, rather than making an attempt to account for the deaths in Jonestown.

The third category comprises nonprofessional conspiracists, like Michael Meiers and Nathan Landau. Meiers answered "yes" to the question posed by the title of his book *Was Jonestown a CIA Medical Experiment?* He blamed the CIA, noting the meticulous medical records kept on each individual in Jonestown, as well as the placement of dead bodies on the ground. The experiment was designed to see whether parents could be conditioned to kill their children. (Meiers also asserted that I "was a communications conduit between the experiment and the faction of the federal government that sponsored it."[32] For the record, I am not and never was a communications conduit for any government agency.) In *Heavenly Deceptor*, Nathan Landau took the opposite view and claimed that Jonestown was a right-wing concentration camp from which Jones planned to launch an attack on the United States.[33] African Americans were kept as slaves, and the community was essentially a prototype kibbutz for small fascist groups that were targeting certain races and religions for elimination.

Laurie Efrein Kahalas approached conspiracies from her perspective as a Jonestown survivor. Like those who died in Jonestown, Kahalas was convinced that a conspiracy existed to destroy Jonestown. The conspirators included members of the Concerned Relatives and agents of the U.S. government. Kahalas published *Snake Dance* in 1998, which outlined her views and presented evidence in support of her belief that the CIA destroyed Jonestown.[34] She maintained a website which reiterated her arguments and received thousands of hits from interested visitors. (The website, jonestown.com, is currently archived on *Alternative Considerations of Jonestown and Peoples Temple*.) Although Kahalas changed her mind on some issues—for example, she no longer thinks that the CIA murdered people in Jonestown—she argues today that a CIA hit squad killed Congressman Ryan and the others at the airstrip.

The appeal of conspiracy theories is that they fill in the gaps that exist in the official story. They reject the notion that Jonestown residents committed suicide, and instead claim that they were either murdered or conditioned to commit suicide—another form of murder based on the premise that no one in their right mind would kill their children or their elders. That means they were drugged, tortured, conditioned, or forced to kill themselves. In the conspiracists' view, the suicide explanation does not do justice to the victims. More importantly, it lets the real perpetrators off the hook by letting them get away with murder. They offer explanations that reassure us of a moral order, though an order that is jeopardized by conspirators. In this regard, the conspiratorial canon is similar to the popular canon by making Jonestown very distant from the everyday world.

THE ARTISTIC CANON

Considering that the deaths in Jonestown occurred more than thirty years ago, it seems somewhat surprising that they continue to interest so many people. This is particularly true of artists—musicians, painters, writers, dramatists, and others—who from the beginning and continuing to the present have found in Peoples Temple, and especially Jonestown, material to incorporate into a variety of works of art. Thus, running parallel the popular canon and the scholarly canon, we can find an artistic canon, that is, a range of artistic representations that address different aspects of Jonestown and Peoples Temple. Some artists adopted "Jonestown" as a shibboleth for pure shock value, such as the Brian Jonestown Massacre, a rock group begun in the early 1990s. But others took it seriously. Frank Zappa's symphonic piece "Jonestown," written within six years of the event, was a serious work that featured a percussive sound throughout that evoked the image of someone repeatedly hitting a galvanized tub of poison. The music was eerie, spectral, and reminiscent of the deaths. Zappa was never easy to listen to, and "Jonestown" was as disturbing as anything he ever wrote.

Jim Jones intrigued, and continues to intrigue, artists on many levels: psychological, theological, pathological, homicidal. An Associated Press photograph of Jim Jones has been reconceptualized in numerous ways, appearing on book jackets, promotional posters, album covers, black velvet paintings, even a T-shirt. These representations capitalize on public memories of Jones in much the same way that images of Adolf Hitler or John Lennon create a thought world with only a glimpse of a moustache or a hint of gold-rimmed glasses. Jones's sunglasses lend an aura of menace and mystery and make him instantly recognizable.

Like the images of Jones, the famous picture of corpses surrounding the Jonestown pavilion has become iconic. A major work of art was Laura Baird's twelve-by-twelve-foot tapestry, "Jonestown Carpet," which recreated the view of the brightly colored bodies. Baird was struck by David Hume Kennerly's photo of the bodies for *Time* Magazine, and initially wanted to analyze the photo itself, rather than Jonestown per se. The death of her sister in 1980, however, strengthened her resolve to actually go forward with the project. It would take ten years to complete (although Baird says she deliberately left one portion unfinished to signify that it will never be finished). The artist wrote that

> it seemed utterly inadequate to participate in and perpetuate the various concurrent discourses on the shortcomings of photography and issues of representation. While such theoretical matters were hard to avoid in art practice in the 1980s, it seemed to me they could not measure up to the task of explaining the unforgettable qualities of those aerial photographs of the Jonestown dead.[35]

Another artist who found Jonestown unforgettable was Andrew Brandou, who completed a compelling series of paintings about Peoples Temple.[36] These paintings featured cute little animals acting out scenes from the history of the movement. Some of the artwork had a menacing skull lurking in the background or in the shadows, but other pieces resembled the illustrations in a children's storybook in their color, tone, and subjects. Brandou explained:

> I am trying to discuss the Peoples Temple, not simply the events of Jonestown, with my paintings . . . I have no interest in mocking anyone, glorifying tragedy, playing into conspiracy theory, or being overtly graphic. As a matter of fact, if you did not know it, you may not even realize the paintings were about the Peoples Temple in particular.[37]

Brandou wrote that his introduction to Jonestown occurred when he was ten years old and attending Catholic school. "The sermons each morning tended to be responses to the tragedy for quite some time." These sermons, coupled with extensive media coverage, drove Brandou "to understand exactly 'what' had taken place." Yet the cheerful, sunny paintings clashed ominously with preconceived notions about Jonestown and Peoples Temple, and made it impossible to understand "exactly 'what' had taken place." They remained troubling, disturbing, and baffling all at the same time.

A number of writers have also found Jonestown worth investigating in poetry and prose. Fred D'Aguiar, a Guyanese poet, read Jonestown through postcolonial eyes in *Bill of Rights*, a collection of poems that suggested Jonestown, but was much larger than a single day, event, or locale.[38] The poems reflected the cultural melting pot of Guyana, with references to Tom and Jerry (the United States), Whitbread and Brixton (the United Kingdom), and Banks Beer (Guyana). D'Aguiar placed Jonestown in the context of the surge and flow of immigrants across continents, always demonstrating an awareness of the legacy of domination, whether by colonialists or by Jim Jones.

> *I see stars you see wounds in that flag*
> *I see red you see blood*

The poems presented oppression and domination as global problems. What happened in Guyana still happens around the world, and a bill of rights was needed for those in the tenements of Glasgow to the slums of Shankhill Road.

D'Aguiar's poems made several references to Quetzalcoatl, one of the most important deities in Mesoamerican religion prior to Spanish contact. This precolonial past was explored in greater detail by Wilson Harris, another Guyanese writer, in his novel *Jonestown*, which moved backward and forward between ancestral Caribbean time and Jonestown time.[39] Wilson tied the deaths in Jonestown to the South American culture of Mayan sacrifices, colonialism, and postcolonial oppression. In his introduction Harris stated that all of the characters in the book were "fictional and archetypal,"[40] indicating his purpose in placing Jonestown and Jim Jones (Jonah Jones in the novel) in an enlarged and expansive drama that transcended time and space, and yet was intimately linked to the reality of colonialism in the Guianas—British, French, and Dutch.

Harris concerned himself with history and memory, especially the gap in the history of precolonial peoples that had been erased due to their extermination. He claimed that it is essential to create a jigsaw in which "pasts" and "presents" and likely or unlikely "futures" are the pieces that multitudes in the self employ in order to bridge chasms in historical memory.[41] Difficult to read, *Jonestown* was not literally about Jonestown. Instead, the author used the events to consider the problems caused by colonialism and to discuss the experiences of people living in a postcolonial world whose history has been erased. In effect, Harris made Jonestown bigger, and more important, than the deaths of 900 Americans.

Another literary treatment of the subject was Fraser Sutherland's book-length poem *Jonestown*.[42] Epic in scope, extremely wellresearched, and complex in its treatment of the subject, it did not take a stand for or against Peoples Temple, its members, or Jim Jones. Like Fondakowski's play, Sutherland laid out all of the characters and let readers come to their own conclusions. The Canadian poet took bits of audiocassettes, sermons, and Temple theology and mixed them into a tale that was both literal and symbolic. He made the easy dismissal of members as cultists difficult by providing particulars about them, such as Larry Schacht, "the Texas art student dented his/brain with psychedelics." The members have names and faces provided by word pictures.

In contrast to these and other literary works, a number of paperback novels capitalized on the juicy aspects of Jonestown: mind control, sex, drugs, murder, and suicide. Potboilers attempted to take advantage of what Gar Wilson's novel called *Terror in Guyana*, with the cover caption reading: "Hitler's legacy is alive in South America."[43] Nick Carter's *Retreat for Death* was "a race against time as Nick tries to prevent another Jonestown massacre."[44] *Cult Sunday* by William D. Rodgers "begins with church bells and ends in terror."[45] Most prescient of the novels with popular appeal was Harold Robbins's book *Dreams Die First*.[46] The book, with a publication date of 1977, described a suicide cult that sounded an eerie note.

I have provided merely a sampling of the better-known works in this brief overview, and have neglected many. A few additional examples would include Henning Mankell's mystery novel *Before the Frost*, which alluded to Jonestown, and Armistad Maupin's *Tales of the City* and *Further Tales of the City*, which incorporated Jim Jones into the plots. Two additional plays, *Jonestown Express* by James Reston Jr. and *Jonestown: The Musical* by Brian Silliman and Larry Lee, have both had public performances. The Jonestown Reenactment occurred in spring 1998 in the United Kingdom. Performance artist Fernando Maneca's one-man show of "Drinking the Kool-Aid" in spring 2006 used the metaphor to critique "believing without questioning" in current politics.[47] Ken Risling's song, "The Unanswered Question," asked a friend who died in Jonestown why she followed Jim Jones.[48] There are many other works to mention, and there will be more artistic representations of Jonestown in the future.

THE ONGOING SIGNIFICANCE OF JONESTOWN

This chapter has introduced the idea of four different canons, or types, of interpretations of Jonestown: popular, scholarly, conspiratorial, and artistic. Most of us will recognize the popular canon, the one that relates a famil-iar story in well-known tropes: brainwashing, madness, coercion, evil. The conspiratorial canon reprises these themes but sets them within the frame-work of a master plan coordinated by unknown forces that seek to control us. Jonestown is the evidence for this conspiracy. The popular canon, on the other hand, tends to blame the charismatic leader, and to exculpate his followers, for all that transpired. There was nothing outside Peoples Temple to influence the course of events, according to the comfortable narrative.

The scholarly canon departs from both of these considerations of Peoples Temple by looking at the institution in distinctly different ways. Academics analyze the movement in its historical context; they look at the individuals and the group; they observe interactions with outside forces; they compare it to other new religions. Rather than ask what is the meaning and message of Jonestown, scholars ask: how did Peoples Temple members make meaning? How did they understand themselves and what they were doing? In addition to trying to understand what happened, they try to assess why it happened. Issues of right and wrong are not at stake; instead, scholars hope to be able to predict when violence might occur and find ways to prevent it.

The emerging artistic canon is expanding, rather than diminishing, as the years pass. This canon differs from other ways of interpreting Jonestown by abandoning previous canons and challenging all preconceptions. In this canon there is no single meaning, there is no single version of the story, but instead multiple layers and levels. Every poem or painting or song displays a unique facet, one never before seen yet in some way recognizable. The creative imagination poses new questions and presents new answers that may shock and amaze us. Artists, writers, and musicians make it difficult to maintain a narrative that asserts that Jonestown was only about crazy cultists. By transgressing, and ignoring, the rituals of exclusion that kept the dead apart from us, they have rewoven Jonestown into the fabric of society.

For Further Reading

Much of the material for this chapter came from several scholarly papers I wrote between 2000 and 2008. The complete citations for the following articles can be found under "Resources" at the end of the book: "Is the Canon on Jonestown Closed?;" "Reconstructing Reality: Conspiracy Theories about Jonestown;" "Drinking the Kool-Aid: The Cultural Transformation of a Tragedy;" and "Jonestown in Literature: Caribbean Reflections on a Tragedy." *The Jonestown Report* carries arts reports in every issue. Artists, writers, and others describe their work and projects in the annual journal, which can be accessed at http://jonestown.sdsu.edu/ AboutJonestown/ JonestownReport/jtreport.htm. A few volumes of poetry to read include Pat Parker's *Jonestown and Other Madness*, Fred D'Aguiar's *Bill of Rights*, and Fraser Sutherland's *Jonestown*. Wilson Harris's novel *Jonestown* is a difficult read, like all of his fiction, but is worth a try, as long as the reader realizes it is nonlinear and nonliteral. Armistead Maupin, whose novels describe life in San Francisco in the 1970s and 1980s, includes some characters from Peoples Temple in *Tales of the City* and *Further Tales of the City* in an imaginative, if unbelievable, way.

A number of conspiracy articles appear on the website *Alternative Considerations of Jonestown and Peoples Temple*, http://jonestown.sdsu.edu. These include Jim Hougan's "Jonestown: The Secret Life of Jim Jones: A Parapolitical Fugue;" Laurie Efrein's "jonestown.com" website in archived form and her current examination of the airstrip shooting, "In Plain Sight;" and Thomas G. Whittle and Jan Thorpe's, "Revisiting the Jonestown Tragedy." Books by Michael Meiers and Nathan Landau are listed under Resources.

CHAPTER 9

Making Meaning after Jonestown

Some tell me I am blessed. I actually don't want that to be the case, since there were so many who were lost, and who should have been so blessed, if there were any justice in this blessing thing.
— Laura Johnston Kohl, *A Temple Member's Odyssey**

It is appropriate that Peoples Temple survivors have the last word in this book. For three decades their voices have been muted, drowned out by a few high-profile defectors who dominated media coverage in the weeks and years immediately following 18 November. These survivors, whose experiences over the past thirty years have varied widely, have only recently been willing and able to come out of the shadows of Jonestown to tell their own stories in their own words. Some have written books that they have self-published; some have appeared on television, in news programs and documentaries; some have been interviewed for *The People's Temple* drama; and a number have written accounts of what happened to them after Jonestown in *The Jonestown Report*, an annual online journal edited by my husband, Fielding McGehee.

I am defining the term "survivor" as anyone whoever belonged to Peoples Temple. It seems more accurate and more descriptive than saying "former member": everyone today is a former member because Peoples Temple no longer exists. Moreover, former member suggests a defection from the movement that may or may not have occurred. Hence the expression "survivor," which does not include relatives who lost family members in Jonestown (although they too have suffered greatly) but does encompass the range of those who once were committed to Peoples Temple.

The late Chris Hatcher, a San Francisco psychologist who counseled dozens and perhaps hundreds of people connected to Jonestown and Peoples Temple, differentiated between defector and loyalist survivors to indicate those who had left the Temple prior to 18 November and those who were part of it on that fateful day.[1] Hatcher believed that both were traumatized by their involvement in the organization, though in different ways.

In the immediate aftermath of Jonestown, three primary groups of survivors faced very different problems. Guyana survivors consisted of people living under house arrest in Lamaha Gardens, the group's residence in Georgetown, and others temporarily staying in various hotels in the capital city. Survivors in San Francisco remained in the Temple headquarters on Geary Boulevard, surrounded by police officers protecting them from angry relatives. Finally, survivors in Berkeley gathered at the Human Freedom Center, a halfway house for Temple defectors founded by Al and Jeannie Mills, themselves former Temple members. The primary difference between the first two groups and the latter was that the general public hated and feared the survivors who were loyalists, while the media and government investigators trusted and relied on the survivors who were defectors.

LOYALIST SURVIVORS

Everyone was a suspect in Guyana, since nobody knew exactly what had happened either at the airstrip in Port Kaituma or in Jonestown or at the third crime scene in Lamaha Gardens, where Sharon Amos and her three children died in a murder-suicide. Laura Kohl, who was there at the time, wrote that:

> The Guyanese military took over the house. They walked around, keeping an eye on us, protecting us from ourselves and from anything unforeseen. They were young kids who became friends, for the most part. Really, they were out of their league, as we were all. We had no direct information then. We heard there were 300 bodies, then 500.[2]

Those who escaped Jonestown and eventually came to Georgetown were met with wariness as well.

It wasn't until December that the Guyana survivors were repatriated to the United States. They encountered hostility from many sides, including from some airline pilots who refused to allow certain survivors on board. The majority of survivors coming from Guyana were flown to New York Kennedy Airport where they were greeted by FBI interrogators who questioned them for as long as fourteen hours in small trailers located on the tarmac.

The interviews were part of the FBI investigation into the assassination of Congressman Ryan. Thirty special agents from the San Francisco field office were assigned to the investigation, and a total of eighty agents worked around the country in the immediate aftermath. The agents interviewed 2,000 individuals, including eighty loyalist survivors who returned from Guyana. Heavily redacted reports of the interviews show that people unconnected with the Temple as well as defector survivors ("ex-members," in FBI parlance) primarily shaped the agents' views. FBI agents wanted to interrogate ex-members, current members, members of the Planning Commission, and the "Angels," who were characterized as members of a purported hit squad. "Ex-members have also indicated the existence of a 'contingency plan,'" which would go into effect if public officials attempted to expose Peoples Temple or if Jim Jones were arrested.[3]

A list of questions that the FBI generated on 22 November guided the questioning of survivors from Guyana. It included queries about a conspiracy to kill Congressman Ryan, weapons and firearms training, a hit squad, hiding weapons or money, and the "contingency plan." Agents repeatedly asked for the names of members of the basketball team and the Jonestown security force, since ex-members had singled them out as particularly dangerous. Results of the interrogations were routinely disappointing, however, since only a handful of survivors seemed to know about the more sensational allegations. Perhaps most dissatisfying to the FBI was the lack of substantive information about weapons training or a stockpile of arms in Jonestown. One survivor asserted that "Jones maintained possibly 50 weapons," the most that anyone ever mentioned. FBI documents included a listing of six Peoples Temple members who took firearms training with the San Francisco Police Department. Ironically, only a single individual who took the training died in Jonestown; the rest quit the Temple long before 1978. Again, Laura Johnston Kohl's narrative illuminated what it was like for the Guyana survivors:

> We were taken off the plane in pairs, escorted to RV's that had been set up on the runway, and interrogated by the FBI. The agents tried "good cop–bad cop" and other tactics. They told me that others had told them that I knew everything that happened. They asked me about a list of other members, a list, as I found out later, which the FBI made of people who allegedly followed the congressional party to the Port Kaituma airstrip and participated in the shootings. I asked to see a lawyer at some point. Then I just sort of went to sleep.

Kohl found it particularly cruel that they were fed McDonald's hamburgers after their healthy diet in Jonestown.

While the Guyana survivors faced the immediate shock and trauma of losing family members and of nearly losing their own lives, the survivors in San Francisco faced a different challenge. At that time, about 150 members lived in San Francisco, 80 members lived in Los Angeles, and 20 members lived in Redwood Valley. The San Francisco contingent had received instructions via shortwave radio from Jonestown and Georgetown to kill themselves, but Stephan Jones's urgent and repeated messages helped to prevent that from happening. When relatives of Temple members began to learn of the deaths in Jonestown, they surrounded the Geary Boulevard facility, with angry crowds swelling to several hundred each afternoon. Archie Ijames, the associate pastor Jim Jones had left in charge of the San Francisco headquarters, made statements to the relatives and to the media but could not quell the rage. A twenty-four-hour police presence was needed to protect the confused and isolated group living in the Temple facility. "If anyone has received death threats, it's us," said Hue Fortson. "We have received phone calls at all hours of the day and night threatening us with murder."[4]

Just nine days after the mass deaths in Jonestown, the mayor of San Francisco and a city supervisor were assassinated. A former city supervisor, Dan White, was charged and eventually convicted of killing Mayor George Moscone and Supervisor Harvey Milk. "The combined effect on San Francisco of the assassinations and Jonestown has been compared to the reactions to the John F. Kennedy assassination on the country as a whole," said Chris Hatcher, the psychologist assigned to counsel survivors.[5] The president of the Board of Supervisors, Dianne Feinstein, became the mayor, and despite the fact that other elected officials were distancing themselves from Peoples Temple, she chose to associate her office with the group in order to prevent any more violence from occurring. Within a matter of days she met with a small group of advisors, including Hatcher and San Francisco Police Chief Charles Gain, and devised a plan to make contact with members living inside the San Francisco Temple. Hatcher and Gain learned that those inside feared retribution from relatives on the outside. They also discovered that the members had virtually no financial resources. As a result, Mayor Feinstein adopted a three-part plan to help Peoples Temple members, that:

(1) assigned public safety resources to prevent violence against or by Temple members;
(2) mobilized job and welfare assistance to members to facilitate reintegration into society; and
(3) provided counseling to survivors.[6]

This plan was never publicly announced, given the fact that a range of public officials experienced harsh criticism for efforts to help Temple survivors—from President Jimmy Carter and Secretary of State Cyrus Vance on down.

Loyalist survivors—both those in San Francisco and those who returned from Guyana—told Hatcher that they did not want welfare but wanted to work at whatever job they could get. They received a cold welcome, however. One member was physically ejected from a job interview, while others found their interviews terminated when they listed Peoples Temple as their former employer. Upon learning that one of his employees had been in the Temple, an employer told the survivor to leave the premises immediately. Even mental health workers had to be carefully screened to work with the survivors, because their own prejudices and fears often interfered with their ability to listen and be helpful. "Some members, unable to find jobs, had been turned away by welfare agencies that refused to deal with 'baby killers'."[7] Mike Carter, who escaped from Jonestown on 18 November, wrote:

> One thing I quickly learned was not to just blurt out at a party or at work that I had lived in Jonestown and survived. People treated me differently after they found out, and usually—okay, always— relationships were affected, colored, tainted by my Jonestown connection. So I adapted and became more selective when sharing my background.
>
> With time I learned. I would let people get to know me for a while, and then I would find an appropriate time to let them know that I was in Peoples Temple. They were always amazed, since I was like them. And then, nearly always, even though they knew me, people would distance themselves from me.[8]

DEFECTOR SURVIVORS

If the San Francisco survivors feared attack from hostile relatives, the Berkeley survivors at the Human Freedom Center (HFC)—all of them defector survivors—feared assault from unknown Temple assailants. Remembering their days in the Temple when Jones boasted of having the parts to make an atomic bomb and having the means to do away with his enemies, they were terrified. Founded in summer 1978, the HFC was housed in a building the Millses had once operated as a licensed nursing home, and functioned as the organizing center for the Concerned Relatives.

Lowell Streiker, who briefly served as Executive Director of HFC after 18 November, wrote that in the weeks and months after the deaths, the building "turned into a maelstrom of confusion as surviving Temple members, earlier defectors, relatives of the dead, and members of the media from every part of the world converged."[9] Streiker especially remarked upon the ongoing presence of media who "interviewed, photographed, tape recorded, and filmed again and again," as everyone jockeyed for the inside story. In addition:

> mental health professionals, seldom hearing what the survivors and defectors actually had to say, offered their own theories of "brainwashing," "mind control," "thought reform," and "systematic manipulation of social influences," thereby enabling Jones' followers to blame everything on "Dad" and nothing on themselves.[10]

Like Hatcher, Streiker counseled a variety of survivors, who all reported having the same dream. They would find themselves in Jonestown, exhausted and disoriented, and would hear Jim Jones's voice on the loudspeaker saying "You will never get away from me! Never!" The dreamer would realize (in the dream) that the mass deaths had not yet occurred but were still inescapably to come.

Most counselors at the Human Freedom Center sought to deprogram former members by instructing them about Jones's manipulative techniques and providing them information they might not have had about incidents that occurred within the Temple. Neva Sly Hargrave was one defector who described the benefits of being voluntarily deprogrammed by the Millses in 1977:

> I can't imagine how I would have reacted to Guyana if I had not been deprogrammed! I had enough guilt as it was, knowing everyone was down there. But the lies we were taught—the brainwashing we went through, because that's what it was—would have kept us in that prison of the mind forever.[11]

A key element of HFC's program was to tell clients they had been brainwashed: how else could they explain the dangerous, immoral, and at times illegal actions they had committed while in the Temple? Counseling sessions—in which people could talk with each other about the experiences they had—also helped to deconstruct the Temple's highly compartmentalized organizational structure. It became clear that most people knew very little about the entire workings of the group: a few people knew everything, while the majority knew next to nothing.

When Al and Jeannie Mills and their daughter Daphene were murdered in February 1980, shock waves reverberated through the defector community. Their deaths seemed to prove the existence of a hit squad, although no evidence was found to link the deaths to anyone connected with the Temple. The reactions were similar to those that occurred after the deaths in Jonestown. Some defector survivors went into hiding again and others refused to discuss their pasts. Hargrave lost her job as a live-in secretary because her employer feared for both of their lives. Jeannie Mills became a martyr to alleged cult violence, with defectors convinced that a hit squad assassinated the family. Others, including the local police, were not so sure. As recently as 2005 police arrested Eddie Mills, the Millses's son who had just returned home after living abroad for a number of years but released him shortly afterwards for lack of evidence.

THE RECONCILIATION OF SURVIVORS

Defectors and loyalists remained suspicious of each other for more than a decade. The Rev. Jynona Norwood, whose mother, along with many cousins and other relatives, died in Jonestown, held a memorial service on 18 November 1979, at Evergreen Cemetery—an observance she has faithfully organized every year since. With its anticult message and its critique of Jim Jones, the service appealed to defectors and the critical relatives of those who died. For many years, only the news media, members of Dr. Norwood's church, and a few others attended. After the tenth anniversary, however, a few loyalists began to attend. A big shift occurred on the twentieth anniversary of the deaths, when more than thirty survivors met at a restaurant following the service. Although both defectors and loyalists expected recriminations and blame, they found only a welcome greeting and the renewal of friendships that had begun more than two decades earlier. Everyone was there to mourn the dead, not to re-create the past.

Another milestone marking reconciliation between defectors and loyalists occurred in January 2002, when a small group of people met at the Z Space in San Francisco—a theater development and production company—to discuss the possibility of developing a play about Peoples Temple. Leigh Fondakowski, the playwright, listened by speakerphone to those assembled: Grace Stoen Jones and Yulanda Williams (high-profile defectors), Leslie Wilson (who had escaped Jonestown on 18 November with her young son), and Laura Johnston Kohl, Stephan Jones, and James Jones Jr. (loyalist survivors). Other defectors and loyalists, including Mike Cartmell, Bryan Kravitz and Kristine Johnston Kravitz, also attended. Kohl spoke for all in attendance when she said that she had never seen her story presented in the media, that no one had documented her own understanding of Peoples Temple and Jonestown. While many books, films, and articles had come out, none seemed to grasp the totality of Peoples Temple. The meeting marked Fondakowski's introduction to just a few of the people she would go on to interview for *The People's Temple* drama.

The most significant step occurred at the twenty-fifth anniversary in 2003, when survivors gathered at Evergreen Cemetery in a private ceremony. Many who had never been to the cemetery came to the private observance. Some loyalists and defectors saw each other for the first time in twenty-five years, or sometimes more. Everyone was older, grayer, and heavier. But no matter who or what one was in the Temple, they all shared a bond that transcended old differences: grief over the loss of loved ones and the death of the communal experiment they so fervently wanted to succeed. That year survivors also began what has become an annual gathering at a private home to mourn and reconnect outside public view.

The California Historical Society (CHS) facilitated the reconnection in 2003 by opening its doors to survivors and sharing its collection in a private showing. Survivors gathered to identify photographs in the collection—to give names to the faces—a process that helped CHS archivists and elicited memories, tears, and smiles. Survivors talked about the past but also about the present as they asked where other survivors were and what they were doing.

The private ceremony at Evergreen Cemetery on the twenty-fifth anniversary, coupled with the session at CHS, fostered conversations about having reunions that would not coincide with the date of the deaths. Survivors found comfort in their mutual experiences and deep friendships. They could exchange stories about their days in the Temple and, by sharing, learn much that had been hidden. Many felt they wanted to get together to socialize and not just to memorialize. These discussions led to the first annual Fourth of July reunion in 2005, and held every year since then. Each year found a few more survivors attending, overcoming the terrible anxiety and guilt they felt about encountering people they may have hurt in the past. Those who had attended found the event life-changing because it provided the opportunity for reconnecting with old friends and finding forgiveness and reconciliation. Terri Buford wrote a poem after she attended the reunion for the first time in 2007, which indicated the depth of emotion that accompanied the trip from the past to the present:[12]

> You...
> Familiar with
> Original pain
>
> Squeezed my hand
> In one brave act
> Of forgiveness
> So please...
> Rock me gently
> In your soul
> Teach me
> The lost art
> Of living
> After death
> Has ruled
> So long

MORE CASUALTIES OF JONESTOWN

For the past thirty years all survivors of Peoples Temple have lived with the guilt that comes with simply being alive while so many others perished. Their endurance has come at a cost. Many have struggled with alcoholism, addiction, and depression. A number dealt with posttraumatic stress disorders, and continue to be plagued with nightmares. Some were fugitives from the law; others became abusive or were subject to abuse. One woman described her marriage to a survivor in this way:

I was married to a Jonestown survivor for 13 years. He never got over it. Often, especially around the anniversary, he would have night-mares. He was very paranoid, sleeping with guns and knives, always suspicious of everyone. He could never become involved in church, although he tried on several occasions[13]

Laurence Mann, Guyana's Ambassador to the United States, had a rela-tionship with Temple member Paula Adams, which began in Georgetown several years before the deaths in Jonestown. In 1983 Mann killed Adams and their young son, and then shot himself. Richard Cordell, whose wife and four children died in Jonestown, also committed suicide that same year. Tyrone Mitchell, whose parents and four sisters died in Jonestown, opened fire on a schoolyard in Los Angeles in 1984, killing one girl and injuring thirteen other children before turning the gun on himself.

Perhaps the most shocking suicide occurred when Mike Prokes, a public relations spokesperson for the group and a close advisor to Jones, killed himself in a Modesto motel room after meeting with reporters at a press conference he had convened in March 1979. Jones had sent Prokes, along with the Carter brothers, away from Jonestown on 18 November, with suitcases full of cash destined for the Soviet Embassy. Although Prokes escaped physically unharmed, he bore the scars of his commitment to Peoples Temple. In the statement he made to the press, he said that he had initially joined the group as an informant but became convinced of the sincerity of Jones and the dedication of its members. "I believe in the basic rightness of the life and work that went on in Jonestown," Prokes told the reporters, "and I can't disassociate myself from the people who died, nor do I want to."[14] Then he went into the bathroom and shot himself.

Greg Pierotti, one of the playwrights for *The People's Temple*, identified a common denominator among survivors. "Each has loved profoundly and suffered profoundly. That is what everyone who was touched by the tragedy of Jonestown seems to share: Profound love and suffering."[15] For some survivors, anguish overcame the will to live.

NEW LIVES

The vast majority of survivors transcended their suffering, however, and made new lives for themselves. Many used the skills they had learned in the Temple in other careers, including operating printing presses, designing graphics, and working in law. A number became public school teachers, social workers, conflict mediators, librarians, artists, musicians, and minis-ters. Others entered government, medicine, business, and law enforcement. Jordan Vilchez, who lost two sisters and two nephews in Jonestown, wrote that the challenge for her "has been remaining vital, functional and produc-tive, not only in the face of our own personal loss, but in the face of the planetary sacrilege and governing bodies who haven't got a clue about how to promote and defend the welfare of the entire earth community."[16] It is impossible to generalize about what a typical survivor does today since they represent a complete cross section of American society.

One generalization that can be made, however, is that survivors have struggled to overcome feelings of anger and guilt. Juanell Smart, whose mother, uncle, and four children died in Jonestown, wrote:

> After November 18, 1978, I was in a state of disbelief. I was mad at my mother. I was mad at my uncle. I wanted Jim Jones to be alive so I could kill him. Then I went through the guilt stage which I have not totally come out of. I have somehow managed to survive even though I wanted to die ... I still go through periods of self-pity, but I no longer hate Jim or my white former sisters and brothers of Peoples Temple.[17]

Neva Sly Hargrave, whose son and husband perished, observed that Jim Jones fueled the anger that Temple members felt about a racist and unjust society.[18] But maintaining that anger served no purpose. She asked: Who could you be angry with? The parents who trusted Jim Jones with their children? Jim Jones?

> But why hold on to anger against someone who was mentally deranged, and now dead for 28 years? Furthermore, you can't hold anger against someone who abused you or your family when they were following and obeying Jim Jones.
> You have to let it go ... and forgive!! [ellipses in original]

Vernon Gosney, whose son died in Jonestown, described his journey back to wholeness. He went from rage to self-hatred to forgiveness, and although it was not a short trip, he concluded, "To forgive is to be free. I could have been Larry Layton or any of the others very easily."[19]

Survivors have adopted a range of religious responses for understanding their life journeys. Some have embraced, or re-embraced, Christianity. Hattie Newell, who lost twelve relatives in Jonestown, including her mother and most of her siblings, said, "My search led me to the one person who could give me new life and strength to face the fact that I may never find the answers to why all of this happened. His name is Jesus Christ."[20] Hue Fortson and David Wise began independent Christian ministries in Los Angeles and Austin. Others turned, or returned, to New Age philosophies or metaphysical beliefs that saw divinity in all persons and self-realization as the goal and purpose of life. Still others rejected any form of religiosity, although it would probably be more accurate to say that they are humanists who believe that working for the good of humanity is the imperative of life on earth.

While the religious beliefs of survivors vary, their political beliefs and commitments seem quite similar, and have only deepened over the past three decades. Kathy Barbour, a loyalist survivor, set three goals for herself after 18 November:

> First, not to ever go back to being "white" and accepting the privileges and favors of society, until poverty and racism became dim memories. The second was to vindicate those who died in Jonestown by validating their ideals. The third was to do my part, whatever it may be, to bring the world to the point where universal brotherhood and equality are attainable goals, not just dreams.[21]

Barbour's dedication to overcoming racism appeared as a common theme among survivors. David Wise noted that, "The Jonestown grave is full of hundreds of unclaimed dead blacks who literally had no one on earth to claim them." He then examined the situation today, describing the incarceration rate for African American men and asked, "Why aren't all of us aware of this?"[22] Patti Chastain Haag, who died of AIDS in 1995, wrote in 1992 that "We lived and worked Black and White together. It was challenging, exhilarating, exhausting."[23]

Survivors today speak nostalgically of the "challenging, exhilarating, exhausting" years they spent in Peoples Temple. They retain a preference for communal living, untempered by the disaster of Jonestown which they blame primarily on Jim Jones. Some have only half-jokingly proposed a communal retirement center.

Family members of those who died in Jonestown have also had to rebuild their lives since the devastating losses of 1978. "I have no grandchildren, no family, absolutely no one to go on after me," wrote Barbara Sines of the loss of her two children Ron and Nancy. "I'm not wanting—or looking—for sympathy. This is just a statement of fact, a statement of loss . . . This is my broken heart talking."[24]

Sines, like other relatives, busied herself in activities not only to keep her mind occupied but also to make meaning out of the events. My mother, Barbara Moore, volunteered for many years at a Catholic Worker hospitality house for the homeless. My uncle, Robert Moore, co-founded the Redlands Peace Center with his wife Doris as a direct response to my sisters' deaths in Jonestown.[25] My husband and I have written books and now manage a website, *Alternative Considerations of Jonestown and Peoples Temple*, which serves as a clearinghouse for information about Peoples Temple and Jonestown, our own way of making meaning. A number of survivors and others have contributed to the website in many ways: writing articles; transcribing audiotapes; providing corrections to a comprehensive listing of who died in Jonestown; and making suggestions and critiques. Much of the information upon which this book is based came from the website.

THE LESSONS OF JONESTOWN

What are the lessons of Jonestown? Writing ten years after the events, Chris Hatcher said that "almost all Temple survivors, defectors, and relatives believe that society has learned little from the mass suicides and murders at Jonestown."[26] My father, John Moore, wrote that:

> The lesson of Jonestown is that good people are capable of evil acts. Those who made the fateful decision to murder their children and take their own lives regarded that decision as tragic, but not evil. We who survive them must be the ones to declare it to be both evil and tragic.[27]

Commentators in the immediate aftermath of the deaths pointed to a number of lessons: an uncaring society, the dangers of socialism, the menace of cults. Writing twenty-five years later, John R. Hall saw Jonestown as a harbinger of our own, post-9/11 era where "countercultural religious conflict is a dialectical process in which each side is labeled by the other as 'evil'."[28] This process leads to ever-escalating confrontations in which the cause of vanquishing evil "can become a crusade that begets evil."

Tim Carter, a survivor, offered a different explanation. He argued that members of Peoples Temple did not know in 1978 what they know today. A lack of information and a failure to communicate trapped people in a world they did not, and could not, fully comprehend. If Temple members had known the whole story, they would have made different choices, according to Carter.[29] In other words, they were more like us than not.

There may be large lessons to learn from the rise and fall of Peoples Temple, but smaller lessons may be just as valuable: the enjoyment of a stroll down the mall, a chocolate sundae, or a new pair of sandals, wrote one relative; the blessing of a new kitchen utensil, as a survivor said. Neva Sly Hargrave has found that an evolution within her spirit has brought her loving and nonjudgmental thoughts and emotions. Juanell Smart observed that, "In spite of losing my whole family, I try to remember that the experience was not all bad. I am a lot more tolerant, a lot more caring, and a whole lot wiser. I go into old age alone, but not bitter and without placing blame on anyone."

"Life asks all of us how we will deal with tragedy," declared John Moore. For most of the world, the story of Peoples Temple ended on 18 November 1978. For the survivors, a part of themselves died that day as well. At the same time, a new self was born from the ashes of the disaster. It was a self that admits the capacity for evil that exists within all of us, but one that also recognizes "the capacity to relieve suffering when we cannot prevent it, to search for truth and create beauty, and to persist in the struggle to bring universal good from out of personal tragedy."[30] That is exactly what Jonestown survivors today are trying to do.

For Further Reading

The website *Alternative Considerations of Jonestown and Peoples Temple* (http://jonestown.sdsu.edu) contains numerous articles by survivors describing their reflections and opinions on a number of different subjects. *The Jonestown Report*, an annual update on research into Jonestown, also includes survivor narratives. *The Need for a Second Look at Jonestown* comprises a collection of essays written ten years after the deaths and includes several survivor accounts and reports by individuals involved in helping people in the wake of the disaster. *New Religious Movements, Mass Suicide, and Peoples Temple* also includes several essays that analyze various responses to Jonestown.

NOTES

AUTHOR'S NOTE

1. More complete accounts of my family's relationship with Peoples Temple appear in *A Sympathetic History of Jonestown* and *The Jonestown Letters*, published by the Edwin Mellen Press in the 1980s. These and other works are listed in "Resources."

2. Ken Risling, "Jonestown: The Unanswered Question," can be heard at: http://www.myspace.com/kenrisling.

INTRODUCTION

* Denis Diderot, *Pensées Philosophiques*, no. 29, 1746. In *Bartlett's Familiar Quotations*, 17th ed., ed. John Bartlett (Boston: Little, Brown, and Company, 2002), 331.

1. For more information, see James D. Tabor and Eugene V. Gallagher, *Why Waco? Cults and the Battle for Religious Freedom in America* (Berkeley and Los Angeles: University of California Press, 1995).

2. John R. Hall, *Gone from the Promised Land: Jonestown in American Cultural History* (New Brunswick, N.J.: Transaction Publishers, 1987, reprint 2004), xxv.

3. Rebecca Moore, Anthony B. Pinn, and Mary R. Sawyer, eds., *Peoples Temple and Black Religion in America* (Bloomington and Indianapolis: University of Indiana Press, 2004).

4. The most helpful comparative analysis in this regard comes from Catherine Wessinger's book *How the Millennium Comes Violently: From Jonestown to Heaven's Gate* (New York: Seven Bridges Press, 2000).

5. Many primary sources, including transcripts of FBI audiotapes, are posted on *Alternative Considerations of Jonestown and Peoples Temple*, http://jonestown.sdsu.edu, henceforth abbreviated as *Alternative Considerations*. Additional primary

texts are housed at the California Historical Society in San Francisco, and the Special Collections at San Diego State University Library and Information Access. See the section on "Resources" for a complete listing.

CHAPTER 1

* Jim Jones, *Notes for Bible Study*, in author's personal collection of papers.

1. Jim Jones's description of his childhood and adolescence appears in FBI FOIA doc. O-1-B (1-19). A discussion of his development as a Marxist occurs in FBI FOIA doc. O-1-A-1 (a-h). Lynetta Jones's account of young Jimba is in FBI FOIA doc. BB-18-Z (2-48). Marceline Jones's description of her life with Jones in Indiana can be found in FBI FOIA doc. BB-18-Z (63–68).

2. Tim Reiterman, with John Jacobs. *Raven: The Untold Story of the Rev. Jim Jones and His People* (New York: E. P. Dutton, 1982, reprint 2008), 13.

3. John R. Hall, *Gone from the Promised Land: Jonestown in American Cultural History* (New Brunswick, N.J.: Transaction Publishers, 1987, reprint 2004), 10. Ellipses in original.

4. FBI Audiotape Q 1058 (Part 2).

5. FBI FOIA doc. O-1-B-11.

6. Hall, 44. Beam's comments appear on FBI Audiotape Q 777.

7. Interview with Rick Cordell, FBI FOIA doc. HH-6-A-3.

8. FBI FOIA doc. BB-18-Z-67; also available in Denice Stephenson, ed., *Dear People: Remembering Jonestown* (San Francisco and Berkeley: California Historical Society and Heyday Books, 2005), 16.

9. Catherine (Hyacinth) Thrash, as told to Marian K. Towne, *The Onliest One Alive: Surviving Jonestown, Guyana* (Indianapolis: Marian K. Towne, 1995), 47–48.

10. "Pastor Jones meets M. J. Divine," *Alternative Considerations*; also in FBI FOIA doc. BB-17-O-1.

11. Bonnie Thielmann, with Dean Merrill, *The Broken God* (Elgin, Ill.: David C. Cook Publishing Co., 1979), 23.

12. FBI Audiotape Q 134.

13. Harold Cordell Jr. letter to Ross Case, 18 February 1965, MS 4062, Folder 2, California Historical Society, San Francisco.

14. Ross Case letter to James Jones, 3 March 1965, MS 4062, Folder 2, California Historical Society, San Francisco. The remainder of the quotations appear in a handwritten draft of the letter.

CHAPTER 2

* Tim Carter, "The Big Grey," *The Jonestown Report* 5 (August 2003), http://jonestown.sdsu.edu/AboutJonestown/PersonalReflections/carter.htm.

1. Shiva Naipaul, *Journey to Nowhere: A New World Tragedy* (New York: Penguin Books, 1980), 209–10. Subsequent quotations in this paragraph come from pp. 297 and 293.

2. Archie Smith Jr., "An Interpretation of Peoples Temple and Jonestown: Implications for the Black Church," in *Peoples Temple and Black Religion in America*,

ed. Rebecca Moore, Anthony B. Pinn, and Mary R. Sawyer (Bloomington and Indianapolis: University of Indiana Press, 2004), 49.

3. Duchess Harris and Adam John Waterman, "To Die for the Peoples Temple: Religion and Revolution after Black Power," in Moore, Pinn, and Sawyer, 105.

4. FBI FOIA doc. FF-1-106-d; also available in Denice Stephenson, ed., *Dear People: Remembering Jonestown* (San Francisco and Berkeley: California Historical Society and Heyday Books, 2005), 20.

5. FBI FOIA doc. FF-1-96-a; also available in Stephenson, 46.

6. FBI FOIA doc. HH-6-A (22–23).

7. Catherine (Hyacinth) Thrash, as told to Marian K. Towne, *The Onliest One Alive: Surviving Jonestown, Guyana* (Indianapolis: Marian K. Towne, 1995), 63–65.

8. FBI Audiotape Q 929.

9. Garrett Lambrev, "What Does 'The People's Temple' Do for Our Understanding of the Real Thing," *The Jonestown Report* 7 (November 2005).

10. The promotional materials quoted throughout this chapter appear in several leaflets and flyers that can be found in folder 1203, "Media Mailings," in Peoples Temple Records, MS 3800, California Historical Society, San Francisco.

11. Jim Jones, "Who Are the Real Radicals?" (October 1970), leaflet in folder 1203, Peoples Temple Records, MS 3800, California Historical Society, San Francisco. See also Stephenson, 32–34 for complete text.

12. Jim Jones, "The Letter Killeth," *Alternative Considerations*.

13. Data compiled using home addresses of those who moved to Guyana, see http://jonestown.sdsu.edu/images/pdf/PTaddressesinUS.pdf.

14. Tanya M. Hollis, "Peoples Temple and Housing Politics in San Francisco," in Moore, Pinn, and Sawyer, 97.

15. MS 3800, folder 2172. California Historical Society, San Francisco.

16. Mary McCormick Maaga, *Hearing the Voices of Jonestown* (Syracuse, N.Y.: Syracuse University Press, 1998), 85.

17. Archie Smith Jr., *The Relational Self: Ethics and Therapy from a Black Church Perspective* (Nashville, Tenn.: Abingdon Press, 1982), 196–97.

18. J. Alfred Smith, "Breaking the Silence: Reflections of a Black Pastor," in Moore, Pinn, and Sawyer, 140.

19. Bea Alethia Orsot, "Together We Stood, Divided We Fell," *Alternative Considerations*; also in *The Need for a Second Look at Jonestown*, ed. Rebecca Moore and Fielding M. McGehee III (Lewiston, N.Y.: The Edwin Mellen Press, 1989), 96.

20. Tim Reiterman, with John Jacobs. *Raven: The Untold Story of the Rev. Jim Jones and His People* (New York: E. P. Dutton, 1982, reprint 2008), 266.

21. Harris and Waterman, 106.

22. Calendar, in Margaret Singer Papers, MS 4123/Peoples Temple Papers, California Historical Society, San Francisco.

23. *Peoples Forum* 1, no. 6, 2d issue (May 1976), 3. Copies of *Peoples Forum* are available at the California Historical Society, MS 4124 and MS 3800.

24. *Peoples Forum* 1, no. 13, 1st issue (December 1976), 1.

25. Edith Roller, Journal, 23 May 1976, FBI FOIA doc. C-2-A-9 (110).

26. John R. Hall, *Gone from the Promised Land: Jonestown in American Cultural History* (New Brunswick, N.J.: Transaction Publishers, 1987, reprint 2004), 54.

27. Patricia Cartmell, "No Haloes Please" (1970) in folder 18, John R. Hall Research Materials, MS 3803, California Historical Society, San Francisco See also Stephenson, 23–24, for complete text.

28. Edith Roller, Journal, 21 April 1976, FBI FOIA doc. C-2-A-8.

29. FBI FOIA doc. EE-3-4-YY; doc. X-1-B-5; and doc. X-1-B-6.

30. David Wise, "Sex in Peoples Temple," *The Jonestown Report* 6 (October 2004).

31. Edith Roller, Journal, 12 May 1976, FBI FOIA doc. C-2-A-9 (58–59).

32. Michael Bellefountaine, *A Lavender Look at Peoples Temple*, unpublished manuscript.

33. Laura Johnston Kohl, "Sex in the City? Make That, The Commune," *The Jonestown Report* 6 (October 2004).

34. Garry Lambrev, "The Board (of Elders)," *The Jonestown Report* 9 (November 2007).

35. Maaga, 65.

36. "Gang of Eight Letter," *Alternative Considerations*; also in Stephenson, 65.

37. Maaga, 66.

38. Jeannie Mills, *Six Years with God: Life Inside Rev. Jim Jones's Peoples Temple* (New York: A&W Publishers, 1979), 231.

39. Lester Kinsolving, "The Original Exposés," on *Jonestown Apologists Alert*, http://jonestownapologistsalert.blogspot.com.

40. Hall, 184–85.

CHAPTER 3

* Zipporah Edwards, in *Dear People: Remembering Jonestown*, ed. Denice Stephenson (San Francisco and Berkeley: California Historical Society Press and Heyday Books, 2005), 87. Also on FBI FOIA doc. EE-1E-10-B.

1. Gordon K. Lewis, *"Gather with the Saints at the River:" The Jonestown Guyana Holocaust 1978* (Río Piedras, Puerto Rico: Institute of Caribbean Studies, University of Puerto Rico, 1979), 31. The remaining quotations from Dr. Lewis come from pp. 30, and 24–25 of his book.

2. FBI FOIA doc. A-31-A-21 (a-c); also on *Alternative Considerations*.

3. Ambassador Maxwell V. Krebs, Memorandum to Mr. Ashley Hewitt (3 December 1978) reprinted in *The Assassination of Representative Leo J. Ryan and the Jonestown, Guyana Tragedy: Report of a Staff Investigative Group to the Committee on Foreign Affairs, U.S. House of Representatives*, House Document No. 96-223 (15 May 1979) 96th Congress, 1st Session (Washington, D.C.: U.S. Government Printing Office, 1979), 135. Henceforth, citations will be called *House Committee Report*.

4. Wade Matthews, Memorandum to Mr. Ashley Hewitt (4 December 1978), reprinted in *House Committee Report*, 141.

5. "Agricultural Mission Offers New Hope for 23 Young Urban 'Incorrigibles'," *Peoples Forum* 2, no. 1, 1st issue (April 1977), 1.

6. Don Beck, "A Peoples Temple Life," *The Jonestown Report* 7 (November 2005).

7. John V Moore, "Notes and Reflections on Our Trip to Guyana," May 1978, *Alternative Considerations*; also in Rebecca Moore, *A Sympathetic History of Jonestown* (Lewiston, N.Y.: The Edwin Mellen Press, 1985), 195.

8. Deborah Layton, *Seductive Poison: A Jonestown Survivor's Story of Life and Death in the Peoples Temple* (New York: Anchor Books, 1998), 164.

9. Affidavit of Deborah Layton Blakey, June 1978, *Alternative Considerations*.

10. Edith Roller, Journal, 17 June 1978, *Alternative Considerations*.

11. Edith Roller, Journal, 4 August 1978, *Alternative Considerations*.

12. FBI Audiotape Q 597.

13. "Instructions from JJ," FBI FOIA doc. EE-1-S-47. Also available in Denice Stephenson, ed., *Dear People: Remembering Jonestown* (San Francisco and Berkeley: California Historical Society and Heyday Books, 2005), 83–84.

14. Douglas J. Bennet Jr., letter to Congressman Clement J. Zablocki, 14 March 1979, *House Committee Report*, 159.

15. Cable from the American Embassy in Georgetown, to the U.S. Secretary of State, 5 December 1978, *House Committee Report*, 144.

16. Stephenson, 86. Similar, though not identical, notes appear in FBI FOIA doc. C-8-A-22a.

17. FBI Audiotape Q 279, possibly from 19 August 1978, according to FBI notes.

18. Harriet Tropp, Memo to Jim Jones, n.d., FBI FOIA doc. EE-2-S-13A. Also available in Stephenson, 101.

19. Carey Winfrey, "Desolate Scene Found at Ruined Jonestown Schoolhouse," *New York Times*, 28 November 1978.

20. Edith Roller, Journal, 13 June 1978, *Alternative Considerations*.

21. Carolyn Layton, letter to John and Barbara Moore (1 November 1977), in Rebecca Moore, *The Jonestown Letters: Correspondence of the Moore Family 1970–1985* (Lewiston, N.Y.: The Edwin Mellen Press, 1986), 198.

22. FBI FOIA doc. FF-11-A-42.

23. FBI Audiotape Q 596a, text edited slightly for clarity.

24. FBI Audiotape Q 134.

25. Duchess Harris and Adam John Waterman, "To Die for the Peoples Temple: Religion and Revolution after Black Power," in *Peoples Temple and Black Religion in America*, ed. Rebecca Moore, Anthony B. Pinn, and Mary R. Sawyer (Bloomington and Indianapolis: University of Indiana Press, 2004), 106.

26. FBI Audiotape Q 182.

27. FBI Audiotape Q 182.

CHAPTER 4

* Friedrich Nietzsche, *Beyond Good and Evil*, IV, 146. In *Bartlett's Familiar Quotations*, 17th ed., ed. John Bartlett (Boston: Little, Brown, and Company, 2002), 589.

1. John R. Hall, *Gone from the Promised Land: Jonestown in American Cultural History* (New Brunswick, N.J.: Transaction Publishers, 1987, reprint 2004), 215.

2. Jeannie Mills, *Six Years with God: Life Inside Rev. Jim Jones's Peoples Temple* (New York: A&W Publishers, 1979), 50.

3. George Klineman and Sherman Butler, and David Conn, *The Cult That Died: The Tragedy of Jim Jones and the People's Temple* (New York: G. P. Putnam's Sons, 1980), 252.

4. Marshall Kilduff and Phil Tracy, "Inside Peoples Temple," *New West Magazine* 17 (1 August 1977): 30–38; also on *Alternative Considerations*.

5. Hall, 233.

6. Unaware of the theft, Moore took the briefcase to the United Airlines ticket counter (because it had a UA luggage tag) at the Oakland Airport. Not surprisingly, Kinsolving later claimed that Temple members seemed aware of the contents of documents contained in the briefcase. He also accused Moore of providing them with the documents.

7. Tim Reiterman, with John Jacobs, *Raven: The Untold Story of the Rev. Jim Jones and His People* (New York: E. P. Dutton, 1982, reprint 2008), 131.

8. Reiterman and Jacobs, 379.

9. Richard A. McCoy, letter to Elizabeth Powers, 18 January 1978, released under the Freedom of Information Act.

10. Hall, 247.

11. FBI FOIA doc. X-4-M-3b.

12. FBI FOIA doc. B-5-B-11b.

13. John V Moore, letter to Rebecca Moore, 12 August 1978, in Rebecca Moore, *The Jonestown Letters: Correspondence of the Moore Family 1970–1985* (Lewiston, N.Y.: The Edwin Mellen Press, 1986), 266–67.

14. FBI FOIA doc. I-1-C-1(a-v).

15. Reiterman and Jacobs, 441.

16. "Accusation of Human Rights Violations by Rev. James Warren Jones against Our Children and Relatives at the Peoples Temple Jungle Encampment in Guyana, South America" (11 April 1978), *Alternative Considerations*.

17. Affidavit of Deborah Layton Blakey, "Re the Threat and Possibility of Mass Suicide by Members of the People's Temple," *Alternative Considerations*.

18. A single page from the three-page report appears on FBI FOIA doc. K-1-A-2, while the complete report is available from the California Historical Society, Moore Family Papers, MS 3802, Box 19, Folder 116, U.S. Customs Service.

19. Documents released under FOIA provide details of the investigation by the Bureau of Alcohol, Tobacco, and Firearms, including a five-page memo dated 12 December 78, a four-page follow-up dated 2 January 1979, and a single page wrapping up the investigation dated 16 January 1979, at *Alternative Considerations*.

20. FCC logs were received under a FOIA request. Copies of audiocassettes—which are of very poor quality—are available from The Jonestown Institute, http://jonestown.sdsu.edu.

21. Jonestown residents were convinced that McCoy was part of the CIA. Kit Nascimento, an official in the government of Guyana in 1978, told me in 2008 that the U.S. Embassy informed Guyanese officials that Richard Dwyer, the Deputy Chief of Mission, was a representative of the CIA stationed at the Embassy. Ambassador John Burke was working for the CIA in 1980, after his return to the U.S. from Guyana.

CHAPTER 5

* Friedrich Nietzsche, *Beyond Good and Evil*, IV, 146. In *Bartlett's Familiar Quotations*, 17th ed., ed. John Bartlett (Boston: Little, Brown, and Company, 2002), 589.

1. John and Barbara Moore, "A Visit to Peoples Temple Cooperative Agricultural Project. Jonestown, Guyana" (June 1978), *Alternative Considerations*; also in Rebecca Moore, *The Jonestown Letters: Correspondence of the Moore Family 1970–1985* (Lewiston, N.Y.: The Edwin Mellen Press, 1986), 236.

2. Denice Stephenson, ed., *Dear People: Remembering Jonestown* (San Francisco and Berkeley: California Historical Society and Heyday Books, 2005), 104; also in FBI FOIA doc. GG-1-C, dated 25 October 1978.

3. Stephenson, 100; also in FBI FOIA doc. BB-10-J.

4. FBI FOIA doc. X-3-E-32b.

5. Deborah Layton, *Seductive Poison: A Jonestown Survivor's Story of Life and Death in the Peoples Temple* (New York: Anchor Books, 1998), 204.

6. Michael Bellefountaine, *A Lavender Look at Peoples Temple*, unpublished manuscript, 121.

7. FBI Audiotape Q 594.

8. Tim Reiterman, with John Jacobs, *Raven: the Untold Story of the Rev. Jim Jones and His People* (New York: Dutton, 1982, reprint 2008), 394.

9. Reiterman and Jacobs, 395.

10. Bellefountaine, 118.

11. Reiterman and Jacobs, 452–53; and FBI Interview on 6 December 1978, FBI FOIA doc. 89-4286-1305, p. 9.

12. "Medical Instructions from Jim Jones," 20 May 1978, *Alternative Considerations*; also in FBI FOIA doc. J-3-E-1a-c.

13. Jim Jones, "Instructions for 16 October 1978," *Alternative Considerations*; also on FBI Audiotape Q 384.

14. "Doctor: Jones Was Close to Death," *The New York Times* (24 December 1978), A14.

15. FBI FOIA doc. FF-11-A-62.

16. Reiterman and Jacobs, 390.

17. "To Whom It May Concern," signed, Carolyn Layton, n.d., FBI FOIA doc. X-3-B-2a.

18. Deborah Layton, 179.

19. FBI Audiotape Q 642. This tape is the second in a series, Q 641-644, of the events of that White Night.

20. FBI Audiotape Q 635.

21. FBI Audiotape Q 636.

22. Jeannie Mills, *Six Years with God: Life Inside Rev. Jim Jones's Peoples Temple* (New York: A&W Publishers, 1979), 231.

23. Reiterman and Jacobs, 294–96.

24. Edith Roller, Journal, 16 February 1978, *Alternative Considerations*. This is probably the one described by Deborah Layton Blakey in her Affidavit of June 1978, since the language is quite similar in the two accounts.

25. Pam Moton, "To All U. S. Senators and Members Of Congress," *Alternative Considerations*; also in FBI FOIA doc. MM-1-27.

26. FBI Audiotape Q 736.

27. FBI FOIA doc. N-1-A-3a-b; doc. N-1-A-6; doc. N-1-A-29c; doc. N-1-A-36b.

28. Carolyn Layton, letter to John and Barbara Moore, 14 September 1978, in Moore, *The Jonestown Letters*, 276.

29. Reiterman and Jacobs, 350–52.

30. John R. Hall, *Gone from the Promised Land: Jonestown in American Cultural History* (New Brunswick, N.J.: Transaction Publishers, 1987, reprint 2004), 216.

31. FBI FOIA doc. S-1-B-7a-c and doc. S-1-B-8a-c.

32. Interview with Joseph A. Mazor and Donald Freed, with Pat Richartz and Mark Lane, 5 September 1978, FBI FOIA doc. S-1-G-2 (1–78).

33. Mark Lane, *The Strongest Poison* (New York: Hawthorn Books, 1980), 24–25.

34. FBI FOIA doc. NN-3-D-3.

35. FBI FOIA doc. S-1-G-5.

36. FBI FOIA doc. S-1-G-1c.

37. Lane, 32.

38. FBI FOIA doc. NN-6-A (1-10), at *Alternative Considerations*.

39. FBI FOIA doc. X-4-M-3b.

40. Annie Moore, letter to Rebecca Moore, October 1978, in Moore, *The Jonestown Letters*, 282.

41. FBI Audiotape Q 245.

42. FBI FOIA doc. EE-1-M-78.

43. FBI FOIA doc. X-3-E-32d.

44. FBI FOIA doc. 89-4286-774.

CHAPTER 6

* Unnamed woman speaking on 18 November 1978, FBI Audiotape Q042, transcript available online at: http://jonestown.sdsu.edu/AboutJonestown/Tapes/Tapes/DeathTape/Q042.html.

1. Catherine Wessinger, *How the Millennium Comes Violently: From Jonestown to Heaven's Gate* (New York: Seven Bridges Press, 2000).

2. Wessinger, 19.

3. Wessinger, 18.

4. State Department Cable, 5 November 1978, from U.S. Embassy to Secretary of State, in *The Assassination of Representative Leo J. Ryan and the Jonestown, Guyana Tragedy: Report of a Staff Investigative Group to the Committee on Foreign Affairs, U.S. House of Representatives*, House Document No. 96-223 (15 May 1979), 96th Congress, 1st Session (Washington, D.C.: U.S. Government Printing Office, 1979), 51. Henceforth, citations will be called *House Committee Report*.

5. FBI Audiotape Q 175.

6. FBI FOIA doc. E-3-A-2(10).

7. FBI Audiotape Q 313.

8. FBI Audiotape Q 323.

9. FBI FOIA doc. 89-4286-571.

10. *House Committee Report*, 100.

11. Ron Javers, "Expedition to Reverend Jones' Refuge," *San Francisco Chronicle*, 15 November 1978, reprinted in *House Committee Report*, 345.

12. FBI Audiotape Q 050.

13. This account of Tim Carter's defection and his report on Tim Stoen's comments comes from Mark Lane, *The Strongest Poison* (New York: Hawthorn Books, 1980), 140–41.

14. This account is drawn from several sources, but the cable dictated by Richard Dwyer on 20 November, and sent to the U.S. Department of State on 22 November 1978 seems the most factual and straightforward. Obviously he was not present everywhere, so I have used other sources as well. See Dwyer's report in Denice Stephenson, ed., *Dear People: Remembering Jonestown* (San Francisco and Berkeley: California Historical Society and Heyday Books, 2005), 116–27.

15. FBI Audiotape Q 048.

16. Stephenson, 123.

17. FBI audiotape Q 042.

18. Michael Bellefountaine, "Christine Miller: A Voice of Independence," *The Jonestown Report*, vol. 7 (November 2005).

19. FBI Audiotape Q 833.

20. Ethan Feinsod, *Awake in a Nightmare. Jonestown: The Only Eyewitness Account* (New York: W. W. Norton, 1981), 195.

21. Feinsod, 198.

22. "Guyana Operations: After Action Report, 18-27 November 1978," prepared by Special Study Group, Office of the Joint Chiefs of Staff, 31 January 1979; in Moore Family Papers, MS 3802, Box 19, Folder 118, Department of Defense FOIA, California Historical Society, San Francisco.

23. Kenneth Wooden, *The Children of Jonestown* (New York: McGraw-Hill, 1981), 184–91.

24. Lane, 176.

25. Transcripts of Doug Ellice's conversations on 18 November 1978 are online at a site created by Josef Dieckman, *Researching the Use of Amateur (Ham) Radio by the Peoples Temple in Guyana, South America*, http://www.geocities. com/josefjoey/peoplestemplehamradio.html. Tapes made by Ellice were released to Dieckman under FOIA by the State Department in December 2007, and appear at http://www.geocities.com/josefjoey/Q1289.html and http://www.geocities.com/ josefjoey/Q1290.html.

26. Peoples Temple Radio Codebook, *Alternative Considerations*.

27. FBI FOIA doc. 89-4286-484.

28. Annie Moore, n.d., *Alternative Considerations*; also in Rebecca Moore, *The Jonestown Letters: Correspondence of the Moore Family 1970-1985* (Lewiston, N.Y.: The Edwin Mellen Press, 1986), 284–86.

29. FBI FOIA doc. X-1-A-54; also at *Alternative Considerations*.

30. Duchess Harris and Adam John Waterman, "To Die for the Peoples Temple: Religion and Revolution after Black Power," in *Peoples Temple and Black Religion in America*, ed. Rebecca Moore, Anthony B. Pinn, and Mary R. Sawyer (Bloomington and Indianapolis: University of Indiana Press, 2004), 112.

CHAPTER 7

* Unnamed undertaker, quoted in Christopher Reed, "Officials Wrangle over 582 Cult Dead," *The Globe and Mail* (Canada), 10 February 1979.

1. David Chidester, *Salvation and Suicide: An Interpretation of Jim Jones, the Peoples Temple, and Jonestown* (Bloomington and Indianapolis: University of Indiana Press, 1988; revised ed. 2003).

2. Jeffrey Brailey, *The Ghosts of November: Memoirs of an Outsider Who Witnessed the Carnage at Jonestown, Guyana* (San Antonio, Tex.: J & J Publishers, 1998), 45.

3. Cyril H. Wecht, "Jonestown, Guyana—November 1978: A Forensic Pathologist's Retrospective Observations," *The Jonestown Report* 10 (October 2008).

4. Jim Hougan, "Jonestown: The Secret Life of Jim Jones: A Parapolitical Fugue," *Alternative Considerations*; also in *Lobster* 37 (Summer 1999): 2–20.

5. Rebecca Moore, *A Sympathetic History of Jonestown* (Lewiston, N.Y.: The Edwin Mellen Press, 1985), 31.

6. Karen Provenza, letter to Judge Robert Peckham, 9 December 1986, in "Petition for Commutation of Sentence—Laurence J. Layton," submitted to the U.S. Pardon Attorney, 1997.

7. "The Performance of the Department of State and the American Embassy in Georgetown, Guyana in the People's Temple Case" [a.k.a. "The Crimmins Report] (Washington, D.C.: U.S. Department of State, May 1979).

8. The Comptroller General, "Guyana Tragedy Points to a Need for Better Care and Protection of Guardianship Children," Report to the Congress of the United States (Washington, D.C.: General Accounting Office, 1980), i.

9. Office of the Attorney General, State of California, *Report of Investigation of People's Temple* (April 1980; reprint December 1981), 61.

10. See Rebecca Moore, "Closing the Books," *Alternative Considerations*.

11. Moore, *A Sympathetic History of Jonestown*, 354.

12. Emergency Relief Committee, "Briefing Notes," 19 January 1979, in Donneter Lane Collection, California Historical Society, San Francisco.

13. Donneter Lane, "The Emergency Relief Committee: An Interview with Rabbi Malcolm Sparer, Donneter Lane, and John Lane," in *The Need for a Second Look at Jonestown*, ed. Rebecca Moore and Fielding M. McGehee III (Lewiston, N.Y.: The Edwin Mellen Press, 1989), 115–16.

14. Emergency Relief Committee, "Legal Documents," 5 March 1979, No. 746571; letter from Carmen A. DiPlacido to Judge Ira A. Brown, 28 February 1979, in Donneter Lane Collection, California Historical Society, San Francisco.

15. These and other items come from the folder, "Religious Responses to Jonestown" in Donneter Lane Collection, California Historical Society, San Francisco.

16. Muhammed Isaiah Kenyatta, "America Was Not Hard to Find," in *Peoples Temple and Black Religion in America*, ed. Rebecca Moore, Anthony B. Pinn, and Mary R. Sawyer (Bloomington and Indianapolis: University of Indiana Press, 2004), 164.

17. Information about the "Consultation on the Implications of Jonestown for the Black Church and the Nation," comes from the Kelly Miller Smith Papers, Box 134, File 23, in the Jean and Alexander Heard Library, Vanderbilt University, Nashville, Tennessee.

18. J. Alfred Smith, "Breaking the Silence: Reflections of a Black Pastor," in Moore, Pinn, and Sawyer, 151.

19. This and other statements from Disciples of Christ leaders can be found in the Donneter Lane Collection, California Historical Society, San Francisco.

20. Quotation is from Karen Stroup, "Jonestown and Disciple-Dom: Effects on a Denomination," *The Jonestown Report* 10 (October 2008). See her earlier article as well: "Could it Happen Again?" *The Jonestown Report* 9 (November 2007).

21. Stroup, "Jonestown and Disciple-Dom."

22. Jon Nordheimer, "Jersey Psychiatrist Studying the Guyana Survivors, Fears Implications for U.S. Society from Other Cults," *New York Times*, 30 November 1978, reprinted in *The Assassination of Representative Leo J. Ryan and the Jonestown, Guyana Tragedy: Report of a Staff Investigative Group to the Committee on Foreign Affairs, U.S. House of Representatives*, House Document No. 96-223 15 May 1979) 96th Congress, 1st Session (Washington, D.C.: U.S. Government Printing Office, 1979), 392. Henceforth, citations will be called *House Committee Report*.

23. *Newsweek*, 4 December 1978, reprinted in *House Committee Report*, 430.

24. *New York Times*, 21 January 1979, reprinted in *House Committee Report*, 467.

25. Chidester, 15–46.

CHAPTER 8

* Senator John McCain, quoted in Associated Press, "Rebel with a cause chases the presidency," 22 August 2008, initially found on: http://ap.google.com/article/AleqM5jbaR_oao57xPq0mOSYRzhrmM6GdAD92NETG80 (25 August 2008), currently offline. The article now appears on: http://climate.weather.com/articles/mccainprofile092301.html?page=10 (11 October 2008).

1. Rebecca Moore, "Drinking the Kool-Aid: The Cultural Transformation of a Tragedy," *Nova Religio* 7, no. 2 (November 2003), 96.

2. Joe Wilcox, quoted by Charles Arthur, "Microsoft 'Mojave' (aka Vista)? It's brilliant! I mean, terrible," *The Guardian* 31 July 2008, web log http://blogs.guardian.co.uk/technology/2008/07/31/microsoft_mojave_aka_vista_its_brilliant_i_mean_terrible.html.

3. Touré, *Never Drank the Kool-Aid* (New York: Picador, 2006), 1.

4. Gary Younge, "Obama and the Power of Symbols," *The Nation* 286, no. 25 (30 June 2008), 10.

5. Patrick Stevens, "Coaches Poll Released," *Washington Times*, 1 August 2008, web log http://washingtontimes.com/weblogs/d1scourse/2008/Aug/01/coaches-poll-released/.

6. Mike Carter, "Drinking the Kool-Aid," *The Jonestown Report* 5 (August 2003).

7. Anson Shupe, David Bromley, and Edward Breschel, "The Peoples Temple, the Apocalypse at Jonestown, and the Anti-Cult Movement," in *New Religious Movements, Mass Suicide, and Peoples Temple: Scholarly Perspectives on a Tragedy*, ed. Rebecca Moore and Fielding M. McGehee III (Lewiston, N.Y.: The Edwin Mellen Press, 1989), 153–78.

8. Thomas Robbins, "The Second Wave of Jonestown Literature: A Review Essay," in Moore and McGehee, 113–34.

9. David Chidester, *Salvation and Suicide: An Interpretation of Jim Jones, the Peoples Temple, and Jonestown* (Bloomington and Indianapolis: University of Indiana Press, 1988; revised ed. 2003), 56–57.

10. Chidester, 62.

11. John R. Hall, *Gone from the Promised Land: Jonestown in American Cultural History* (New Brunswick, N.J.: Transaction Publishers, 1987, reprint 2004).

12. Mary McCormick Maaga, *Hearing the Voices of Jonestown* (Syracuse, N.Y.: Syracuse University Press, 1998).

13. Archie Smith Jr., "We Need to Press Forward: Black Religion and Jonestown, Twenty Years Later," *Alternative Considerations*. The substance of this article reiterates and elaborates upon Smith's earlier writings, which are listed in "Resources."

14. Denice Stephenson, ed., *Dear People: Remembering Jonestown* (San Francisco and Berkeley: California Historical Society and Heyday Books, 2005).

15. Josef Dieckman, "One Misconception Down, Countless to Go," *The Jonestown Report* 7 (November 2005).

16. Jonestown Audiotape Project, *Alternative Considerations*.

17. Paul Schmutzok, "A Lesson for us All," *The Jonestown Report* 9 (November 2007).

18. Tina Columbus, "Jonestown Tapes Reveal Disturbing Contradictions," *The Jonestown Report* 9 (November 2007).

19. Dean Coughlan, "Questioning Jonestown, Questioning Faith," *The Jonestown Report* 8 (November 2006).

20. The title, *The People's Temple*, included an apostrophe in "Peoples" to differentiate the theatrical event from the actual group.

21. Greg Pierotti, "Theater Team Shows Complexity of Jonestown Interviews," *The Jonestown Report* 5 (August 2000).

22. Bryan Kravitz, quoted by Stephen Wangh, "Theater Team Shows Complexity of Jonestown Interviews."

23. Leigh Fondakowski, "Theater Team Shows Complexity of Jonestown Interviews."

24. Michael Guillén, "Stanley Nelson: Nobody Joins a Cult," *GreenCine*, 20 October 2006, http://www.greencine.com/article?action=view&articleID=347.

25. Pat Parker, "Jonestown," in *Jonestown and Other Madness* (Ithaca, N.Y.: Firebrand Books, 1985), 56.

26. *The Assassination of Representative Leo J. Ryan and the Jonestown, Guyana Tragedy: Report of a Staff Investigative Group to the Committee on Foreign Affairs, U.S. House of Representatives*, House Document No. 96-223, 15 May 1979, 96th Congress, 1st Session (Washington, D.C.: U.S. Government Printing Office, 1979), 21.

27. A discussion of *McGehee v. CIA* is online at *Alternative Considerations*.

28. Jim Hougan, "Jonestown: The Secret Life of Jim Jones: A Parapolitical Fugue," *Alternative Considerations*; also in *Lobster* 37 (Summer 1999): 2–20.

29. Rebecca Moore, "Reconstructing Reality: Conspiracy Theories about Jonestown," *Alternative Considerations*; also in *Controversial New Religions*, ed. James R. Lewis and Jasper Aagaard Petersen (New York: Oxford University Press, 2005), 61–78.

30. John Judge, "The Black Hole of Guyana: The Untold Story of the Jonestown Massacre," in *Secret and Suppressed: Banned Ideas and Hidden History*, ed. Jim Keith (Portland, Ore.: Feral House, 1993), 127–65; also online at http://www.ratical.org/ratville/ JFK/JohnJudge/Jonestown.html.

31. Matthew Farrell, "Kool Aid, Hot Tape," *World Domination Update*, http://www.branchfloridians.org/wdu45.html#jones.

32. Michael Meiers, *Was Jonestown a CIA Medical Experiment? A Review of the Evidence* (Lewiston, N.Y.: The Edwin Mellen Press, 1988), 509.

33. Nathan Landau, *Heavenly Deceptor* (Brooklyn, N.Y.: Sound of Music Publishing, 1992).

34. Laurie Efrein Kahalas, *Snake Dance: Unravelling the Mysteries of Jonestown* (New York: Red Robin Press, 1998).

35. Laura Baird, "Notes on Jonestown Carpet, 2004," *The Jonestown Report* 6 (October 2004).

36. The images can be seen on Brandou's website under the title "As A Man Thinketh, So He Is," at http://www.howdypardner.com/slideshow/slideshow .html.

37. Andrew Brandou, "Artist Depicts Jonestown Lessons in Children's Animals," *The Jonestown Report* 9 (November 2007).

38. Fred D'Aguiar, *Bill of Rights* (London: Chatto and Windus, 1998).

39. Wilson Harris, *Jonestown* (London: Faber and Faber, 1996).

40. Harris, *Jonestown*, 3.

41. Harris, *Jonestown*, 5.

42. Fraser Sutherland, *Jonestown* (Toronto, Ontario: McClelland and Stewart, 1996).

43. Gar Wilson, *Terror in Guyana* (New York: Gold Eagle, 1990).

44. Nick Carter, *Retreat for Death* (New York: New York: Charter, 1982).

45. William D. Rodgers, *Cult Sunday* (Denver: Accent Books, 1979).

46. Harold Robbins, *Dreams Die First* (New York: Pocket Books, 1977).

47. Fernando Maneca, email to Fielding McGehee, 26 June 2006. For more information visit Fernando Maneca's website, http://www.manoiseca.org/upcomingperf .html.

48. Ken Risling, "Jonestown: The Unanswered Question," can be heard at: http://www.myspace.com/kenrisling.

CHAPTER 9

* Laura Johnston Kohl, "A Temple Member's Odyssey," *The Jonestown Report* 5 (August 2003), online at: http://jonestown.sdsu.edu/AboutJonestown/PersonalReflections/kohl.htm.

1. Chris Hatcher, "After Jonestown: Survivors of Peoples Temple," in *The Need for a Second Look at Jonestown*, ed. Rebecca Moore and Fielding M. McGehee III (Lewiston, N.Y.: The Edwin Mellen Press, 1989), 130.

2. Laura Johnston Kohl, "A Temple Member's Odyssey," *The Jonestown Report* 5 (August 2003).

3. FBI FOIA doc. 89-4286-300, p. 2, dated 22 November 1978.

4. "Coast Cultists are Still in Shock," *New York Times*, 24 November 1978, A15.

5. Hatcher, 132.

6. Hatcher, 134.

7. Hatcher, 135.

8. Mike Carter, "Drinking the Kool-Aid," *The Jonestown Report* 5 (August 2003).

9. Lowell D. Streiker," Reflections on the Human Freedom Center," in Moore and McGehee, *The Need for a Second Look at Jonestown*, 154.

10. Streiker, 155.

11. Neva Sly Hargrave, "A Story of Deprogramming," *The Jonestown Report* 6 (October 2004).

12. Terri Buford, "Jonestown Survivor 9," *The Jonestown Report* 9 (November 2007).

13. Anonymous, "The Trauma of Marriage to a Temple Survivor," *The Jonestown Report* 5 (August 2003).

14. Mike Prokes, Statement, 14 March 1979, *Alternative Considerations*.

15. Greg Pierotti, "Theater Team Shows Complexity of Jonestown Interviews," *The Jonestown Report* 5 (August 2003).

16. Jordan Vilchez, email correspondence, 7 July 2008.

17. Juanell Smart, "My Life In—and After—Peoples Temple," *The Jonestown Report* 6 (October 2004).

18. Neva Sly Hargrave, "What Good Is Anger?" *The Jonestown Report* 8 (November 2006).

19. Vernon Gosney, "The Voice," *The Jonestown Report* 5 (August 2003).

20. Hattie Newell, "Who Guided My Life?" *The Jonestown Report* 5 (August 2003).

21. Kathy Barbour, "Life Ten Years after Jonestown: The Peoples Temple Legacy," in Moore and McGehee, *The Need for a Second Look at Jonestown*, 198.

22. David Wise, "25 Years after Jonestown," *The Jonestown Report* 5 (August 2003).

23. Patti Chastain Haag, "Shade," *The Jonestown Report* 5 (August 2003).

24. Barbara Sines, "The Pain That Never Leaves," *The Jonestown Report* 6 (October 2004).

25. Barbara Moore, "The Deaths of Two Daughters: Grieving and Remembering," and Robert B. Moore, "Jonestown: Catalyst for Social Change," in Moore and McGehee, *The Need for a Second Look at Jonestown*.

26. Hatcher, 146.

27. John V. Moore, "Remembrance, Identification and Tragedy: Jonestown, The Mirror," in *New Religious Movements, Mass Suicide, and Peoples Temple: Scholarly Perspectives on a Tragedy*, ed. Rebecca Moore and Fielding M. McGehee III (Lewiston, N.Y.: The Edwin Mellen Press, 1989), 240.

28. John R. Hall, *Gone from the Promised Land: Jonestown in American Cultural History*, 2d. ed. (New Brunswick, N.J.: Transaction Publishers, 1987, reprint 2004), xiii.

29. Tim Carter, "The Big Grey," *The Jonestown Report* 5 (August 2003).

30. John V. Moore, 241.

RESOURCES FOR UNDERSTANDING JONESTOWN AND PEOPLES TEMPLE

Primary Sources

Primary source documents—that is, materials generated by Peoples Temple members, government agencies, relatives and family members, and others directly connected to the historical events of Peoples Temple and Jonestown—are available through several venues.

The website *Alternative Considerations of Jonestown and Peoples Temple* http://jonestown.sdsu.edu has published numerous primary sources online, including audiotape summaries and transcripts; documents generated by Peoples Temple, the Concerned Relatives, and government agencies; a journal prepared by Temple member Edith Roller; and articles written by Temple survivors and others. Sponsored by the Department of Religious Studies at San Diego State University, this source is cited throughout the book as *Alternative Considerations*.

Researchers will find online catalogue records for primary source materials relating to Peoples Temple in Worldcat, http://www.worldcat.org. Guides or finding aids to larger collections that provide more detailed information may be searched in the Online Archive of California (OAC) at http://www .oac.cdlib.org.

The California Historical Society (CHS) is the chief repository for materials related to Peoples Temple. These materials include organizational and personal papers, legal documents, financial records, and photographs.

CHS currently holds many individual collections that form the Peoples Temple Collection. The California Historical Society http://www.california historicalsociety.org is located at 678 Mission Street, San Francisco, California 94105. The North Baker Research Library is open to the public, but researchers are encouraged to email or call ahead for hours prior to visiting. Contact the Library by email at reference@calhist.org or call 415-357-1848 ext. 220.

The Special Collections at San Diego State University Library and Information Access has the Peoples Temple Collection, MS-0183. A "Biographical and Historical Note" prepared by Jennifer Martinez describes the collection at http://scua2.sdsu.edu/archon/index.php?p=collections/findingaid& id=106&q=. The SDSU Special Collections maintains a complete archive of all transcripts and audiotapes, and maintains other documents and papers, some of which are unique to the collection, and some of which duplicate materials held at the California Historical Society. Contact Special Collections by email at scref@rohan.sdsu.edu, or call 619-594-6791.

A final place to find primary sources about Peoples Temple and Jonestown is the American Religions Collection (ARC) at the Donald C. Davidson Library of the University of California, Santa Barbara, http://www.library. ucsb.edu/speccoll/research/arc.html. J. Gordon Melton gathered items that were generated by Peoples Temple, which include church bulletins, newsletters, flyers, and correspondence. For more detailed information on materials in ARC, call the Special Collections office at U.C.S.B. 805-893-3062.

Government Documents (presented in chronological order)

"Information Meeting on the Cult Phenomenon in the U.S." Transcript of Proceedings, U.S. Senate, February 5, 1979, 96th Congress, 1st Session.

The Assassination of Representative Leo J. Ryan and the Jonestown, Guyana Tragedy: Report of a Staff Investigative Group to the Committee on Foreign Affairs, U.S. House of Representatives, House Document No. 96-223, May 15, 1979, 96th Congress, 1st Session. Washington, D.C.: U.S. Government Printing Office, 1979. [Cited throughout as *House Committee Report*.]

"The Death of Representative Leo J. Ryan, People's Temple, and Jonestown: Understanding a Tragedy." Hearing by Committee on Foreign Affairs, U.S. House of Representatives, May 15, 1979, 96th Congress, 1st Session. Washington, D.C.: U.S. Government Printing Office, 1979.

"Findings of GAO study on California placement and federal funding of foster children under guardianship of members of Peoples Temple religious group in Jonestown, Guyana." In *Abuse and Neglect of Children in Institutions*, 1979 Hearings before the Subcommittee on Child and Human Development, U.S. Senate Committee on Labor and Human Resources, May 31, 1979.

"The Performance of the Department of State and the American Embassy in Georgetown, Guyana in the People's Temple Case" a.k.a. "The Crimmins Report." U.S. Department of State, Washington, D.C., May 1979.

"Investigative Report on Peoples Temple." Department of Social Services, State of California, Sacramento, Calif., November 1979.

"Report of Investigation of Peoples Temple." Office of the Attorney General, State of California, Sacramento, Calif., April 1980.

"Cult Awareness Week," House Joint Resolution 390, 100th Congress, 1st Session. Washington, D.C., 1988.

Scholarly Resources

Ahlberg, Sture. *Messianic Movements: A Comparative Analysis of the Sabbatians, the People's Temple and the Unification Church*. Stockholm: Almqvist and Wiksell, 1986.

Anthony, Dick and Thomas Robbins. "Religious Totalism, Exemplary Dualism, and the Waco Tragedy." In *Millennium, Messiahs, and Mayhem: Contemporary Apocalyptic Movements*. Ed. Thomas Robbins and Susan J. Palmer. New York: Routledge, 1994, pp. 261–84.

Barker, Eileen. "Religious Movements: Cult and Anticult Since Jonestown." *Annual Review of Sociology* 12 (1986): 329–46.

Bromley, David G. and Anson D. Shupe Jr. *Strange Gods: The Great American Cult Scare*. Boston: Beacon Press, 1981.

Chidester, David. "Rituals of Exclusion and the Jonestown Dead." *Journal of the American Academy of Religion* 56, no. 4 (Winter 1988): 681–702.

———. *Salvation and Suicide: An Interpretation of Jim Jones, the Peoples Temple, and Jonestown*. Bloomington and Indianapolis: University of Indiana Press, 1988. Revised ed. titled *Salvation and Suicide: Jim Jones, the Peoples Temple and Jonestown*, 2003.

———. "Saving the Children by Killing Them: Redemptive Sacrifice in the Ideologies of Jim Jones and Ronald Reagan." *Religion and American Culture* 1, no. 2 (Summer 1991): 177–201.

Crist, R. E. "Jungle Geopolitics in Guyana." *American Journal of Economics and Sociology* 40 (1981): 107–14.

Hall, John R. "The Apocalypse at Jonestown." In *In Gods We Trust: New Patterns of Religious Pluralism in America*. Ed. Thomas Robbins and Dick Anthony. New Brunswick, N.J.: Transaction Books, 1981, pp. 171–90. Reprinted from *Transaction/Society* 16, no. 6 (September/October 1979): 52–61.

———. "Collective Welfare as Resource Mobilization in Peoples Temple: A Case Study of a Poor People's Religious Social Movement." *Sociological Analysis* 49, Supplement (December 1988): 645–775.

———. *Gone from the Promised Land: Jonestown in American Cultural History*. New Brunswick, N.J.: Transaction Publishers, 1987; reprint 2004.

———. "The Impact of Apostates on the Trajectories of Religious Movements: The Case of Peoples Temple." In *Falling From the Faith: The Causes, Course, and Consequences of Religious Apostasy*. Ed. David G. Bromley. Beverley Hills, Calif.: Sage Publications, 1988, pp. 229–50.

———. "Jonestown in the 21st Century." *Transaction/Society* 41, no. 2 (January/February 2004): 9–11.

———. "Peoples Temple." In *America's Alternative Religions*. Ed. Timothy Miller. Albany, N.Y.: State University of New York, 1995, pp. 303–11.

———. "Public Narratives and the Apocalyptic Sect: From Jonestown to Mt. Carmel." In *Armageddon in Waco: Critical Perspectives on the Branch Davidian Conflict*. Ed. Stuart A. Wright. Chicago: University of Chicago Press, 1995, pp. 205–35.

Hall, John R. and Philip Schuyler. "Apostasy, Apocalypse, and Religious Violence: An Exploratory Comparison of Peoples Temple, the Branch Davidians, and the Solar Temple." In *The Politics of Religious Apostasy: The Role of Apostates in the Transformation of Religious Movements*. Ed. David G. Bromley. Westport, Conn.: Praeger, 1998, pp. 141–69.

Hall, John R., with Philip D. Schuyler and Sylvaine Trinh. *Apocalypse Observed: Religious Movements and Violence in North America, Europe, and Japan*. New York: Routledge, 2000.

Harding, Vincent. "My Lord, What a Mourning: Jonestown Is America." In *The Other American Revolution*, by Vincent Harding. Atlanta: Institute of the Black World, 1980.

Introvigne, Massimo. *Idee che uccidono. Jonestown, Waco, il Tempio Solare*. Milan: Pessano MIMEP-Docete, 1995.

Johnson, Doyle Paul. "Dilemma of Charismatic Leadership: The Case of The Peoples Temple." *Sociological Analysis* 40 (1979): 315–23.

Levi, Kenneth, ed. *Violence and Religious Commitment: Implications of Jim Jones' People's Temple Movement*. University Park, Penn.: Pennsylvania State University Press, 1982.

Lewis, Gordon K. *"Gather with the Saints at the River:" The Jonestown Guyana Holocaust 1978*. Río Piedras, Puerto Rico: Institute of Caribbean Studies, University of Puerto Rico, 1979.

Lincoln, C. Eric and Lawrence H. Mamiya. "Daddy Jones and Father Divine: The Cult as Political Religion." *Religious Life* 49 (1980): 6–23. Reprinted in *Peoples Temple and Black Religion in America*. Ed. Rebecca Moore, Anthony B. Pinn, and Mary R. Sawyer. Bloomington and Indianapolis: University of Indiana Press, 2004, pp. 28–46.

Lindt, Gillian. "Journeys to Jonestown: Accounts and Interpretations of the Rise and Demise of People's Temple." *Union Seminary Quarterly Review* 37, nos. 1 & 2 (Fall–Winter 1981–1982): 159–74.

Maaga, Mary McCormick. *Hearing the Voices of Jonestown*. Syracuse, N.Y.: Syracuse University Press, 1998. Chapter available at http://jonestown.sdsu.edu/AboutJonestown/Articles/three.htm.

———. "'No One Commits Suicide': The Need for a Sociology of Knowledge for the Women of Peoples Temple." Paper given at the Annual Meeting, Society for the Scientific Study of Religion, 6-8 November, 1992, Washington, D.C.

McCloud, Sean. "From Exotics to Brainwashers: Portraying New Religions in Mass Media." *Religion Compass* 1, no. 1 (2007): 214–28.

Melton, J. Gordon. *Peoples Temple and Jim Jones: Broadening Our Perspective*. New York: Garland, 1990.

Moore, Rebecca. "'American as Cherry Pie:' Peoples Temple and Violence in America." In *Millennialism, Persecution, and Violence: Historical Cases*. Ed. Catherine Wessinger. Syracuse N.Y.: Syracuse University Press, 2000, pp. 121–37. Available online at http://jonestown.sdsu.edu/AboutJonestown/Articles/cherrypie.htm.

———. "A Demographic Study of Black Involvement in Peoples Temple: What the Numbers Say." In Moore, Pinn, and Sawyer, 57–80.

———. "Drinking the Kool-Aid: The Cultural Transformation of a Tragedy." *Nova Religio* 7, no. 2 (November 2003): 92–100. Available online at http://jonestown. sdsu.edu/AboutJonestown/Articles/koolaid.htm.

———. "Is the Canon on Jonestown Closed?" *Nova Religio* 4, no. 1 (October 2000): 7–27.

———. "Jim Jones." Article in *The Encyclopedia of African American Folklore*. Ed. Anand Prahlad. Westport, Conn.: Greenwood Publishing, 2005.

———. "Jim Jones." Article in *The Encyclopedia of Religion*, 2d edition. Ed. Lindsay Jones. New York: Macmillan Reference, 2005.

———. "Jonestown in Literature: Caribbean Reflections on a Tragedy." *Literature and Theology* 23, no. 1 (March 2009).

———. "Peoples Temple." Article in *The 21st Century Encyclopedia of the World Religions*. Ed. J. Gordon Melton and Martin Baumann. Santa Barbara: ABC-Clio, 2002.

———. "Peoples Temple." Article in *Encyclopedia of Millennialism and Millennial Movements*. Ed. Richard Landes. New York and London: Routledge, 2000, pp. 305–8.

———. "Peoples Temple: A Typical Cult?" In *Introduction to New and Alternative Religions in America*, Vol. 2. Ed. Eugene V. Gallagher and W. Michael Ashcraft. Westport, Conn: Greenwood, 2006, pp. 113–34.

———. "Peoples Temple Revisited: A Review Essay." *Nova Religio* 10, no. 1 (August 2006): 111–18.

———. "Reconstructing Reality: Conspiracy Theories about Jonestown." In *Controversial New Religions*. Ed. James Lewis and Jesper Aagaard Petersen. New York and London: Oxford University Press, 2005, pp. 61–78. Reprint of article in *Journal of Popular Culture* 36, no. 2 (Fall 2002): 200–20. Also online at http://jonestown. sdsu.edu/AboutJonestown/Articles/conspiracy.htm.

———. "The Sacred and the Profane in Wilson Harris' *Jonestown*." http://jonestown .sdsu.edu/AboutJonestown/JonestownReport/Volume10/Moore1.htm.

———. *A Sympathetic History of Jonestown*. Lewiston, N.Y.: The Edwin Mellen Press, 1985.

———. "The Transformation of Peoples Temple in California: From Pentecostal Church to Political Movement." In *Pacific Beliefs: Religious and Cultural Transformations in California*. Ed. Brian Froese. Logan: Utah State University Press, accepted for publication.

Moore, Rebecca and Fielding M. McGehee, III, eds. *The Need for a Second Look at Jonestown*. Lewiston, N.Y.: The Edwin Mellen Press, 1989.

———. *New Religious Movements, Mass Suicide, and Peoples Temple: Scholarly Perspectives on a Tragedy*. Lewiston, N.Y.: The Edwin Mellen Press, 1989.

Moore, Rebecca, Anthony B. Pinn, and Mary R. Sawyer, eds. *Peoples Temple and Black Religion in America*. Bloomington and Indianapolis: University of Indiana Press, 2004.

Pozzi, Enrico. *Il carisma malato. Il People's Temple e il suicidio collettive di Jonestown*. Naples: Liguori, 1992.

Richardson, James. "Peoples Temple and Jonestown: A Corrective Comparison and Critique." *Journal for the Scientific Study of Religion* 19, no. 3 (1980): 239–55.

Robbins, Thomas. "Reconsidering Jonestown." *Religious Studies Review* 15, no. 1 (January 1989): 32–37. (This article was expanded into "The Second Wave of Jonestown Literature," noted below.)

———. "Religious Mass Suicide Before Jonestown: The Russian Old Believers." *Sociological Analysis* 47, no. 1 (Spring 1986): 1–20.

———. "The Second Wave of Jonestown Literature: A Review Essay." In Moore and McGehee. *New Religious Movements, Mass Suicide, and Peoples Temple*, pp. 113–34.

Robbins, Thomas and Dick Anthony. "Sects and Violence: Factors Enhancing the Volatility of Marginal Religious Movements." In *Armageddon at Waco: Critical Perspectives on the Branch Davidian Conflict*. Ed. Stuart A. Wright. Chicago and London: University of Chicago Press, 1995, pp. 236–59.

Smith, Archie, Jr. "An Interpretation of the Peoples Temple and Jonestown: Implications for the Black Church." *PSR Bulletin* Occasional Paper 58, no. 2 (February 1980). Reprinted in Moore, Pinn, and Sawyer, pp. 47–56.

———. *The Relational Self: Ethics and Therapy from a Black Church Perspective*. Nashville: Abingdon Press, 1982. (The last chapter discusses Peoples Temple.)

———. "We Need to Press Forward: Black Religion and Jonestown, Twenty Years Later," published online 1998; online at http://jonestown.sdsu.edu/AboutJonestown/Articles/smith.htm.

Smith, Jonathan Z. *Imagining Religion: From Babylon to Jonestown*. Chicago: University of Chicago Press, 1982.

Smith, Karin A. "A Taxonomy of Jonestown." M.A. Thesis. San Francisco and Oakland: California College of the Arts, 2007.

———. "A Taxonomy of Jonestown: What Isn't in the Envelope Just Before It Isn't." *Sightlines*, online journal of California College of the Arts, http://sites.cca.edu/currents/sightlines/index.html.

Stephenson, Denice, ed. *Dear People: Remembering Jonestown*. San Francisco and Berkeley: California Historical Society and Heyday Books, 2005.

Weightman, Judith. *Making Sense of the Jonestown Suicides*. Lewiston, N.Y.: The Edwin Mellen Press, 1983.

Wessinger, Catherine. *How the Millennium Comes Violently: From Jonestown to Heaven's Gate*. New York: Seven Bridges Press, 2000.

———. "1978—Jonestown," chapter from *How the Millennium Comes Violently* online at http://jonestown.sdsu.edu/AboutJonestown/Articles/jt1978.htm.

———. "How the Millennium Comes Violently: A Comparison of Jonestown, Aum Shinrikyo, Branch Davidians, and the Montana Freemen." *Dialog* 36, no. 4 (Fall 1997): 277–88.

———. "How the Millennium Comes Violently," chapter from *How the Millennium Comes Violently* online at http://jonestown.sdsu.edu/AboutJonestown/Articles/millennium.

———. "Thoughts on the 25th Anniversary of Jonestown," online at http://jonestown.sdsu.edu/AboutJonestown/Articles/25wessinger.

Psychological Analyses

Black, Albert. "Jonestown: Two Faces of Suicide: A Durkheimian Analysis." *Suicide and Life Threatening Behavior* 20, no. 4 (Winter 1990): 285–306.

Brown, Norman R., Lance J. Rips, and Steven K. Shevel. "The Subjective Dates of Natural Events in Very Long-term Memory." *Cognitive Psychology* 17, no. 2 (April 1985): 139–77.

Bynum, Jack E. and William Thompson. "November 18, 1978 in Jonestown: Statistical Effects of Micro Demographic Event." *Free Inquiry in Creative Sociology* 7 (1979): 45–57.

Dunning, Christine M. and Milton N. Silva. "Disaster-Induced Trauma in Rescue Workers." *Victimology* 5, no. 2 (supp. 4) (1980): 287–97.

Dwyer, Philip M. "An Inquiry into the Psychological Dimensions of Cult Suicide." *Suicide and Life-Threatening Behavior* 9, no. 2 (Summer 1979): 120–27.

Harrary, Keith. "The Truth about Jonestown." *Psychology Today* 25 (March 1992): 62–69; reprinted in *Religious Cults in America*. Ed. Robert Emmet Long. New York: H. W. Wilson Co., 1994, pp. 10–20.

Hochman, John. "Miracle, Mystery, and Authority: The Triangle of Cult Indoctrination." *Psychiatric Annals* 20, no. 4 (April 1990): 179–84, 187.

Hoyt, Michael F. "Observations Regarding Patients' Reactions to the Jonestown Massacre and the Moscone-Milk Assassinations." *Journal of the American Academy of Psychoanalysis* 9, no. 2 (April 1981): 303–9.

Jones, David R. "Secondary Disaster Victims: The Emotional Effects of Recovering and Identifying Human Remains." *American Journal of Psychiatry* 142, no. 3 (March 1985): 303–7.

Jorgensen, Danny. "The Social Construction and Interpretation of Deviance: Jonestown and the Mass Media." *Deviant Behavior: An Interdisciplinary Journal* 1 (1980): 309–32.

Kroth, Jerry. "Recapitulating Jonestown." *Journal of Psychohistory* 11, no. 3 (Winter 1985): 383–93.

Lasaga, Jose I. "Death in Jonestown: Techniques of Political Control by a Paranoid Leader." *Suicide and Life-Threatening Behavior* 10, no. 4 (Winter 1980): 210–13.

Nesci, Domenico Arturo. *The Lessons of Jonestown: An Ethnopsychoanalytical Study of Suicidal Communities*. Rome: Società Editrice Universo, 1999.

Osherow, Neal. "Making Sense of the Nonsensical: An Analysis of Jonestown." In *Readings about the Social Animal*, 7th edition. Ed. Elliot Aronson. New York: W. H. Freeman, 1995. Available online at http://www.academicarmageddon.co.uk/library/OSHER.htm.

Stack, Steven. "The Effect of the Jonestown Suicides on American Suicide Rates." *Journal of Social Psychology* 119, no. 1 (February 1983): 145–46.

Ulman, Richard B. and D. Wilfred Abse. "The Group Psychology of Mass Madness: Jonestown." *Political Psychology* 4, no. 4 (December 1983): 637–61.

General Resources

Bellefountaine, Michael. *A Lavender Look at Peoples Temple*. Unpublished manuscript in private collection.

Coser, Rose L. and Louis Coser. "Jonestown as Perverse Utopia." *Dissent* 26, no. 2 (1979): 158–62.

Curran, William J. "The Guyana Mass Suicides: Medicolegal Re-evaluation." *New England Journal of Medicine* 300, no. 23 (7 June 1979): 1321.

The Disciple: Journal of the Christian Church (Disciples of Christ) 131, no. 7 (July 1993) has three articles which look at the Disciples of Christ's relationship with Peoples Temple.

DisciplesWorld 7, no. 9 (November 2008) has five articles and an editorial commemorating the thirty-year anniversary of the deaths in Jonestown.

Eco, Umberto. "The Suicides of the Temple." In *West of the West: Imagining California.* Ed. Leonard Michaels, David Redi, Raquel Scherr. San Francisco: North Point Press, 1989, pp. 311–15.

Kilduff, Marshall and Phil Tracy. "Inside Peoples Temple." *New West Magazine* 17 (August 1, 1977): 30–38. Available online at http://jonestown.sdsu.edu/About Jonestown/PrimarySources/newWestart.htm.

Naipaul, Shiva. *Journey to Nowhere: A New World Tragedy.* New York: Penguin Books, 1980.

Reiterman, Tim, with John Jacobs. *Raven: The Untold Story of the Rev. Jim Jones and His People.* New York: E. P. Dutton, 1982.

Reston, James, Jr. *Our Father Who Art in Hell.* New York: Times Books, 1981.

Reston, James, Jr. and Noah Adams. "Father Cares: The Last of Jonestown." National Public Radio Education Services, Audiocassettes. Washington, D.C.: National Public Radio, 1981.

Rose, Steve. *Jesus and Jim Jones: Behind Jonestown.* New York: The Pilgrim Press, 1979.

Witten, Manley. "Guyana: The Autopsy of Disbelief." *Lab World* (March 1979): 14–19.

First-Person Accounts

Brailey, Jeffrey. *The Ghosts of November: Memoirs of an Outsider Who Witnessed the Carnage at Jonestown, Guyana.* San Antonio, Tex.: J & J Publishers, 1998.

Feinsod, Ethan. *Awake in a Nightmare. Jonestown: The Only Eyewitness Account.* New York: W. W. Norton, 1981. (Information provided by Odell Rhodes.)

Kahalas, Laurie Efrein. *Snake Dance: Unravelling the Mysteries of Jonestown.* New York: Red Robin Press, 1998.

Kern, Phil and Doug Wead. *People's Temple, People's Tomb.* Plainfield, N.J.: Logos International, 1979.

Klineman, George and Sherman Butler, and David Conn. *The Cult That Died: The Tragedy of Jim Jones and the People's Temple.* New York: G. P. Putnam's Sons, 1980.

Krause, Charles, with Laurence M. Stern, Richard Harwood and the staff of the *Washington Post. Guyana Massacre: The Eyewitness Account.* New York: Berkley Publishing, 1978.

Lane, Mark. *The Strongest Poison.* New York: Hawthorn Books, 1980.

Layton, Deborah. *Seductive Poison: A Jonestown Survivor's Story of Life and Death in the Peoples Temple.* New York: Anchor Books, 1998.

Mills, Jeannie. *Six Years With God: Life Inside Rev. Jim Jones's Peoples Temple.* New York: A&W Publishers, 1979.

Moore, Rebecca. *In Defense of Peoples Temple.* Lewiston, N.Y.: The Edwin Mellen Press, 1988.

———. *The Jonestown Letters: Correspondence of the Moore Family 1970–1985*. Lewiston, N.Y.: The Edwin Mellen Press, 1986.

Thielmann, Bonnie, with Dean Merrill. *The Broken God*. Elgin, Ill.: David C. Cook Publishing Co., 1979.

Thrash, Catherine (Hyacinth), as told to Marian K. Towne. *The Onliest One Alive: Surviving Jonestown, Guyana*. Indianapolis: Marian K. Towne, 1995.

Wooden, Kenneth. *The Children of Jonestown*. New York: McGraw-Hill, 1981. (Cites Stanley Clayton extensively.)

Wright, Lawrence. "The Sons of Jim Jones." *The New Yorker* 69, no. 39 (22 November 1993): 66–89.

Yee, Min S. and Thomas N. Layton. *In My Father's House*. New York: Holt, Rinehart and Winston, 1981.

Miscellaneous Resources

Alinin, S. F., Antonov, B. G. and A. N. Itskov. *The Jonestown Carnage: A CIA Crime*. Moscow: Progress Publishers, 1987.

Appel, Willa. *Cults in America: Programmed for Paradise*. New York: Holt, Rinehart and Winston, 1983.

Bacon, Margaret. *Journey to Guyana*. London: Dobson Books, 1970.

Boyle, James J. *Killer Cults*. New York: St. Martin's Paperbacks, 1995.

Carpozi, George, Jr. *The Suicide Cults*. New York: Manor Books, 1978.

Cawthorne, Nigel. *The World's Greatest Cults*. London: Chancellor Press, 1999.

Daniels, Elam J. *An Exposé of the King of the Cults*. Orlando, Fla.: Christ for the World, 1979.

De Angelis, Gina. *Jonestown Massacre: Tragic End of a Cult*. Berkeley Heights, N.J.: Enslow Publishers, 2002.

Dieckmann, Ed, Jr. *Beyond Jonestown: 'Sensitivity Training' and the Cult of Mind Control*. Torrance, Calif.: Noontide Press, 1981.

———. *The Secret of Jonestown: The Reason Why*. Torrance, Calif.: Noontide Press and Decatur, Ga.: Historical Review Press, 1981

Endleman, Robert. *Jonestown and the Manson Family: Race, Sexuality and Collective Madness*. New York: Psyche Press, 1993.

Hamilton, Sue L. *The Death of a Cult Family: Jim Jones*. Bloomington, Minn.: Abdo and Daughters, 1989.

Hougan, Jim. "Jonestown: The Secret Life of Jim Jones: A Parapolitical Fugue." *Lobster* 37 (Summer 1999): 2–20. Also online at http://jonestown.sdsu.edu/AboutJonestown/Articles/hougan-lobster.htm.

Judge, John. "The Black Hole of Guyana." In *Secret and Suppressed: Banned Ideas and Hidden History*. Ed. Jim Keith. Portland, Ore.: Feral House, 1993, pp. 127–65. Also online at http://www.ratical.org/ratville/JFK/JohnJudge/Jonestown.html.

———. "Jonestown, CIA, Assassinations, Drugs and Mind Control." *Critique: A Journal of Conspiracies and Metaphysics* 6, no. 1, 2 (Spring/Summer 1986): 39–63.

Landau, Nathan. *Heavenly Deceptor*. Brooklyn, N.Y.: Sound of Music Publishing, 1992.

Kilduff, Marshall and Ron Javers. *The Suicide Cult: The Inside Story of the Peoples Temple Sect and the Massacre in Guyana*. New York: Bantam, 1978.

Knerr, M. E. *Suicide in Guyana*. New York: Belmont Tower Books, 1978.

Maguire, John and Mary Lee Dunn. *Hold Hands and Die.* New York: Dale, 1978.

McBirnie, W. S. *The Untold Story of Jonestown.* Glendale, Calif.: Community Churches of America, 1979.

McCoy, Alan W. *The Guyana Murders.* San Francisco: Highland House, 1988.

Meiers, Michael. *Was Jonestown a CIA Medical Experiment? A Review of the Evidence.* Lewiston, N.Y.: The Edwin Mellen Press, 1988.

Nichols, Norma. *Pot-Pourri with a Taste of Cult.* n.p., n.d.

Nugent, John Peer. *White Night: The Untold Story of What Happened Before—and Beyond—Jonestown.* New York: Rawson, Wade Publishers, 1979.

White, Mel. *Deceived.* Old Tappan, N.J.: Spire Books, 1979.

Whittle, Thomas G. and Jan Thorpe, "Revisiting the Jonestown Tragedy." *Freedom Magazine* n.v. (August 1997): 4–11. Available online at http://jonestown.sdsu.edu/JonestownPDF/CSI_FreedomRGB.pdf.

Literary Works Based on Peoples Temple and Jonestown

D'Aguiar, Fred. *Bill of Rights.* London: Chatto and Windus, 1998.

Fondakowski, Leigh, with Greg Pierotti, Stephen Wangh, and Margo Hall. *The People's Temple.* Minneapolis, Minn.: The Guthrie Theater, 2005/2006.

Harris, Wilson. *Jonestown.* London: Faber and Faber, 1996.

Hirschman, Jack. *The Jonestown Arcane.* Los Angeles: Parentheses Writing Series, 1991.

Parker, Pat. *Jonestown and Other Madness.* Ithaca, N.Y.: Firebrand Books, 1985.

Reston, James, Jr. "Jonestown Express." *Plays in Process* 5, no. 10 (1984).

Sutherland, Fraser. *Jonestown.* Toronto, Ontario: McClelland and Stewart, 1996.

Websites of Interest

Baird, Laura. "Jonestown Carpet." http://www.umanitoba.ca/schools/art/content/galleryoneoneone/laurab.html.

Brandou, Andrew. "As a Man Thinketh, So He Is." http://www.howdypardner.com/slideshow/slideshow.html.

CESNUR. "Scholars Present Request to Declassify Jonestown Documents." 18 November 1998 http://www.cesnur.org/testi/guyana_doc.htm.

Federal Bureau of Investigation. "Jonestown (Summary)." http://foia.fbi.gov/foiaindex/jonestown.htm.

Guyana News and Information. "Features on Jonestown." http://www.guyana.org/features/jonestown.html.

Howard, Lela. Homepage for The Mary Pearl Willis Foundation. http://www.mpwfoundation.org/home.

International Cultic Studies Association. http://www.icsahome.com/. (Search the site for "Jonestown" articles.)

Kahalas, Laurie Efrein. "Jonestown.com." Archived at http://jonestown.sdsu.edu/Jonestown_com/home.htm.

Kinsolving, Tom. "Jonestown Apologists Alert." http://jonestownapologistsalert.blogspot.com/.

Layton, Deborah. Homepage for *Seductive Poison.* http://www.deborahlayton.com/.

National Public Radio. "Father Cares: The Last of Jonestown." http://www.npr.org/programs/specials/jonestown.html.

————. "Remembering Jonestown," by Melissa Block. http://www.npr.org/templates/story/story.php?storyId=1509317.

Norwood, Jynona. "Jonestown Memorial." http://www.jones-town.org/modules/content/index.php?id=1.

Ontario Consultants on Religious Tolerance. "The People's Temple led by James Warren (Jim) Jones." http://www.religioustolerance.org/dc_jones.htm.

Osherow, Neal. "An Analysis of Jonestown." http://www.guyana.org/features/jonestown.html. Rural People's Party. http//ruralpeople.atspace.org.

Sterling, Robert. "The Jonestown Genocide." http://www.konformist.com/vault/jnstwn.htm.

University of Virginia, The Religious Movements Homepage Project. "Peoples Temple (Jonestown)." http://web.archive.org/web/20060828030228/religiousmovements.lib.virginia.edu/nrms/Jonestwn.html.

Wise, David. "Jonestown Legacy Website." http://jonestownlegacy.com/.

INDEX

About the Author

REBECCA MOORE is Professor and Chair in the Department of Religious Studies at San Diego State University. She is co-editor of *Nova Religio: The Journal of New and Emergent Religions*, and served on the Steering Committee of the New Religious Movements Group of the American Academy of Religion for six years. She has published extensively on Peoples Temple, her interest stemming, in part, from the loss of three family members in the mass deaths in Jonestown, Guyana, in November 1978. Her last book about Peoples Temple was as co-editor of a volume titled *Peoples Temple and Black Religion in America* (2004).